CW01216747

Bringing Desegregation Home

Palgrave Studies in Oral History

Series Editors: Linda Shopes and Bruce M. Stave

The Order Has Been Carried Out: History, Memory, and Meaning of a Nazi Massacre in Rome, by Alessandro Portelli (2003)

Sticking to the Union: An Oral History of the Life and Times of Julia Ruuttila, by Sandy Polishuk (2003)

To Wear the Dust of War: From Bialystok to Shanghai to the Promised Land, an Oral History, by Samuel Iwry, edited by L. J. H. Kelley (2004)

Education as My Agenda: Gertrude Williams, Race, and the Baltimore Public Schools, by Jo Ann Robinson (2005)

Remembering: Oral History Performance, edited by Della Pollock (2005)

Postmemories of Terror: A New Generation Copes with the Legacy of the "Dirty War," by Susana Kaiser (2005)

Growing Up in The People's Republic: Conversations between Two Daughters of China's Revolution, by Ye Weili and Ma Xiaodong (2005)

Life and Death in the Delta: African American Narratives of Violence, Resilience, and Social Change, by Kim Lacy Rogers (2006)

Creating Choice: A Community Responds to the Need for Abortion and Birth Control, 1961–1973, by David P. Cline (2006)

Voices from This Long Brown Land: Oral Recollections of Owens Valley Lives and Manzanar Pasts, by Jane Wehrey (2006)

Radicals, Rhetoric, and the War: The University of Nevada in the Wake of Kent State, by Brad E. Lucas (2006)

The Unquiet Nisei: An Oral History of the Life of Sue Kunitomi Embrey, by Diana Meyers Bahr (2007)

Sisters in the Brotherhoods: Working Women Organizing for Equality in New York City, by Jane LaTour (2008)

Iraq's Last Jews: Stories of Daily Life, Upheaval, and Escape from Modern Babylon, edited by Tamar Morad, Dennis Shasha, and Robert Shasha (2008)

Soldiers and Citizens: An Oral History of Operation Iraqi Freedom from the Battlefield to the Pentagon, by Carl Mirra (2008)

Overcoming Katrina: African American Voices from the Crescent City and Beyond, by D'Ann R. Penner and Keith C. Ferdinand (2009)

Bringing Desegregation Home: Memories of the Struggle toward School Integration in Rural North Carolina, by Kate Willink (2009)

I Saw it Coming: Worker Narratives of Plant Closings and Job Loss, by Tracy K'Meyer and Joy Hart (2010)

Speaking History: The American Past through Oral Histories, 1865-Present, edited by Susan Armitage and Laurie Mercier (2010)

Women Survivors of the Bhopal Disaster, by Suroopa Mukherjee (2010)

Stories from the Gulag, by Jehanne Gheith and Katherine Jolluck (2010)

Bringing Desegregation Home

Memories of the Struggle toward School Integration in Rural North Carolina

Kate Willink

palgrave
macmillan

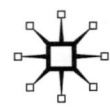

BRINGING DESEGREGATION HOME
Copyright © Kate Willink, 2009.

All rights reserved.

First published in 2009 by
PALGRAVE MACMILLAN®
in the United States—a division of St. Martin's Press LLC,
175 Fifth Avenue, New York, NY 10010.

Where this book is distributed in the UK, Europe and the rest of the world, this is by Palgrave Macmillan, a division of Macmillan Publishers Limited, registered in England, company number 785998, of Houndmills, Basingstoke, Hampshire RG21 6XS.

Palgrave Macmillan is the global academic imprint of the above companies and has companies and representatives throughout the world.

Palgrave® and Macmillan® are registered trademarks in the United States, the United Kingdom, Europe and other countries.

ISBN: 978–0–230–61135–1

Library of Congress Cataloging-in-Publication Data

Willink, Kate.
　Bringing desegregation home : memories of the struggle toward school integration in rural North Carolina / by Kate Willink.
　　p. cm. — (Palgrave studies in oral history)
　Includes bibliographical references and index.
　ISBN 0–230–61135–4
　1. School integration—North Carolina—Camden County. 2. Camden County (N.C.)—Race relations. I. Title.

LC214.22.N66W55 2009
379.2'6309756—dc22   2009006417

A catalogue record of the book is available from the British Library.

Design by Newgen Imaging Systems (P) Ltd., Chennai, India.

First edition: October 2009

10 9 8 7 6 5 4 3 2 1

Printed in the United States of America.

*To my family,
especially Dad,
with love and gratitude.*

Contents

Series Editors' Foreword ... ix

Acknowledgments ... xi

Map 1   Camden region ... xiii

Map 2   Camden County ... xiv

Introduction ... 1

CHAPTER 1
"Learn 'em to Work" ... 11

CHAPTER 2
"Wait a Minute…I'm a White" ... 33

CHAPTER 3
From Social and Cultural Capital to Social Change ... 51

CHAPTER 4
The Ghost of Whittier Crockett Witherspoon ... 73

CHAPTER 5
The Gentle Rebel ... 99

CHAPTER 6
Pedagogy and Social Change ... 119

CHAPTER 7
"You Forget This Is a Democracy" ... 133

CHAPTER 8
Working toward Integration: White-School Cafeteria Worker by Day, a Black Mom for Integration by Night ... 157

CHAPTER 9
Memory, Pedagogy, and Social Change ... 167

CONCLUSION
    Moving On   183

Notes   187
Bibliography   211
Index   219

Series Editors' Foreword

Oral history has been essential for telling the story of the modern Civil Rights Movement in the United States: It's a dramatic story, well suited to the sort of vivid narratives oral history records; it's also a story of complex motivations, shifting relationships, local organizing, and political maneuvering, for which first-person accounts rather than official records are the best—often the only—source. And while some participants have written memoirs of their experiences in the movement, many more—activists rather than memoirists—have not.

Kate Willink's *Bringing Desegregation Home: Memories of the Struggle toward School Integration in Rural North Carolina* brings a unique focus, approach, and voice to the growing body of oral history based work on the Civil Rights Movement. Hers is not a progressive narrative, nor does it focus on well-known leaders; rather, it centers on the still-incomplete process of school desegregation in one small rural southern county, in which, she suggests, African Americans have lost as much as they have gained. She wraps her account around the narratives of (or in one case, about) six participants—principals, teachers, and parents, black and white—using each individual's stories to consider ways school desegregation has played out on the ground, not in courtrooms, as individuals made choices—and explained the meaning of those choices—within very specific historical circumstances. And, while Willink's assessment of the process of change is not especially optimistic, she finds in oral history itself a source of optimism: Oral history is, for her, a social act, as individual narrators, first through her gentle prodding and now through the medium of this book, lay out their experiences and their views for others to consider in a manner that, hopefully, creates understanding and goodwill.

For both its conscientious appraisal of school desegregation and its regard for the social value of oral history, we are pleased to include *Bringing Desegregation Home* as the seventeenth book in the Palgrave Studies in Oral History series. It joins two previously published works on the subjects of the

Civil Rights Movement and education: Kim Lacy Rogers' award-winning *Life and Death in the Delta: African American Narratives of Violence, Resilience, and Social Change* (2006); and Jo Ann Robinson's *Education As My Agenda: Gertrude Williams, Race, and the Baltimore Public Schools* (2005). Volumes in the series are deeply grounded in interviews and also present those interviews in ways that aid readers to more fully appreciate their historical significance and cultural meaning. Their aim is to bring oral history interviews out of the archives and into the hands of students, educators, scholars, and the reading public. The series also includes work that approaches oral history more theoretically, as a point of departure for an exploration of broad questions of cultural production and representation.

Linda Shopes
Carlisle, Pennsylvania

Bruce M. Stave
University of Connecticut

Acknowledgments

This book has truly been a collective endeavor, primarily reliant on: a group of scholars outstanding in their contributions to their various fields as well as in their generosity to me; a number of families in Camden County who have graciously opened their lives and taught me volumes; and my own family and friends who have supported me with unwavering love. I am forever grateful for this embarrassment of riches, which this book has brought home to me.

Friend and mentor Della Pollock's generous spirit, well-tuned ear, and superb editing have touched me as well as this book. For all of this and much more, I am forever grateful. Many thanks to D. Soyini Madison who provided me with wisdom and support to do the kind of work I care passionately about. George Noblit's good humor, warm heart, and sage advice steered me in directions that I would never have imagined and have thoroughly enjoyed. I benefited greatly from the mindful listening and guidance of Julia Wood. Robbie Cox's boisterous enthusiasm and encouragement advanced this research. Jacquelyn Hall's insightful readings from the beginning of this project have been influential in shaping this book. Bland Simpson, who showed me the best of North Carolina hospitality, opened new worlds in northeastern North Carolina and inspired me to try to bring the place alive in words. Thank you all for your guidance, inspiring expectations, and generous readings.

This book comes from numerous conversations with the people of Camden County, North Carolina, and its surroundings. It is indebted to and inspired by their work, struggles, and commitments to create a better educational system and community. I am particularly indebted to Mr. Charlie Hughes, Mr. Alex Leary, Mrs. Fannie Lewis, Mrs. Vivian Jones, and Mr. Billy and Mrs. Earlene Revelle. In addition, I would like to thank: Ms. Jean Bischoff, Mr. Thomas Butchko, Mrs. Barbarette Davis, The Elizabeth City State University Archives, The Elizabeth City Bed and Breakfast, Mr. Fred Fearing, Mr. Clay and Mrs. Nancy Ferebee, Ms. Freshwater, Mrs. Joyce Gallup, Mr. Mark Harnley, Mrs. Sylvia Holley, Mr. Sherick Hughes, Mr. Scott Jones, Mrs. Vivian Jones,

Mrs. Malco, Mrs. Irene McCoy, Ms. Linda McMann, The Museum of the Albemarle, Ms. Christine Otmani, Mr. Vann Pannell, Mr. Don Pendergraf, Ms. Linda Perry, Mrs. Melba Purquette, Mr. J. R. Spence, Mr. Bobby Vaughn, and Mr. Whittier Crockett Witherspoon. I will always hold Camden County and its residents close to my heart.

I am forever grateful to my spouse, Tim Willink, for his untiring support and love. And for all the intimacies of which I write, I would not understand the journey of love if it were not for him. Deepest gratitude to my sons Pablo and Aiden Willink for their unfailing love and patience during this arduous process. They provided me with laughter, joy, and hope for the next generation. Alan Ternes, my father, was a patient, wise, and generous travel companion and editor. I am grateful beyond measure for his camaraderie and his consul. Deepest gratitude and love to Suzanne Ferrari, my mother, who provided steady support and love during this long process. Special thanks to Barbara Ternes and George Willink for their untiring editorial and emotional support. Many of my family members provided invaluable love and support: Aime Ferrari, Marie Ternes, Paul Ternes, Margaret Textor, Clinton Textor, Gwen Willink, Randy Willink, Patrick Willink, and Roseann Willink. Much love and thanks to you all.

I am blessed with good friends who supported me along the way. Deepest thanks to Christina Foust, outstanding friend and colleague, for her companionship and support throughout this process. Special thanks to my friends and colleagues Bill Balthrop, Kip Bobroff, Paula Becker-Brown, Bernadette Calafell, David Cecelski, Frank Coyne, Ken Coates, Nick Cuttforth, Diana Denton, Eric Fretz, Karen Foss, Hava Gordon, Darrin Hicks, Dan Lair, Andrew Meyerson, Chandra Seki, Kelly Smyer, Kersti Tyson, Wannie Womble, Roy Wood, and many others. My students and research assistance have also inspired me and contributed to this project. Special appreciation to Charla Agnoletti, Russell Cole, Jolene Collins, Auravelia Colomer, Curtis Darling, Craig Garbe, Cameron Lewis, Jacquelynn McDaniels, Kim Roesch, Natai Shelsen, and Scott Stoneman.

Finally, I am profoundly grateful to the Spencer Foundation, the University of Waterloo, and the Center for Multicultural Excellence at the University of Denver, whose generous support was vital to the success of this project. Palgrave's oral history series editors, Linda Shopes and Bruce Stave, along with Christopher Chapell, Sam Hasey, and an anonymous reviewer, guided this manuscript from conception to completion with careful insight and generosity. Heartfelt thanks one and all.

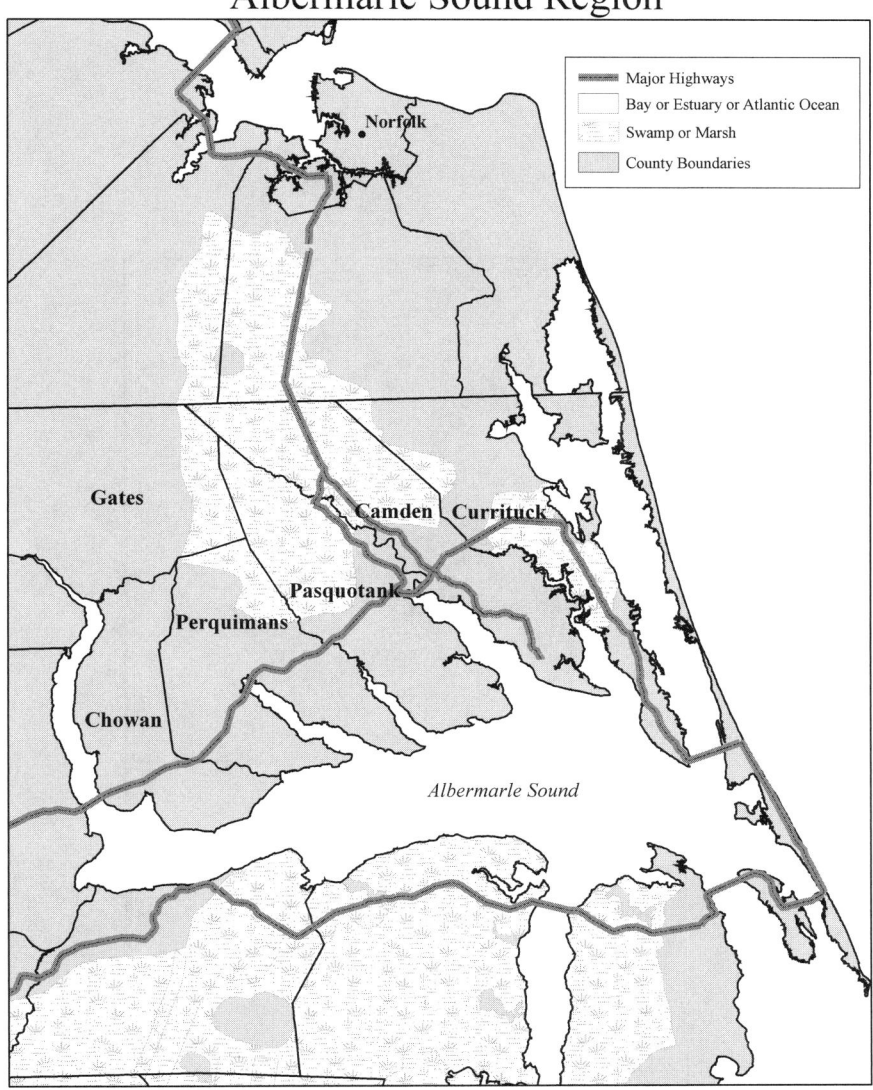

Map 1 Camden region.

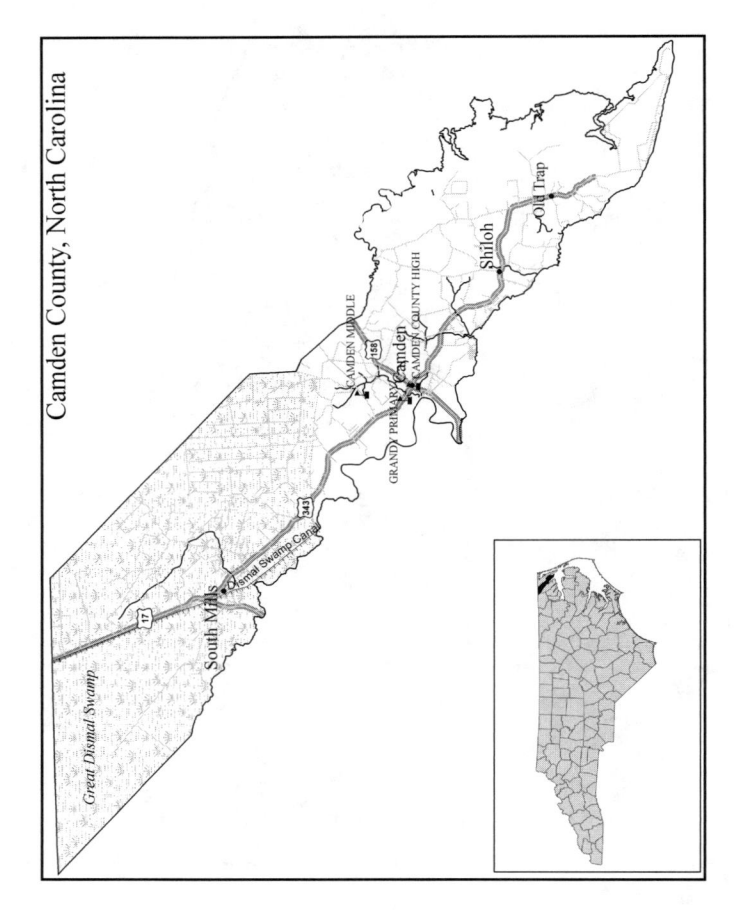

Map 2 Camden County.

Introduction

The landmark U.S. Supreme Court decision of *Brown v. Board of Education* (1954) swept aside the doctrine of separate-but-equal schools for blacks and shook the cultural foundations of the South. The well-intentioned goals of the mandate and the attendant state and local educational policies of school desegregation were catalysts for social change. But the success or failure of these policies depended on their implementation on the local and family levels. As a result, desegregation across the nation was an uneven and incomplete process.

Far from the epicenters of the Civil Rights Movement, residents in Camden County and North Carolina in general seemed caught by surprise by the *Brown* decision: "On the eve of the great civil rights struggles of the 1950s and 1960s, few whites seemed to sense that a half a century of segregation—customs, laws, and traditions their politicians promised would never end—teetered on the brink of destruction."[1]

Mandated from afar, the impact of desegregation filtered down slowly to this rural tidewater county. When it arrived its impact touched not only the schools but also the community and everyday family life. De jure desegregation closed black schools and forced the integration of public education. The narrow de jure policies mandated change of the education system, but could control neither the prejudices or predilections of the people, nor the myriad ways de facto segregation persisted in the schools and throughout the community.

Revisiting Camden County reveals how much de facto segregation continues in the community and its schools a half century later. For example, the talented black athletes were quickly integrated into the Camden High School football team but, as decades of yearbook pictures testify, the cheerleaders remained all white. School administrations and teachers added students from black schools into their classrooms but discarded the black curriculum. Even when the schools eventually decided to celebrate Martin Luther King Jr.'s birthday, white students were allowed to skip school on that day. U.S. Supreme Court decisions and federal policy statements alone cannot overcome the broad, deep-seated resistance to racial integration.[2]

School Desegregation and Camden County, North Carolina

The rural tidewater county of Camden, North Carolina, has long been overshadowed, almost hidden, by the dynamic communities that surround it. Its nearest neighbor, a few minutes west across a small causeway, is Elizabeth City, which—with its narrow brick roads, historic Ku Klux Klan claverns, and black social clubs—is a typical small southern port city. The Pasquotank River that separated Camden County from Pasquotank County has contributed to the historic sense of division that continues to this day. There was no bridge between the two counties until the construction of what locals called the "Floating Road" in 1923. The river, which widens as it reaches Albemarle Sound, was well known for being difficult to cross. Subsequently, the neighboring communities have followed different developmental paths—Elizabeth City modernized as Camden remained largely rural and agriculture-based.

An hour by car north of Camden is the city of Norfolk, Virginia, which has long served as "the sprawled-out Navytown queen of Tidewater Virginia" and the urban center for northeastern North Carolina.[3] Newly expanded State Highway 343 makes the northern Camden County—with its small schools and high-achievement rates—an affordable alternative for those working in the growing metropolis. Long before this highway expansion, Camden residents had begun traveling north on the narrow, notoriously dangerous road that borders the Dismal Swamp Canal in search of better opportunities, generally in the form of well-paying union jobs as longshoremen.[4]

An hour's drive east of Camden, the Outer Banks beaches remain a nationally known tourist destination. Home to the Wright Brothers' early attempts to fly and the site of many shipwrecks, these commercially developed barrier islands attract tens of thousands of visitors each year. Many Camden residents journey to such Outer Banks towns as Duck and Kitty

Hawk to clean and maintain the million-dollar properties that overlook the tempestuous Atlantic Ocean.

In between these destinations lie the flat roads and farm fields of Camden County. If you don't stop for a red light (Camden recently added a second stop light, bemoaned by many locals as an inconvenient sign of development), you hardly notice one of North Carolina's smallest counties with some seven thousand people. The county projects like a long narrow finger in the brackish waters of the Albemarle Sound.

Sheltered from the Atlantic Ocean's larger tides and storms by the sand dunes of the Outer Banks, the county has also been sheltered from political and social changes that have roiled the nation. In Camden County tidal pools of memories preserve the past in ways that have been washed away in dynamic urban areas of America. The county residents remember historical events on the national level—*Brown v. Board Education*, Martin Luther King's "I have a Dream" Speech, and Malcolm X and the black power movement. Yet the events that rocked Camden County include the black community's loss of their schools, the white school's loss of the rebel mascot, and the fates of the first brave children that chose to go to a white school.

Until recently, Camden's overall population remained remarkably stable. An important element of its social history is the exodus of people in search of economic opportunities, particularly blacks, who in 1950 comprised two-fifths of the total population and now make up one-fifth.[5] Prior to this, for more than a century, the county's population was virtually unchanged.

A growing wave of suburbanization is overwhelming Camden's traditionally agricultural economy. The U.S. Commerce Department recently ranked Camden as the seventh fastest growing county in the nation. Grandy Elementary School has added mobile trailers to accommodate the growing number of students; and Camden County was one of seven North Carolina counties to receive a grant from the Gates Foundation to create a technology-themed high school. De facto racial segregation, though rarely mentioned, influences many of these changes. For example, the schools require portables because white families are moving from predominantly black inner city school neighborhoods in Norfolk to the increasingly white Camden school system.

Why study a place that time forgot for awhile and now is being overwhelmed by modernity? With the recent conservative Supreme Court decisions, changing political attitudes about school desegregation, white-led urbanization, and changing generations, Camden's pools of memory are disappearing. In contrast to much of the nation, local Camden families and memories continue to span generations, tied geographically to a place where reputations of "good" or "bad" families still benefit or burden the new generation and where the stories of the past continue to influence people's daily lives.

Micro-Level Social Change

The drama of the quiet places has frequently been ignored in studies of desegregation. Yet oral history in rural places highlights elements of desegregation that are obscured by the many complex changes in dynamic urban settings. For example, echoes of a county clerk's statement a century ago that blacks should not be educated because it makes them "uppity" continue through the acts of erasure of the black educational accomplishments[6]: the name of the famous black opera singer Marian Anderson was removed from the middle school; pictures from the black graduating classes disappeared; the name of the generous black farmer who donated the land for the middle school is forgotten; and the white administration has failed to understand the black community's strong desire to use the historic black school for public events.

Elements of integration's complexity[7] can only be captured in fine-grained analysis of intensive oral histories.[8] The prominence of such urban-based leaders in the Civil Rights Movement as Martin Luther King Jr. and Rosa Parks—emblazoned in our collective memory—is a mixed blessing. Their iconic nature often obscures social change on micro-levels and the vital roles of the small players in the movement. The crowning moments of the Civil Rights Movement support a national narrative of racial progress.[9] This timeline has many heroic and tragic characters, yet everyday social changes in race relations have often been overlooked. The battles in a tradition-bound, rural community over small changes, such as whether or not a newly integrated school would keep a rebel mascot from the white school, were emotion-filled and vital symbolic statements of race relations.

Camden County is part of North Carolina's "black belt," a region mistakenly characterized as "bypassed by the Civil Rights Movement."[10] Like many rural communities, Camden's civil rights struggles have been understudied and unappreciated. Outside of limelight and media attention, conservative rural communities were neither sites of black power nor of dramatic white resistance. Camden's civil rights struggles manifested themselves as whites and blacks made slow and small changes in institutional and everyday race relations. The conflicts were not dramatic, choreographed civil rights events that drew national media, but this does not diminish the significance of these local human struggles.

Small change, initiated by one person or a few individuals, often appears insignificant, unlikely to bring about long-lasting transformation. For example, the decisions to terminate rather than integrate the white-run PTA kept black parents from influencing school policy; a white principal choosing not to respond in an authoritarian way to displays of black students' anger at integration during the first years of desegregation represents a change in traditional black-white power relations; and the mundane act at a graduation ceremony of a black mother choosing to shake the hand of a white principal that she felt had wronged her son reverberated throughout her family as different generations negotiated their meanings of forgiveness and racial justice.

The impact of small change is difficult to measure in the short term and is often not counted as change at all. Yet over time, small changes, presented in everyday detail in this book, accumulate power and transform communities, even if the process is slow, iterative, incomplete, and sometimes regressive. These changes occur where educational and legal policies stumble over barriers of human prejudice and racism. They are a vital part—often unrecognized—of nationwide social transformation. Small changes often shaped the long-term successes and failures of local school integration.

Social constructions of race complicated educational practices and policy a half century ago...and continue to do so. In Camden County, close daily contact fostered interracial childhood friendships, while sexual anxieties made integration of the high schools difficult, even lethal. Local school integration, which did not begin in the county until 1969, destroyed the close relationships between the black schools and families and their mutual approval of strong discipline. The process of desegregation highlighted the ways that informal education continues to transfer feelings about race across generations. The assumed inferiority of blackness and superiority of whiteness persists and overwhelms many important black values—such as pride and discipline.

Selective and often faulty memories the Civil Rights era influence both white and black Camden residents' assessment of racial equality today.[11] In Camden, and across the nation, many whites consider desegregation accomplished. For most blacks (and some whites), it is far from complete. The tensions of these different viewpoints undermine ongoing movements toward racial equality.

Some of the consequences of the largest national effort ever made to address education, race, and equality—such as racial underachievement and racially segregated schools—are the result of how this effort was implemented.

For example, contemporary concerns about the lack of discipline and perceived lack of parental involvement of people of color are partly the result of the white power brokers of integration ignoring how black segregated schools operated. We must look—with careful attention to detail—at our experiences with desegregation over the last half century in order complete the task.

Ethnographic Oral History

In a spotless kitchen, in an aging trailer, in a snug den with gun-lined walls, I have listened to the stories of people who have lived through the everyday consequences of school desegregation. This book considers in depth the memories from selected individuals who provide unique insights into the process of school integration—including former students, teachers, administrators, parents, and community members. Their stories reveal how federal and local public education policies and pedagogies were implemented in everyday practice. These individual memories touch on events, attitudes, and emotions that are missing from most versions of school desegregation. The oral histories of this small, tradition-bound, agricultural county address intimately the complex social and historical constructions of racial difference in education, including student-teacher relations, discipline, extracurricular activities, and parent-child interactions.

The interviews are semi-structured, informal conversations grounded in an inductive storytelling approach. They also include repeated visits and growing trust and friendship. The interviews contain histories of dialogue and oral traditions, anecdotes, proverbs, and folk narratives.[12] The narrators not only tell their own stories but also the versions they recall of their parents and grandparents.

Interwoven with the oral histories are significant insights into theoretical and methodological concerns including the power and politics of story; whiteness and blackness; collective memory; different perspectives of educational equity; the emotional qualities of history; and persistent racism. The stories of individuals' pasts and prejudices are ultimately about people remembering and reinventing community, education, race relations, and democracy on a day-to-day basis. Taken together they comprise not only a history, but are an untapped resource for successful education policy, democratic change, and substantive racial integration.

The collected oral histories are practices of democratic citizenship. Citizens[13] at a local level are given the opportunity to present their differing viewpoints. Individual memories often challenge standard histories, opening doors to "spaces for a radical cultural politics that…will help us to imagine a more humane, pluralistic, and just racial order."[14] *Parents Involved in Community Schools v. Seattle School District No. 1* (2007)—the recent Supreme Court decision that forbids student assignments to public schools solely to ensure racial integration and refuses to acknowledge "racial balance" as a compelling state interest—underscores that these topics are unsettled and are an ongoing part of our national agenda.

The Book Structure

This book is organized around the oral histories of six individuals whose lives were touched by school desegregation. The narratives are coupled in sets of two chapters, followed by a bridge chapter that addresses the broader theoretical issues of the preceding chapters.

Chapter one addresses the segregated education of farmer and father-of-ten Charlie Hughes, and the segregated and desegregated education of his children. The stories Hughes tells highlight the importance of formal and informal education where he "learned" his children to work. His narratives provide both a black historical framework from which to understand race and public education in Camden County and a wider view of what Jacquelyn Hall calls "the long Civil Rights Movement"—including both the treacherous trail leading up to *Brown v. Board of Education* in the twentieth century and the unfinished road toward full integration in the twenty-first.

The early steps of mandated school desegregation, during the freedom of choice period (1965–1969), began with black teachers going into all-white schools and white teachers going into all-black schools. Chapter two takes up the oral history of Alex Leary, one of the first white teachers in the all-black Marian Anderson School. His stories provide insights into how whites negotiated the transition to de jure school desegregation and the persistence of de facto segregation.

Chapter three explores the roles of social and cultural capital that sustained vital and often under-examined networks both in the segregated and the integrated schools.[15] Leary's narratives show how white privilege and the dominant networks controlled Camden County. Hughes' stories introduce the under-recognized forms of black social and cultural capital.

Whittier Crockett Witherspoon, the black principal of Marian Anderson segregated school, is the focus of chapter four. Witherspoon was a powerful advocate for black education, cultivating a wealth of community support and resources despite its second-class treatment and financing. The year before mandatory desegregation, he crossed the bridge to Elizabeth City to work at the traditionally black Elizabeth City State University, to higher challenges and greater acclaim. From across this narrow river, he continued to be an iconic example of a positive view of segregated black education and a strong disciplinarian.

Billy Revelle, the first white principal at the all-black Marian Anderson School during desegregation, has dedicated his life to economic and social justice. Chapter five reveals how white supporters of integration were subjected to stigmatization and exclusion, albeit often in subtle ways. A traveler between his white neighborhood and an all-black school, Revelle offers a road less taken by white leaders at the time—a potential path for addressing issues of race, education, and equity today.

The narratives of black education success embodied in Witherspoon as well as the challenges and sense of failure Revelle endured during desegregation raise questions about the way *Brown* was implemented. Desegregation in Camden County resulted in a sense of loss for the white and black Camden communities. Chapter six addresses the struggles of Witherspoon and Revelle through the process of school integration and the limits of education as a vehicle for social change.

Chapter seven looks at the memories of Vivian Jones, a black community activist, and what "was lost in the translation of integration." Her black activism started in her teens and her expertise made her a valued county worker, where she continued to work for the interests of the black community. An avid supporter of education and democracy, Jones fought for her own rights, her children's, and her neighbors'.

In chapter eight Fannie Lewis's narratives dramatize how emotions, including pride and fear, travel through stories to propel future generations' achievement and activism. Lewis, whose six children went through the Camden schools, worked for the school system for many years as a bus driver and a cafeteria employee. As a parent, she fought against ongoing community practices to keep her children segregated. Her stories reveal the challenges of parenting in a society with many residual prejudices.

Chapter nine addresses the various roles of memories, their often-ignored power in social change, and the unanticipated consequences of educational policies that memories uncover. The black and white attempts to make meaning from the experience of school desegregation offer insights into the segregated nature of racial memory. They also suggest a need for increased understanding in the present.

The short final chapter looks at the broad implications of the findings from these detailed oral histories. The social and cultural insights into racial inequality that arise from this humanistic study are often ignored from the political and economic-based evaluations of integration. It argues for a more inclusive understanding of the storied past to inform contemporary education in order for more America to move toward a more just and equitable society.

The recent Supreme Court decision—*Parents Involved in Community Schools v. Seattle School District No. 1*—also shows that foundational legal decisions can be undermined. Many of the solutions to issues of residual segregation and unrealized integration highlight the limitations of the law and educational policy to achieve change and the necessity of people to make decisions on a daily basis that forward racial and economic equality.

As Dr. Martin Luther King noted, "Too long has our beloved Southland been bogged down in a tragic effort to live in monologue instead of dialogue."[16] Segregation resulted in monologues of powerful voices instead of a dialogue of all those involved in the choices that faced the nation. Segregation has also distorted the identities of blacks and whites and has left both groups with impoverished languages and an inability to address one another on issues of race: "Though no longer inscribed in law, the awful consequences of racial segregation and separation continue to undermine the possibility of our achieving the 'beloved community' that King hoped for."[17] This book addresses the deep divisions and obstacles caused by residual segregation. It explores possibilities of increasing interracial understanding through oral histories and memories as we travel along the arduous road toward a more democratic society.

Figure 1 Charlie Hughes at the Elizabeth City Farmers Market. Photo by Alan Ternes.

CHAPTER 1

"Learn 'em to Work"

> The storyteller joins the ranks of teachers and sages. He has counsel—not for a few situations, as the proverb does, but for many, like the sage.
> —Walter Benjamin, *Illuminations*

Charlie Hughes was one of the few black farmers in Camden County who still owned their family land.[1] Until Hughes' death in his late eighties, he continued to farm five acres. With a cell phone on his belt, he drove his tractor through the fields of watermelon, potatoes, onions, and green beans—which he harvested by hand, sold at the local farmers' market, and bartered for basic goods and services.

His house—with a sparkling white Cadillac in the carport—was gently worn from the ten children he and his wife raised. For more than a decade Hughes and his grown children cared for his ill wife until her passing, a year before him. With a couple of his children close-by to lend a hand, his comfortable home exuded a feeling of support from family, neighbors, and church members.

Throughout his life, Hughes remained a powerful influence in the community—an active member and former chairman of the Shiloh community's Democratic Committee. As he traveled the county, he encountered friends wherever he went. Agile, quick, and slight in frame, Hughes—with a youthful grin and sparkling eyes—lit up a room. In Camden and the neighboring Pasquotank County, Hughes was a renowned storyteller and local farmer, often quoted in the newspapers.

Seen from a distance, Hughes' life appears to run with a beautiful ease, guided by an unfailing ethic of good works. Yet like a world-class athlete, Hughes' achievements are undergirded by sustained effort—held together by a carefully considered philosophy, shrewd economic decisions, gentle humor, strong moral and physical fiber, and an unfailingly positive attitude. His success is also the result of lifetimes of family labor—his own and his children's. This patriarch of the black community employed wit, work, and good will to lead a long and prosperous life.

School and the Farm

Hughes started school in Camden County, North Carolina, in the 1920s. He attended a rural one-room elementary school for black children. The school was a long walk down a red-dirt road from his family farmhouse and nearby community church. Growing up on a farm, Hughes was well-learned in agricultural work. The farm work and the church were rich sources of informal education for his fertile mind.

Hughes' father Elijah owned the land his family farmed, unlike many sharecroppers. Because his father had a debilitating illness, his eldest brother stayed home to work the land: "My daddy got sick and he was living with us. He got sick two years, and I was about ten or twelve years old. And there wasn't no welfare then."

At the time farmers with disabling illnesses often relied on their children to support the family. Hughes explains: "He sent my older brother back in the fields to work the mules then. Got him back in the field working. And one day he hitched the mules (*he chuckles*) to the other end of the field and kept on walking." On that day, Hughes' life changed.

"Yeah, I had to go get 'em because mama come to school, got me to go get the mules to bring them to the house. And the next day it was my job to work 'em. And I got them mules and went to work with 'em. In the two years that I stayed out of school, I forgot everything that I ever learnt. I lost my education." Hughes left school to do what needed to be done—support his family and maintain the farm.[2]

A few years later, after his father recovered, Hughes tried to go back to school: "When I went back to school and the teachers weren't like they is now. And they would kind of slurring on me, you know. And the students were telling me, 'You've got everything on your pants, cotton pants.' 'Ain't your throat scratched from eating cornbread?' Because we had to eat about what we could eat. Just imagine somebody twelve years old taking care of a family. And that's how it had to go then. There wasn't no help out there for you. And I done it." Instead of his peers recognizing his remarkable achievements, they made fun of his clothing that revealed his work on the farm and the food he provided to sustain his family. He left school for good and worked on the farm.

In his late teens, another turning point in his life occurred: "My daddy came o'er one morning, and he said to me said, said, 'Me and your mama have been talking about you.' I thought maybe that he'd been talking about, found out something that I had done because back in those days if you give 'em any slack they'd go out on you. So I said, 'What have you been talking about?!'"

"He said, 'You ain't never left home.' Said, 'And I want you to have that farm down there.' I said, 'I ain't got no money to pay for no farm.' He said, 'I'm going to fix it up for you to pay for it.' I said, 'What do you want for it?' He told me, he said, 'I want a thousand dollars now and five hundred dollars a year as long as I live.' Five hundred dollars at that time was a piecely living,[3] and I didn't have no thousand dollars. I said, 'I don't got no thousand dollars.' He said, 'Well, I'll tell you what I'm going to do.' He said, 'I'm going to the bank to sign a note with you...' So he did. Signed a note at the bank... and I gave him the money. He said the rest would pay for the five hundred dollars. I said, 'Yes, it will.'"

A shrewd investor, not wanting to buy what he could not afford, Hughes negotiated with his father. He knew from the beginning that he would work for what he would get, not counting on inheritance, despite the fact that he had supported his family in his childhood. Hughes was more than good to his word because their financial agreement eventually didn't cover the costs: "As the time went on, five hundred dollars wouldn't even pay taxes on it. I had to give him whatever it took to live with. If you do right, things will come to you." Hughes did "whatever it took" to take care of his parents, not because he expected direct reciprocation but because it was the right thing to do. Hughes' investment yielded valuable land, self-sufficiency, and later a way to support his wife and ten children.

Because his older children attended segregated schools and the younger ones went to desegregated schools, his life has been profoundly touched by school desegregation. The stories Hughes tells, as a student, a farmer, a parent, and a community member, highlight the importance he attributes to formal and informal education. All but one of Hughes' ten children are college graduates, four with master's degrees.

Hughes' life story fits into the broader historical narrative of interracial progress through alternative economic and educational arrangements. But he does not tell his story in the traditional narrative arc of starting poor and arriving at prosperity. He never participates in what Solorzano and Yosso call "deficit storytelling," crafting a narrative of cultural, economic, or racial deficit that improves with the national progress narrative of the Civil Rights Movement and desegregation.[4]

While Hughes may be an unusual character for any era, he is not free from historical conditions. His narratives provide both a black historical framework from which to understand race and public education in Camden County and a wider view of "the long Civil Rights Movement."[5]

Segregated Education in North Carolina

With the ratification of the Thirteenth Amendment and the abolition of slavery in 1865, the concept of wage labor began to gain currency in the South. Former slaveholders went from being "laborlords" to landlords; debt-burdened freedmen farmed cash crops or sold their labor for wages.[6] On the heels of emancipation, the railroad steamed into North Carolina. Workers laid out fifteen hundred miles of track by 1880, which increased to around five thousand by the turn of the century, opening new markets across the state.[7] In the same period in the Albemarle region the Dismal Swamp Canal brought boatloads of commercial opportunities to Camden and the surrounding counties. The "money age," as L.L. Wright of Thomasville told a group of teachers, had arrived in North Carolina.[8]

In 1875 a state constitutional amendment legislated racial segregation in the classroom and required separate but equal facilities.[9] For many people at the time, school made up a small portion of a child's education.[10] The other components included, for example, work skills learned on the farm, civic lessons gained from conversations about local politics, and moral education acquired in church. Book learning was considered a poor substitute for common sense and practical experience in the daily lives of most rural North Carolinians.

Around 1890, approximately 58 percent of school-aged North Carolinians, black and white, were enrolled in school.[11] Alex Leary, the local historian of Camden County, provides an overview of early education: "The Civil War came along and that about destroyed our educational system for a long time. Then in the 1880s they began to provide these one-room schools.

About 1900 we had twenty-two schools in Camden County, throughout the county."

In North Carolina, as in all areas of the country, the massive social and economic changes of the late nineteenth century required a "radical readjustment" in the education of all children. The common school system was gradually replaced by the graded school system.[12] Common schools in Camden were one-room schoolhouses with one teacher for all levels, and a commitment to local control, often scheduled around the agricultural calendar. In the common school system, teachers used "the language of politics and morals...to make 'GOOD CITIZENS,'" of their students.[13]

In contrast, the new graded education model, while still pursuing education for citizenship, used "the language of markets and competitive individualism."[14] Along with new multiple-room school buildings, separate grades, and bureaucratic administrative control, graded education changed schools from a nexus of community relations to a training ground for pupils to become lifelong participants in a competitive market economy.

Graded schools emphasized professionalism and standardization. The curriculum focused increasingly on reading, writing, and arithmetic as ways to improve efficiency on the farm and in commercial relations. Particularly in cities, the money age brought a shift away from intimate economic interactions based on family, neighborhood, and community to a calculating, competition-driven world of business transactions.[15]

In North Carolina, where schools were segregated, black and white schools experienced this educational and economic change in markedly different ways. After 1900, when blacks lost the right to vote, state funding for black schools dropped by more than half.[16] City schools received more money than rural schools, especially in rural eastern areas of the state with larger black populations.[17] For example, in the 1920s, school buildings for a rural white child averaged to $65.76 a year compared to $13.78 for a rural black child. In cities black and white school children received about four times as much funds as their rural counterparts.[18] Nathan Carter Newbold, the director of the Division of Negro Education at the time, noted that local officials "seem to have the idea that it will not be possible to do anything in the matter of providing respectable school buildings for Negroes until they have provided a good school building of standard type for every white school district in the county."[19] In order to partially redress the inequities and the poor funding for black schools, black parents and community members frequently contributed funds and in-kind support, a practice called "double taxation."

White political rhetoric at the time reinforced the importance of maintaining segregated education. In the fall of 1901 at the Negro State Fair, Governor Charles Aycock announced his position on the neglected issue of black education. Advocating separate schools for the races, he declared, segregation "is well for you; it is well for us; it is necessary for the peace of our section."[20]

Starting in 1900, with little possibility of recourse, the black community worked "within the crevices of white supremacy for every opportunity for black power and self-determination."[21] Education became an increasingly important focus for blacks seeking equality and improvement of their social and economic conditions.[22] From this time on, black teachers, most of them women, continued to help "place education at the center of a much broader context of race, justice, and citizenship in a democratic society."[23] The black community used education to promote equality and to instill awareness of citizens' rights as well as the drive to achieve equality. The black schools, along with the black churches, were later important foundations of the Civil Rights Movement in rural North Carolina and throughout the South.

In the first two decades of twentieth-century North Carolina, black schools fared differently from their white counterparts: The state began to fund secondary schools for whites in rural areas in 1907, while black public elementary schools were funded in 1910 for the first time, and the first black secondary school in 1918.[24] By 1920 Camden County had four high schools—all white.[25] Local historian Alex Leary recalls with some pride,

> In early 1900s we began to build high schools. One of the first high schools built is, well,...we had a high school in South Mills that I thought matched any school around...that was built in 1913. Then Old Trap built a school. Shiloh built a school, and then Camden built a school. So by 1920 they had four high schools in Camden County. No black high school...Blacks went mostly to the elementary grades. They had schools, but eighth grade was as high as they went, from what somebody told me.

With time the disparity in expenditures between North Carolina and the rest of the Nation became part of the rationale for a campaign across the state to improve education. Yet the state was slow to catch up with national standards. The transition from common schools to graded schools was late in some parts of North Carolina, and in fact, the common school continued into, and beyond, the 1920s in rural North Carolina communities, which lacked funding to add teachers, extend the school year (from three months to thirty-two weeks), and renovate classrooms.

A decade after Governor Aycock's speech, another trend affecting the black community in North Carolina began, when black people started migrating North at a rate that alarmed many white businessmen. With the start of World War I and the subsequent drop in foreign immigrant labor in the North, many black people left the South in search of higher wages and a reprieve from the oppressive, at times terrorizing, world of Southern racist practices. Nearly half a million blacks joined the "great migration" northward between 1914 and 1920. Almost twice that number left the South in the following decade.[26]

During the same period other blacks enlisted to serve their country in World War I. This prompted Professor D.J. Jordan of Dudley's A & M College in Greensboro to ask President Woodrow Wilson—based on the president's position on race relations in the United States versus the rights of Europeans—in an open letter printed in the *Independent*: "Is this the kind of Democracy I am asked to give my fortune and my life to make safe in the world?"[27]

Across the nation and in the South particularly, white officials and businessmen sought ways to cool the "migration fever" that threatened to drain the South of its low cost labor pool and, some feared, to spread "racial problems" northward. When state officials met during the summer of 1917 in Raleigh to discuss solutions for the labor shortage, they assumed blacks "would prefer to remain in the land of their birth if guaranteed a living wage... and proper instruction for their children."[28] As a result, "Negro" education increased in importance for white politicians, although this sentiment did not translate quickly into identifiable changes in black classrooms. In 1921, when the legislature overhauled the public school laws, Nathan Carter Newbold persuaded the legislators to create a separate division of Negro education.

Despite white public resistance to improvements in education for black North Carolinians, the state became the southern leader in education and peaceful race relations. This was in part due to the state politicians' growing attention to the education of black people and the support of black education in North Carolina by northern philanthropists such as Julius Rosenwald. Camden County was one of the counties with a Rosenwald school.

The states rural schools were already a decade into broad social and institutional reform when Charles Hughes was born in 1919 in Shiloh, North Carolina, to Elijah and Rebecca Hughes.[29] The first public secondary school for blacks had opened its doors in North Carolina a year earlier. Graded education, which was gaining favor, had not reached rural and black communities in many parts of North Carolina. In order to keep black people like Hughes' father from leaving, southern officials realized that they had to alleviate some of the oppressive conditions of everyday life. Federal officials doing research on the "exodus movement" identified "the inadequacy of the school facilities" as one of the primary reasons black Americans headed north.[30] In response, North Carolina turned its attention to improve black education.

However, in the rural one-room schoolhouse for black children that Hughes attended, the traditions of the common school still prevailed. Education emphasized the agrarian community, good citizenship, and African American liberation. These teachings became part of Hughes' life and values. His close-knit black community had its values and its own economic system based on bartering that he mastered and used for his entire life. And the nearby church became the source for his evolving literacy and deep ethical values.

Despite the relative inequality of the black school facilities and funding, segregated education in the state persisted in an environment of relative calm. In 1928, North Carolina's reputation for civil race relations, limited conflict, and thinly cloaked paternalism earned the state a visit from the British Colonial Office. The increasing cries for self-determination in the British colonies after World War I prompted this visit from British officials in search of educational models that would promote good labor and race relations to maintain the British Empire.[31] As this connection between worried authorities of two ruling nations illustrates, the deep interlocking roots of education, race relations, and struggles for freedom were developing throughout the world, from the crowded streets of Calcutta to the rural lanes of Hughes' Camden County.

Despite the state's good international reputation, black citizens in the state continued to fight for better educational opportunities in North Carolina. The disparities continued, however. In 1927, around the time Hughes first attended school, the average state expenditure for education was 19 cents a day for a white child and 11 for a black child; white teachers earned $800 a year, almost twice the salary of their black counterparts.[32]

In 1929, North Carolina's Institute for Research in Social Science and the School of Public Welfare surveyed one hundred North Carolina counties about the welfare of black children, including their education. Segregationists claimed that the state was meetings its obligations to provide "separate but equal" schooling. Yet a remark made at the same time by Camden's court clerk suggests that this was not the case. In fact, he objected to any education for blacks, saying: "'It makes them too biggety and they forget their places.'"[33] For a public official to make such a racist statement certainly raises doubts that North Carolina was even abiding by its legal obligation under *Plessy v. Ferguson* (1896) to provide "separate but equal" education for blacks.

"I Make More off of That There Five Acres Than I Do on a Hundred Acres"

From the 1920s onward, Camden County began a gradual process of consolidation of both the schools and the economy. The county gradually shifted away from truck farming and intimate economic interactions based on family and community relations toward the mechanized world of large corporate farming. Local historian Leary points out the gradual evolution of farming in the country, "I'd say, 1930s–40s, a lot of people in this area probably farmed 50–60 acres and could have made a living on it. By the late sixties that's gone. Because of modernized equipment you can do more. Today if a farmer doesn't have eight to twelve hundred acres he can't make it." As the area's economy moved toward mechanization and capital-intensive large farms, most small farms, facing severe competition, declined and many fell into bankruptcy. The schools, which had been scattered throughout the county, were consolidated in the early 1950s so that by the late 1960s when desegregation occurred, only three schools remained.

Hughes recounts his story of economic transformation in the face of the modern logic based on the assumption that increasing capital always yields increased profit. "You go broke (*chuckling*) in that big time farming. It don't take you long to be broke. We have about a hundred and ten acres. I mess with that and if I don't do any more off of that than pay taxes, I don't even worry about it. But it ain't any money out there in that big time farming…Anything that you can't set your price, they ain't going to let you make no money off it."

Hughes began working at the farmers' market in 1987, when he stopped large-scale farming. He laughs: "A lot of 'em, a lot of them boys are going out of business, big boys. If I am the middleman, I ain't going to set the price that the farmer can make a whole lot of money if I'm the one setting the price. So that's just the way it is." Hughes knows Camden farmers, his friends and neighbors, who have no control over prices, which are set by middlemen and fluctuate with shifts in the larger global markets. Farmers can't control the price of their inputs either (e.g., farm equipment, fuel, and seeds and fertilizer). They sink into debt under the relentless and merciless pressures of equipment manufacturers and banks.

Hughes explains how he avoids this trap: "When I set the price, I make more off of that there five acres than I do on a hundred acres. That looks strange, don't it? But I do. I set my own price on that. If I carry some collards out there, if I say fifty cent a pound, they give 'em to you. And my potatoes, I put my own price on it. I sell it. I usually go to the store. I look and see what their prices is. And I try to be about two or three cents under them. And then mine is fresh too. And theirs has done rode down the highway for weeks. So I sell it... But it looks strange how you can take a little bit of land and make more than you can on a big quantity (*laughing*). So I definitely make more off of that there five acres than I do a hundred acres. Then if you lose, you don't have a lot lost on that five acres."

Hughes demonstrates his pride in both his product—fresh and local— and his business process, carefully monitoring the market and setting his own price. He shares his resistive strategy against big growth: the return to small-scale market farming. Hughes has demonstrated inventiveness and ingenuity in the face of larger capitalist forces, showing that you can make do with less (i.e., a smaller farm) and still make money. In the face of consolidation, big farming, and the endless pursuit of higher tech solutions, Hughes scaled down, although as he points out, not quickly enough. "Back there in the seventies we made some money on the farm. But in the eighties come and there was no money to find. Wasn't none out there. I tried to stay in it as long as I could, and if I got out earlier, I had some, in the seventies all my bills were paid up. And I had about fifty thousand dollars in the bank that I hadn't spent. And the eighties come I spent that. And I had a tract of land, thirty acres, I got sixty thousand dollars for that and I spent that. I reckon I'd have kept right on going if it hadn't have been for my wife. And at that time I got old enough to get my social security. And I was spending that right back in there."[34]

Hughes remembered his dialogue with wife, showing how it moved him to make a major life change: "Because she tells me what it was. Getting into something like... that is just like alcohol."

"My wife asked me, said, 'You crazy?' (*We laugh*). I said, 'No. Why?' She said, 'Looks like you might be. Because all your peddling money going back in the farm.' I was peddling a little bit back then. She said, 'And all our social security money was going back in there.' And said, 'You ain't getting it back.' I said, 'No, we sure aren't getting it back.' So then I went to see a lawyer to see what, how could I quit because when you get in heavy debt, you can hardly quit. He told me how I could quit and I done it. I quit."

During a subsequent interview, when Hughes and I again sat around his kitchen table, I returned to the idea of the profitability of garden farming, curious to know if this form of downsizing to avoid bankruptcy was common practice in Camden. He replied, "Nooooo. There ain't many. Most of them want to go big. And I try not to tell them (We laugh). And you can get hurt bad when you go big. I know that in the seventies I had about fifty or sixty thousand dollars in the bank that I didn't need...had all my bills paid...And I reckon it's hard to quit...I said, 'Must have been crazy.' Because if you keep right on (he laughs)...you know...keep right on going deeper and deeper...But it was just 'bout like gambling for me. It gets in your blood. And you don't want to quit."

Hughes, echoing the comments of his wife, reflects on how hard it was to give up big farming. Yet Hughes didn't quit farming. Instead he restructured his relation to labor and land and continued without sacrificing what he loved to do. At age eighty-six he was still an active farmer, putting in close to a full day of work every day: "Well...I changed. I changed...I've been having pretty good luck after I quit that big mess. Wasn't nothing to me—working for the fertilizer folks, and the tractor folks, and I didn't have nothing for myself. And the tractor salesman don't mind calling you, 'When you going to come in?' And you ain't got nothing, no money to come in with (*he chuckles*). And it's a mess. It's a stress on you...I believe I'd be dead if I stayed out there."

Hughes remembers the "mess," in part to take pride in his choice to give up big farming and in part as a talisman against future temptation. By making the choice to stay small Hughes saved his farm, including one hundred acres he holds as an investment for the next generation. Hughes' story offers lessons on economies of scale that counter contemporary trends. In the modern industrial business world, there is a strong movement toward horizontal integration—specializing in a part of business and feeding into systems of other specialists and bigger operations (e.g., Wal-Mart). Hughes went vertical by going back to integrated market gardening. The challenge to this approach is the necessity of performing many time-consuming tasks in a limited time and space, while specialized competitors farm more extensively—and often more comfortably in air-conditioned cabs—with large, expensive laborsaving machines. Hughes' ability to sustain a vertically integrated small business was a result of his broad informal education: a strong work ethic; the social skills to relate to and barter with others; practical wit; and an engaging smile. By going in the opposite direction from the "big boys," he had to become his own agronomist, laborer, foreman, wholesaler, and retail merchant.

When a farmer scales down, his labor input goes up. Expansion relies on capital (often borrowed) and expensive laborsaving equipment. In return for his "sweat equity," Hughes can avoid debt and does not "work for the man": "Wasn't nothing to me. Working for the fertilizer folks, and the tractor folks, and I didn't have nothing for myself."

Hughes believes working for himself has another long-term benefit: "Well, yeah, I still don't have to take no medicine. I'm eighty-five years old and I still don't have to take no medicine. And that's a good thing. 'Cause most of the eighty-five-year-old people that I talk to, they got to take medicine. And I try not to get around them old folks that grumbling and stuff like that. 'Cause I'm scared some of it may rub off on me. 'Cause I know whole lot of folks, you say, 'How you doin?' 'I ain't doing good today. I feel bad (*in a moany tone*).' I get away from them folks (*he laughs*). Get away from them."

He continues with a smile: "Think positive. I think that that's a good thing to think positive. I think things won't happen to you as quick if you think positive. But you always think negative, some of those negative things going to rub off on you. I try to think positive. Anybody ask me how I feel, 'I'm doin good!' And I'm not going to say, 'I didn't rest good last night and I don't feel good today.' I don't even say it! And you get it programmed in your mind that you doin' all right and a lot of times you'll be doin' all right. I don't have to take no medicine and I hardly be sick and it's something that's programmed in my mind...You got to think positive." His daughter, sitting nearby, echoes Hughes, "Don't have time for negative thought. Too busy."

Barter Economy

Hughes' views on the shift from communal agrarian economy to a money-based capitalism make him a critic of so-called progress. He embraces past practices, long valued in rural, and particularly black, communities. Hughes' life outside of formal education prepared him for barter exchange; schools didn't teach him to be a good consumer or a reliable worker in a communal economy.

Hughes' barter system fills an often-unheralded position rarely taught in schools. It is different from both the "black" market economy (illegal transactions) and the white market economy (a legal form of capitalism that is rife with privileges for whites and discrimination against blacks). A white market economy incorporates paid labor, monetary transactions, and burdensome credit practices. It is subject to taxes and regulations. A black market economy transacts in illegal goods or labor, is not part of the gross national product, and evades government taxes and regulation.

Barter works as a gray market economy. It functions largely outside the capitalistic economy. Accordingly, Hughes remains less influenced by the dominant ideology of opportunity and competition. In a gray economy, goods and services are based on trade, not monetary compensation. People engaging in the gray market determine the terms and methods of exchanges.

Hughes explains: "It's changing hand. I carry them boys sausages up there and they give me any milk and orange juice and cream, and we make butter. They give me their stuff, and I give them what I got on the truck. I go to the farmers market three days a week. I'll stop by there if they need something from me and they do."

Hughes identifies barter with a gift economy that encompasses both products and human relations: "They give me what they got, and I give them what I got. That's just the way it worked about fifty years ago. Didn't nobody have any money and...we traded. If I had some molasses and you had sweet potatoes (*he smiles*), we would trade it. That's how folks, we got along. It would be a whole lot better if it would be like that now. But folks were friendlier back in those days. And they ain't no more friends now. If you ain't got no money, you ain't got no friends (*he begins to chuckle*) most of the time."

"But me and the fellows up there are good friends. We trade with each other. I go out there. I like meeting people too. That's what I like. That helps me. I love to talk and meet people. A lot of people come through that farmers' market and that gets right there in my heart. I enjoy it."

Hughes distinguishes between the human relationships that modern capitalism engenders and those characteristics of the past in which "changing hand" was not based on money. Fifty years ago, Hughes claims, people "got along"—in both the sense of getting what they needed to survive and of living in a friendlier, more fully interdependent community, based on intimate economic interactions rather that the anonymity of the supermarket aisle. In contrast, according to Hughes, such friendships are now scarce. Instead human relationships are calculated increasingly in the same market logic rewarded in graded classrooms—"If you ain't got money, you ain't got no friends."

Hughes develops friends through mutual exchange relationships. The ethics of reciprocity and friendship is an important part of a barter relationship. This relationship is based on collaboration, not competition and individual advancement. Doing things for other people is not entirely altruistic, but also comprises a form of insurance. It is a part of the social contract that sustains many rural black communities.

Farming enabled Hughes to support himself, his birth family, and later his wife and ten children. They subsisted on food that he grew or traded. Money rarely mediated these exchanges; one thing was just traded for another. He and his wife continue to live this way, spending about four or five hundred dollars a year on the few items they can't obtain through barter (e.g., sugar, flour, and cooking oil). Hughes' way of living is a political as well as an economic act that gives him more control over his life and his relationship to the prevailing modes of production.

For Hughes education is not a gateway to consumer capitalism. His teaching and learning builds on his everyday life and participation in the barter economy, similar to the vision advocated by Giroux that offers "historically and contextually specific knowledge, skills, and tools... to participate in, govern, and change, when necessary, those political and economic structures of power that shape their everyday lives."[35] As a parent, Hughes passed on this knowledge, philosophy, and work ethic to his children to ensure their success, not depending on formal education alone to secure a successful future for his children.

Learning Them to Work

Hughes did not delegate the responsibility to teachers or schools for all of his children's education. He saw the home as the place where children learn to work, to be disciplined, and to develop moral grounding. Hughes remembers: "We didn't have... there wasn't no money much along then [in the 1940s], but I'll tell you what, we always had a... made a right good living. We worked our kids. I let them go to school. When school was out, I didn't let them ride the bus back. I had a car up there waiting for them to bring them back to work (*laughter*). I think that helped."

He continues with pride: "I got four that got their master's, and I helped them with the college education, but I didn't help them with the master's. They got that working. I had one girl she finished college for a computer programmer, and she went to Durham. She couldn't find no job in computers, and she found a job laying tile. And she laid tile for about two months and a job come through. Most of the college people wouldn't have took no job laying tile (*we laugh*)... But I think you ought to learn them how to work and I did mine."

He speaks of the rewards of this family pedagogy: "And I tell you I don't want no closer family. Don't want no closer because they don't let us want for nothing. If anything, all of them have good jobs. All, we had ten. We had eight of our own, and her sister got burned out in New York, and we went and got two of hers and raised them. Neither one of them were old enough to go to school so we raised them. The whole ten of them got good jobs. And they don't let us want for anything. If they think we need something, they do it."

Hughes highlights that book learning is not enough. He ensured that all his children received good educations by teaching them first and foremost to work. He insisted to his children that manual and intellectual labor are both important and go hand in hand. Hughes instilled in his children a work ethic that drove both their educational and career successes. But Hughes' homespun pedagogy emphasized strategies for making a living, as opposed to the formal education model that has trained them to fit into the workforce. His pride in their achievements may be racially inflected—that his ten children have been able to navigate an oppressive, white capitalist system successfully through the skills he and his wife taught them.

The lessons have been carried to Hughes' grandchildren, particularly in terms of a barter economy. When I asked him how his children raised their children, he replied proudly: "She [his daughter] raised one of 'em just about how I was raised. That boy cut my grass for about four or five years and I would go out there and ask him, 'What, what do I owe you?' He said, 'I'm all right.' And I didn't rub nothing off on him. If he was all right, I was all right. And I told Brenda, 'You go ahead and have the papers fixed up. I want him to wash my car and cut my grass as long as I live. And when I'm dead, he gets the house.' And he gets the house! And it'll pay off pretty good."

Through this act Hughes continues a different kind of education and reward system in his family.[36] His passing the farm to his grandson contains echoes of one of the most important events in his own childhood. This broader tradition of vernacular knowledge both complemented and challenged the teachings of formal education.

Discipline on the Farm

"Let me tell you about the daughter we had that went to second grade. The teacher got ready to go to the bathroom and had to carry her to a teacher in another room. So one of my kids come home, one of the older ones, and was talking about it one night. I asked her, I said, 'Why do they have to carry her in a room with another teacher?' She said, 'She bad.' I said, 'Well, you go back and tell that teacher try her one more time.' I said, 'Then if she gives her any trouble, write me a note.' And I said, 'She won't never give that teacher no more trouble.'"

When he got the subsequent note, he had Betty come to him: "And I asked her, I said, 'Betty, do you know what your daddy is going to do to you?' She said, 'Yes sir.' I said, 'What?' 'Going to beat me.' I said, 'Nuh uh. Uh uh.' I said, 'I'm not going to beat you.' I said, 'But I'm going to better tell you what I'm going to do you before you do it again.' I said, 'I'm taking you to the woodpile, and take an ax, and cut your head right off.'"

We laugh. "Did she believe you?" I ask. "Yes, she believed it. And I'll tell you another thing. I think that you don't need to play with your kids when they're growing up. Don't play with them because they'll think you're partners with them (*he chuckles*). I didn't play with them, but I told them, I done it and I think they believed it. I think that girl believed. Let me tell you what she done now. She went right on through that little school."

With pride, Hughes recounts an encounter with Betty's teacher: "I met Miss Shaw downtown one day, one afternoon and she said, 'What did you do to her?' (*We laugh*). I said, 'Nothing, why?' Said, 'She was a changed girl' (*we laugh again*). That girl went on through that little school, went on through the high school, and she went on through college. She was so good in college they gave her a two-year scholarship in Ohio to get her master's (*he laughs*). She finished in about two years her master's." The operative secret of his disciplinary logic is that Betty had seen him cut chickens' heads off many times.

"I tell her now." Hughes adds with a chuckle. I say, "Girl, you wouldn't have never went through the school if I hadn't have stepped in there." As boastful and ironic as Hughes became in regaling his role in Betty's success, he quickly adds an economic perspective. Only half-joking and in a raucous sense, he adds: "I told her, 'You owe me some money!'" (*Another round of laughter*).

"At that time she was building house... built about a two-hundred-thousand dollar house. At that time where she built a house near—I remember looking at the man last night and he's on the television in trouble—Sugar Ray Robinson. She built a house in his neighborhood. The house would've been cheaper if she'd gotten in a poor neighborhood (*he laughs*). But she got in a neighborhood with some money in it (*continues to laugh*). Folks charge you for being in a neighborhood like that. So if she'd have made and build a house now, he done killed his reputation now (*we laugh*). The house would've been cheaper if she'd been in another neighborhood. She's in there good. And she would've never done it (*pause*) if I hadn't have gotten her in there and straightened her out. And didn't hit her a lick."

"And I don't think it's wise for parents to play with their kids. Do what you tell them you're going to do. Give 'em, make them work, and then don't go out there and play with them because they won't pay you much mind if you're playing with them (*he smiles*). Mine paid me some mind (*his tone is not authoritarian but slightly mournful as he looks back on that relationship, reflects on its strength, and marvels at its outcome*) ... mine paid me some mind."

Whatever Happened to Discipline?

In a subsequent conversation by which time Hughes felt more comfortable and obliged to "learn" me, I invite Hughes to reflect more broadly on school desegregation. In this context, he recalls the power of corporal punishment—with some laughter, some insistence, and a sense of strong disciplinary practices in black schools. Here Hughes argues with another daughter who was in and out of the kitchen (and who wished to remain unnamed) about a past and about a future that worries them both.

I asked him, "So, 1954 is when the Supreme Court said schools needed to be integrated but it wasn't, like your daughter was saying, until 1969 ... 15 years later ... that this actually started to happen in Camden. What it was like to live through that time and what did people think about integrating the schools?"

Hughes replied, "Some were thinking it ought to happen and some were thinking it shouldn't happen. And I really think that it mostly harmed the schools to do that. Cause at that time and after they integrated them, then they didn't want nobody to whip their kids. And that was the wrong thing to do. What they should have done is to hired somebody to whip them kids. Because if they do wrong they don't need to wait until they get home to get a spanking. I know that some of them people ain't qualified now to do it. But there are qualified people out there that can do it. And it ought to be the sort of the person that's respected for that."

His daughter interjected, "No they shouldn't have hired a person especially for it. The teachers should have been able to discipline them." Hughes counters, "Well, some of the teachers ain't qualified to do it. Some of them on drugs, and you know." She replied, "Well, that kind just don't need to be in there." He concurs, "No, don't need to be in there but how you going to know it until it's too late?" (*laughing*).

"It's been a mess, I tell you. That schools be getting in a mess now. They took things out that ought not to be took out. The whip, they took that out. They took pride out. And put guns in there. Guns in school there. But when my kids was going, they had pride. That was the first thing they done: But they took that away. But they going to be sorry if the world lasts fifty more years and keep on going down, they ain't going to be able to get a teacher."

While Hughes does not offer solutions, he does issue general warnings about the future of education. Based on conversations I have had with others in Camden, he is not alone in his convictions that discipline, respect, and pride are gone from the schools and that these problems began with desegregation. Although Hughes' praise of corporal punishment appears anachronistic when judged by contemporary school practices and social norms, a strong belief in discipline resonates with a common phrase in some families, "Spare the rod, spoil the child."

Hughes' apparent nostalgia for segregated schools mirrors that of a number of black students and educators across the South, who use story as a way to resist a diverse range of public memories about the pejorative descriptions of segregated black schools and the simplistic glorification of desegregation.[37] These stories serve as a way to critique contemporary education and the discriminatory process of desegregation, while also revaluing black education.[38] Like integration itself, the complex problems of discipline, morale, and violence in schools have not been resolved. "It's been a mess," Hughes insists.

"Do Whatever Is Right. And Things Will Fall Right in Place for You"

Hughes continues with his propensity to help others by parables and stories: "If it don't help but one than it be worth my time..." As an example of the rewards of doing right, Hughes finishes the story of his purchase of some family land from his father.

"About six or seven years ago I was offered a half a million dollars for the land. So if you do right I'm a living witness good things will come to you. I've never did thought at that time that farm would sell for a half million dollars. So I reckon it would probably sell for a million now because the road runs through there. I sold the right of way through there for the road to run through the farm now, so it would sell for a million dollars now. But if you do right, things will come to you. Fall right in place."

He turns to me: "And that's a good lesson for you young'uns (*he laughs*) because you young. Do to other people like you wish to be done by and everything will fall right in place for you. And it did with me. I done business with no education. I've talked to people. I know people thought that I had a college education, but I dealt with all the Farm Fresh stores. I furnished them with watermelon, cantaloupes and potatoes, all the Farm Freshes had about ten or twelve of their stores. Earl's Supermarkets, I furnished them and S & R, and I know them boys probably thought I had a college education. Didn't have it."

While the avenue to advancement through education may have closed early in his life, his common sense, practical knowledge, and way of treating others provided Hughes with what he needed to make a good living. He prides himself on doing business with "them boys" [larger retail companies]—navigating the complex wholesale farm business without a middleman.

Hughes does not credit his own ingenuity and intelligence alone for his success, but instead looks to his faith and morality in helping him learn what he wanted to know when he needed to know it. Hughes arrives, late in our conversation, at the story of how he did eventually return to school.

"But the Lord gave me what it took to go onward...I liked to go to Sunday school. Sitting up there, couldn't read as good as the other folks. I asked the Lord, I said, 'Lord if you'll just help me to read your word' and he did. I don't have to ask nobody now what a word is. I was seventy-two years old when I started school [enrolled in a local college]. My wife told me, said, 'All your young'uns are grown now and gone. What do you need it for now?' I said, 'Because I want it.' And I went back to school, seventy-two years old and I don't have to imagine what a word is. I can look at it and tell what it is (*he laughs*)."

"So everything just fell right in place for me. The school, they fell right in place for me. I was lucky enough to have a Sunday school teacher. He's my teacher and they let me carry the Bible to school every night. And me and him, before we do anything else, we'd read the Bible first step. The Lord just put everything right in place for me. And it will, will for you too (*he laughs*) if you do what's right. These older fellows, they've already got things in place for them. But you've got a looooong time to go. Take my advice. Do whatever is right. And things will fall right in place for you. It did me...I go four nights a week. And I'm not going for no job...I don't need no education to live with" (*he laughs*).

Hughes returned to the lesson of "doing right" in one of our later conversations: "It will pay off for you. If it pay off for me, it will sure pay off for someone else (*We laugh*). 'Cause I'm dumb!" I know he is *playing* me for a fool. He laughs. "Nooooooo! I don't think so," I respond playfully. He counters, "And if it pays off for a dumb person, it ought to pay off for somebody that's got some sense." "I don't believe you," I said. "I think you have a whole bunch of sense." "Well," he responds with certainty, "I know how to get along in this world. I know how to treat people. And when you do that, you 'bout done what you need to do."

If school officials, teachers, and parents had followed farmer Charlie's ethic on "how to treat people," I believe the process of school integration in Camden County would have evolved more easily toward Professor Jacquelyn Hall's vision of an "equitable, democratic, multiracial, and multiethnic world."[39] Instead school desegregation became a unilateral process of integration into white forms of knowledge, white teachers, and white symbols (e.g., white school colors and mascots), largely silencing pedagogies cultivated in segregated black schools.

Mr. Charlie's narratives highlight connections between capitalism, education, and white privilege, frayed by locally resistant memories and community practices—from barter relationships to his own success at avoiding overwhelming debt and successfully competing with supermarkets without a formal education. His memories challenge the hegemony of graded education—characterized by separate classrooms for each grade, competition between individuals, and market-oriented pedagogy. These stories also reveal a broader pedagogical practice of memory "as a form of critique that addresses the fundamental inadequacy of official knowledge in representing marginalized and oppressed groups along with...the deep-seated injustices perpetuated by institutions that contain such knowledge."[40]

At the age of eighty-six, Hughes took evening classes at the College of the Albemarle and farmed five acres. Selling the produce he grows at the Elizabeth City farmers' market, he earned more income than he did previously farming one hundred acres. Hughes' story challenges the capitalist-education system as we know it. He succeeded by not buying the dominant capitalist "bigger is better" "progress" narrative that drives the dominant economic and educational systems. Through stories, he teaches his children, grandchildren, and near and distant listeners to do the same.

Hughes' narratives of formal and informal education highlight the ways capitalist economics are inherent in this white pedagogy and dominant forms of schooling. White pedagogy simultaneously reinforces racial systemic inequality and buttresses hegemonic white power. Pedagogy, often presented as color-blind,[41] is "a form of political and cultural production deeply implicated in the construct of knowledge, subjectivities, and social relations." It reifies white themes and disguises fundamental cultural and social biases through the rationale of meritocracy.[42] Yet whiteness is neither natural nor normal; it is a socially constructed set of relational processes that secures privileges of power through property, spatial relations, political control, and economic practices.[43] Whiteness also involves language and ideologies that benefit whites while systematically oppressing others.[44] The designation also involves ways of thinking, acting, and knowing. White pedagogy dominates our schools, as it has done so since desegregation when white pedagogies and educational practices gained ascendancy for black and white children.

Segregated black schools focused on black history and often taught through culturally based maxims. Integrated schools conventionally teach a white history, celebrating a narrow segment of the population and reifying canonical knowledge. This white pedagogy crafts a larger cultural narrative of white accomplishment and power.

Hughes does not tell "majoritarian" stories.[45] Such stories come from "a legacy of racial privilege" and make this privilege look like the natural order of things.[46] These stories sustain white pedagogy. His memory performances actively create alternative narratives to many majoritarian stories about segregation, desegregation, and the glories of capitalism. Alternative pedagogies and memories can resist the powerful cultural forces of individualism and capitalism that shape our contemporary educational institutions and perpetuate racial segregation. His narratives are a form of resistance to white dominance—passing on the ongoing value of labor and relational obligations to his children and grandchildren.[47]

The style of Hughes' homespun narratives is fascinating, but they are not unique. Vernacular stories and parables permeate rural black communities where strong family ties persist. These stories constitute a part of a larger national experience of how white philosophy has dominated formal education and lost the values of vernacular knowledge from virtually all oppressed communities.[48] While people of color have been teaching outside of white pedagogy for centuries, their ways of teaching and learning resistance to the status quo and dominance have not been included in the integrated curriculum. School desegregation was one of the first national attempts to address substantively the issues of race, public education, and equality. Yet the integration shaped dominant knowledge systems to conform to the white ideologies of education and the economy.

Figure 2 Alex Leary at home. Photo by Alan Ternes.

CHAPTER 2

"Wait a Minute...I'm a White"

On May 31, 1955, a little more than a year after the *Brown* ruling, the Supreme Court in *Brown II* turned down the National Association for the Advancement of Colored People's request for immediate and complete school desegregation in favor of a more gradual approach. The Warren Court delegated the task of deciding the pace of desegregation to local federal judges, requiring only that "a prompt and reasonable start" to desegregation begin "with all deliberate speed." In the nation, in North Carolina, and in Camden, this ruling resulted in what Peter Irons in *Jim Crow's Children* (2002) called, "too much deliberation and not enough speed."[1]

Camden County went with the national reactionary tide that did whatever tactically possible to evade the de facto implementation of school desegregation. In the state both white power brokers and popular sentiment opposed school desegregation. In 1955 the North Carolina General Assembly and Governor Luther H. Hodges backed the education committee recommendation that:[2]

> The mixing of races forthwith in the public schools throughout the state cannot be accomplished and should not be attempted. The schools of our state are so intimately related to the customs and feelings of the people of each community that their effective operation is impossible except in conformity with community attitudes. The committee feels that a compulsory mixing of the races in our schools on a statewide basis and without regard to local conditions and assignment factors other than race would alienate

public support of the schools to such an extent that they could not be operated successfully.

In addition to supporting the committee report, the General Assembly passed a resolution to the Supreme Court denouncing the *Brown* decisions.

Despite North Carolina's initial reactionary stance, Tar Heel politicians and businessmen alike realized that the inflammatory rhetoric used by some southern states could "harm the state's reputation for racial moderation, forestall new economic development, and invite judicial intervention in the operation of the schools."[3] As a result, North Carolina, as it had historically done, took a more "moderate" approach to race relations and education. North Carolina won national acclaim as a beacon of moderation as its white leaders promoted a code of civility that put a premium on peaceful race relations and managed incremental change—a policy called the "progressive mystique," by some skeptics.[4] This strategy of gradualism resulted in an integration rate of North Carolina schools even lower than the diehard states of Alabama, Mississippi, and Arkansas.[5]

Of the number of obstructionist plans attempted, the Pearsall Plan, named after North Carolina's speaker of the House Thomas J. Pearsall, was most significant. In July 1956, in an extra session of the General Assembly convened to deal with the issue of school desegregation, the assembly adopted the Pearsall Plan. This legislation basically stated that parents not wishing to send their children to school with children of another race were not required to do so. A legal tactic included in the plan shifted the power to implement desegregation to the local school boards. This was in step with the national strategy to avoid federal class-action suits. Like many rural, conservative counties across the South, the all-white Camden school board welcomed this maneuver that gave them control over the pace of implementing desegregation.

The *Greensboro Daily News* wrote in an editorial supporting the legislation: "North Carolina wants no violence and North Carolina wants no abandonment of its public school system. The path is tortuous and narrow. But with moderation, goodwill, understanding, and wise, sound, and far-seeing statesmanship, we can and shall tread it safely."[6] The Pearsall Plan became an amendment to the state constitution by popular referendum in September 1956.[7]

Despite the outspoken resistance to desegregating with "all deliberate speed," moderate Terry Sanford ran on a gubernatorial platform that made public education his top priority. Sanford publicly supported *Brown v. Board of Education* and sent his children to integrated schools. In 1960 North

Carolinians elected Terry Sanford in his race against segregationist I. Beverly Lake. Despite the sanctimonious words of editorial comments, and state legislation, and the election of a moderate leader, the foot dragging throughout the South (of which North Carolina was particularly adept) did not go unnoticed at the federal level. A decade after the *Brown* decision, Supreme Court Justice Thurgood Marshall remarked on the slow national progress, "Desegregation obviously has not proceeded as fast as we would have liked."[8] After claiming in March 1954 that "come hell or high water we'll be free by '63," he acknowledged a decade later that it will take "at least a generation to bring about any social change" in segregated schools.[9] In the South, a decade after *Brown,* only one in a hundred black children went to an integrated school; in moderate North Carolina, the rate was one black child in two hundred.[10]

The paucity of results brought about increasing nationwide pressures for de facto integration. In 1960 in Greensboro, North Carolina, four college students began with a lunch counter sit-in that quickly spread throughout the South. In 1963, before two hundred and fifty thousand marchers for civil rights, Rev. Martin Luther King became an icon of the movement with his moderate but inspirational "I Have a Dream" speech. With the passage of the Civil Rights Act of 1964 and the Elementary and Secondary Education Act of 1965, the Department of Health, Education, and Welfare (HEW) gained the power to penalize segregated schools by withholding federal funds. The growing governmental pressure for desegregation created a backlash that confirmed some of the segregationists predictions of trouble—bombs in churches, police attacks on marchers, and increased Klan activities. But the march toward integration went on.

Faced with increasing pressures and financial threats, North Carolina joined other southern states in a last ditch effort to circumvent desegregation by adopting "freedom of choice" plans in 1965. The early steps of de facto desegregation, during the freedom of choice period (1965–1969), began with the token desegregation of teachers and school choice for students. In practice, this meant a mandated exchange of a few black and white teachers. Not a single white child chose to go to an all-black school in Camden, or in the rest of North Carolina.[11] Fewer than ten black children elected to go to Camden's white schools.[12] Crosses were burned in front of the homes of three of the black children whose families made this choice.[13]

Alex Leary became one of the first white teachers in Marian Anderson School not because of his free choice—but in order to meet the mandated requirements to keep federal funding flowing. His token presence at Marian

Anderson was a last ditch foot-dragging effort by the superintendent and school board to forestall full desegregation. Leary was an unlikely candidate for the small vanguard of Camden's white teachers who made the first substantive move toward the desegregation of the county's schools.

Leary would have been expected to drag his feet when faced with racial integration because he hails from an influential Camden County family that still speaks with pride of its Confederate roots. He grew up playing ball on the dusty roads of Old Trap, one of the county's oldest communities. Old Trap owed its past growth in part to its borders on Albemarle Sound, which encouraged contact with the outside world, and even trade with the West Indies.[14] Leary describes "The way Old Trap got its name...All the men would carry their farm goods—a bunch of potatoes or whatever—to the wharf and bring other goods back. In the way back they would stop at a local store and tavern and stay so dern late the women began to call it 'the trap.' And that tradition went on until five years ago." The name stuck, the decaying store building still stands, and a few posts of the pier where the trading ships docked still protrude from the briny water.

On hunting and fishing adventures with his brothers, the young Leary explored the rivers, creeks, and forested lands of Camden. As a member of a long-standing white family, he moved freely throughout the county. He knows the territory and the white history of Camden like the back of his hand. Traveling on boats, evading water moccasins, Leary's childhood adventures taught him not only survival, but also to be a better local historian.

In 1965 after graduating from the all-white Camden High School in 1961 and segregated Eastern Carolina University, Leary returned to his family farmland in Old Trap to teach at Camden High School. He then became one of the first white teachers to work in an all-black school for one year, until all schools were desegregated. He worked as a history and physical education teacher for his entire career. In retirement he volunteers one day a week at the Dismal Swamp Canal Welcome Center, competes in a basketball league, participates in living history events with students, and, when his schedule allows, joins in Civil War reenactments. The past plays a vital role in Leary's present.

Besides his knowledge of the land, Leary is renowned for his collection and interpretation of historical artifacts. He is the muse for these mute objects—the self-anointed interpreter. These relics work as bridges to a more distant past and to a particular memorialization (with a markedly militaristic bent). Nowhere is this more apparent than in Leary's den, where our first conversations took place. The wood-paneled room is lined with guns (most of them properly marked with small plaques) from the American Revolution to the Civil War period, as well as sport shooting guns. There are bullets from the Civil War, and Confederate and Camden money mounted in a large display case, upon which he rests the remote control for his big-screen television. He often sits there, where his favorite pastimes are chatting with his buddies and watching the History Channel and Duke basketball games. Behind Leary's blue armchair stands a frightening mannequin dressed in a Confederate Civil War Militia uniform.

For the two hours of our initial meeting, I toured the collection in his den and two outside structures: a red shed with a "Leary Branch Museum" sign that contains memorabilia from World War I and World War II; and a one-room house he built called "the Leary Buzzard Bay home" that is part colonial-style home and part storage area. Leary regularly packs his collections—battle helmets, war posters, mess kits, uniforms, and other memorabilia—into his van and takes them to schools, where his presentations encourage the next generation of local historians. As often occurs in oral histories, this time spent on seemingly unrelated topics allowed us to build the rapport necessary for a Yankee from New York City to have a meaningful discussion on race relations with him.

The First White Teacher in a Black School

In the spring of 1967, when Camden County could forestall government-mandated desegregation no more, Leary attended a faculty meeting that changed his life: "The administration said we're going to send a white teacher to the black school. I'll be honest with you. Most people did not want to go. They asked for volunteers. I think nobody volunteered. They are good people, but would you want to be the only one in the black community?" Like all white teachers at that meeting, Leary did not volunteer at that point. "So Superintendent Burgess said he was going to send his wife [a teacher] over to the black school."

But the thought of a white woman being forced by her husband to teach in an all-black school bothered Leary: "I went to him. I said, 'Mr. Burgess, don't do that.' I said, 'Let me go because I don't mind.'" For a white person to volunteer to teach at a black school at that time required a rationale acceptable to most white people in the community. But, Leary had a gallant excuse: "I thought it would be better for a man to be over there than a woman." Superintendent Burgess accepted his offer.

Leary volunteered out of chivalry rather than as an advocate of racial integration. Saving a white woman from going to a black school could be seen as a respectable response to a difficult situation. This chivalry fits into a long-standing, well-respected Southern tradition. As the only volunteer to teach at the black school, Leary had felt the scrutiny of the white community: "I mean I got some criticism...I took a lot of lip, you know...some of 'em done it in jest. But some of them were kindly serious.[15] Not fellow teachers, but people in the community. I did get a lot of comment. But I remember one guy told me one time [sarcastically], 'We're going to put a statue of you being the first white teacher in the black school.'" As a historian, Leary knew this type of symbolic memorialization was intended to stigmatize him. He had grown accustomed to fellow whites' sarcasm toward his role as one of the first bridges between white and black education.

His buddies had teased him about his new job, "How do you eat in the cafeteria with all those blacks preparing your food? Do you eat with the same forks?" Leary, knowing the realities of the segregated South, retorted wryly, "When you go to a restaurant, guess who prepares most of your meals for you?" In replies to his friends' critiques veiled in humor, Leary responds in jest by pointing out his friends' faulty logic. Master of the double-edged sword of humor himself, he felt both edges of his friends' sword acutely.

Yet unlike advocates of desegregation, Leary did not fear any violent repercussions, which others faced during the early moves toward desegregation. He never feared for his safety: "Oh! Never felt that! Well, I was bigger than a lot of people and I was well respected in the community, and my father was the County Commissioner, and everything." His stature made him an ideal candidate. As he recalls now, "Especially during that time period, it was a big decision of mine. But I always told people that it's one decision that I'm always glad that I made." As Leary pointed out, "I know that it probably was tougher on that black teacher going to the white school than it was on me."

The Sound of the Paddle

Early in the fall semester of 1968, white history teacher Alex Leary felt he was beginning to know his black students and his new setting. But one day early in the fall semester of 1968 he had cause to doubt his understanding. His students, especially the boys, appeared restless—for reasons he couldn't understand.

Then, suddenly, the voice of black principal Whittier Crockett Witherspoon on the public announcement system broke into his classroom: "He said,

'Can I have your attention?'" "The kids in my class did like this." Leary noticed a number of boys in his classroom strangely bow their heads. They knew what was coming. An ominous silence on the public address system, and then the sound of: "Whomp!" A second "whomp!" from the paddle. A third "whomp and that kid hollering out" with a painful cry: the principal was disciplining a student in his office and he wanted all the other students to hear the punishment.

Leary laughs, "I guarantee you it made an impression on the students over there. They knew what happened and he was being punished, and the whole school knew he was being punished. I want to tell you one thing. It was quiet in that school for a while. You didn't have to worry about a student saying, 'Yes, sir or no, sir' after that...I think what that student...I think he had been disrespectful to a woman teacher somewhere in that school, and Witherspoon put the example out there." The power of this incident, as it has traveled across generations, can also be heard in the recollections of those staff and students that attended the segregated Marian Anderson School the year before full desegregation. As his white successor Billy Revelle told me, "Mr. Witherspoon used to spank boys over the PA system." But many students and their parents remember Witherspoon's disciplinary actions as part of his dedication to educational excellence.

Leary was beginning to learn something the kids already knew—that strict discipline was a powerful element of black education. This incident of paddling over the intercom stands out in Leary's memory in a marked contrast to discipline in the white segregated schools where he had previously taught. He marvels, "It just, it just hit me, you know. I've never seen that done before." Leary considers the implications of this disciplinary action, "If that happened in a white school or in an integrated school today, the man would've been crucified. He'd lose his job and everything probably, but that was a different time period." On the contrary, many black parents approved of Witherspoon's disciplinary approach: when one of their children was disciplined in school, they would spank him again at home to make sure the lesson was not lost—young people should not waste their educational opportunities.

The Union and the Buffalos

Leary guided me along the main highway version of white history. His stories did not include the unpaved side roads and cul-de-sacs of black communities, the sharecropper and migrant laborers' life experiences, and the important influences of the black churches and other black culture. Yet, as I returned numerous times to visit him (including an eight-hour trip from one tip of the county to the other), I was struck by how much of the local white history of Camden County he did show me. As we became friends, he and his wife treated me more like one of their children than as a visiting researcher.

This was about the time Leary realized that even though I was a Yankee, I was not a damn Yankee. Simply put, Leary's definition of a Yankee is a Northern visitor to Camden, while "damn Yankees" are the ones who come to live in Camden: "They are the ones that come down here and stay and tell everyone else what to do" (*we laugh*).

As we moved beyond our prejudices, Leary began to share with me some of Camden's hidden history and geography, which is invisible to newcomers, but remains evident to residents, such as the boundary between Old Trap and Shiloh. As we drove from Old Trap into Shiloh, Leary pointed out, "We're crossing the line now. Used to be blacks and Camden residents from outside Old Trap knew not to come down here after dark." This was one of my first hints of Camden's racist geography of fear. Leary continues, "I heard that a black man once went into the Old Trap bar after dark some time ago. They beat him and threw him out onto the street. He never came back." These symbolic boundaries still define the realities of Camden residents, as few black families live farther south than Shiloh.

As I traveled through Camden County, I became increasingly bound to it. Leary's stories about the past, as far back as the Civil War, peopled every corner of his county. While this history seems far removed from school desegregation, the Civil War remains a strong presence in Leary's life and it is part of the powerful folklore that continues to feed the roots of struggles over race relations and social change. Leary, a walking treasure trove of stories of places throughout the county, filled the landscape with ghosts from the past, and I found myself wanting to trudge through the swamps to find the secret hideaway of the Confederate sympathizers.

"We had a lot of people in this area [specifically Old Trap] that also joined the Union Army and they were known as the Buffalos.[16] You ever heard that?...The [black] Buffalo soldiers were out west later on, but these [white] Buffalos here were Union sympathizers and joined the Union Army. But they were not liked. So we had a Civil War within the Civil War. Had neighbors fighting against each other some time. It was mostly in the lower end of this county, right here. We had one man, who got demoted by the Confederate Army [known locally as the Guerillas], and he got so mad he joined the Union Army. His name was Peter T. Burgess...that's a big name around here...But this Peter T. Burgess joined the Union Army and was part of the First North Carolina Volunteers, the Union regiment. A lot of southerners, they didn't get along. They'd attack each other and kill each other sometimes."

Leary tells the story of Tom Jones, a Guerilla who killed a white baby. "Well, the story goes...they went into the Buffaloes' home one night, and they were killing everybody in the house. But when they went to one room there was a little baby in the crib. One guy said, 'Uh-uh. We aren't killing this baby.' Well, this Tom Jones, they claimed he went in there with a knife and took the baby up and stabbed and killed the baby. Now that's, that's a story to tell," he says, raising his eyebrows and underscoring the horror of the story. He adds, "I don't know if this is true, but so many people know this story." In this sense, whether or not it is true, the story told and retold, remembered in the community, exerts a powerful force on the way the community thinks about itself and its traumatic past filled with internecine warfare.[17] The white segregationists have long used fear and violence to maintain dominance and power in community struggles over racial equality. This tactic continued through the period of school desegregation.

Tom Jones fought through the war and after that was a highly respected person. "[He] had a right good-sized farm, but they always claimed that the child-killing bothered him. The day he was about to die, maybe he was thinking about it. I don't know what he was thinking. But he told them, 'The devil is down there. The devil is going to get me! Don't you bury me in the ground!' So he got his family to promise to bury him above ground. See that grave right here? (*pointing to a photograph of a church with a solitary tomb in the foreground*). He's the one that killed that baby...Tom Jones is. He was the one that killed that Buffalo family and killed the baby. But when he was dying, that's when he started hallucinating, saying the devil was going to get him. He's buried at our church. This is our church that we have down here" (*proudly pointing out*), "and he's buried above the ground."

Through the story Leary suggests how this horrific past touches the present, and then begins using his favorite strategy to bring the listeners away from the horror: "And what was so ironic to me, this became the main place for kids to play at. Because when we got out of church, this was home base. We played King of the Mountain! And we all played on Tom Jones' grave!"

"The legend was Tom Jones...you know I told you he killed this baby...When you go down to Tom Jones' grave, wait until that sun hits the trees."

I imagine the tomb at sunset.

"And you knock on the side of that grave and say, 'Uncle Tom, Uncle Tom what are you doing in there?'" He pauses.

I wait.

"And within thirty seconds he'll say 'nothing.'"

My mouth is agape.

He takes a dramatic pause. "Cause that's true," he assures me in a serious tone.

My eyes are wide open. "You can wait all day long, and he'll still say nothing."

Finally, I catch on and burst into laughter. "You had me there for a minute," I concede. I release another round of laughs, relieved by a reprieve from the gruesome stories of war. I am struck momentarily by the complex undercurrents of Civil War that weave through contemporary discussions of desegregation and the North and South. Leary's stories reveal how segregation—maintained by such horrendous acts as brutal whippings, mutilation, and even lynching—is part of a larger violent history. Just a few generations earlier, in the Civil War, whites fought for different social orders with similar grizzly and inhumane acts.

At the same time, Leary's humor changes my simplistic Yankee interpretation of race and the Civil War. His memories contain intra-racial not inter-racial fighting. Leary, a master storyteller and comedian, comes out of these horrible stories by pulling a joke on me. He takes pleasure in this strategic ambiguity. As a historian, he recalls some of what is left out of *history*, the stories one never reads in the schoolbooks. He brings to life the struggle between history, searching for the *truth* of the past, and story, which regardless of its factual nature may be more real to the life of the community. Leary becomes what one scholar has described as a "teller of silly tales which of course no kind of history keeps track of," and shows me "the pleasures and entrapments of lived history."[18]

In the past, I had easily distanced myself from the complexities of race relations, historical injustice, and contemporary social and economic inequities. As a liberal northerner, I simply embraced the commonplace ideas that the Civil War is about slavery and the Confederate flag is about racism. That was the end of the story. Coming from the North, I thought somehow that I was born on the right side of history. I accepted this narrative on blind faith, passively, as a kind of birthright. I attributed a similar blind faith to those Southerners still committed to supporting the Confederacy. Then came Camden County—Leary's love of the South, of his rough and tumble Old

Trap, and his home with more signs of the confederacy than I had ever seen—which made me confront my own simplistic rendering of these deeply entrenched issues of region, race relations, and historical interpretation.

I found my interpretation and the official historical views both failed to capture many elements of the struggle—particularly the human ones. This also became evident when I examined school desegregation. I possessed high school textbook understandings of integration—as a Southern phenomenon, a fait accompli, and a social change achieved primarily through legal edict. While the grand narrative I learned generally reflected the white public memory of the time, I also accepted a one-sided look at the desegregation story that lacked any substantive understanding of what the experience meant to white communities. Both the Civil War and school desegregation battles were fought differently and took on varied meanings in different local communities. I also began to understand that absolving the North from the maintenance of a racist past limits our potential to learn from this history in which we are all implicated.

Segregated Lives

Like many members of small Southern agricultural counties, Leary grew up knowing more than a lily-white world. Working side-by-side on the farm, and on boating and fishing trips, he had close informal contact with blacks all the time. He played with black children and enjoyed interracial childhood friendships—outside of school hours. He recalls one experience in the early 1950s: "I remember when I went to eat one time, you know, we had a section for the blacks to eat. I had a friend of mine who was black. We went to town. When we'd go to eat, he'd go in the black section. I'd go in the white section. We'd get our hot dogs, and we'd go outside and sit and eat, but we couldn't do it inside." As Leary recalls the lengths to which he and his friend went to eat together, he begins to realize how blinded he'd been to accept what he didn't realize were the illogics of segregation. "That just shows you. But I really didn't think all that much about it, but it was idiotic when you think about it."

Leary appreciates the irony of this situation because we can see in hindsight how ridiculous it was. Yet like any good historian, Leary knows not to judge the past only through the lens of the present. He must also explain his lived experience of the time. In this case, sardonic humor becomes an analytical tool for him to reach a kind of peace with a segregated past that haunts all of Camden's members—a peace necessary to continue to live in a relatively closed community like Camden. Using humor to explain the past eases the way for a more integrated present.

Leary did not simply accept segregation. He provides insight into ways people got around it, in this instance by eating outdoors where the patterns of segregation were not enforced. The tactical ease with which these two boys avoided the cultural scripts requiring blacks and whites to eat separately points to reasons that many parents and school administrators were quick to oppose integration of children in schools. His story reminds me that children can undo barriers adults have worked hard to construct.

Although Leary graduated high school seven years after the *Brown* decision, he still attended a segregated school because Camden, unlike some North Carolina counties, had delayed integration. He remembers his experience at the time, "You come home, you might play with some of the blacks, but you didn't ride the school bus with 'em. It's so long ago I can't remember all of it, but I can think back... When I was in high school, I'll be very honest with you, I did not go to town with black students or anything. As a young'un I remember playing with black friends and all that."

By the time students entered high school and adults began to fear their children's more intimate—even sexual—relations, the early childhood friendships that transgressed societal norms of segregation were tightly restricted. Social segregation persisted in the integrated school. Until 1978, Camden High School crowned two sets of homecoming kings and queens, one black, one white, but never an interracial couple. Social segregation was strengthened as children became adolescents, perpetuating de facto segregation well into de jure school desegregation.

Separate but Unequal

Leary's experience as a teacher and long-time white Camden resident did not prepare him for the existing inequality of school segregation: "Truly it wasn't equal because when they integrated the schools, I was the first white teacher in the all-black school. It opened my eyes." In certain ways, his pioneering entry into Marian Anderson showed him first-hand the privileges whiteness provided, those he had long taken for granted.

Soon after his arrival at the school, the black students asked Leary, the renowned athlete, why they didn't have a football team. Leary explained the persistent inequalities to his black students: "And I was very honest with them.

I said, 'Because the white population bought the lights, spent the money, and established a field.' Where the government didn't do it. And being honest, 'The black population didn't have the money to do that. But as the government begins to put more money, schools could do more.' See, a lot of the time the state didn't supplement all that stuff…The school was almost as good as Camden School, but they did not have the baseball teams and the football teams that the whites had, because a lot of that had to be financed locally. The blacks didn't have the money. And I understood that."[19] His students, however, did not.

They did not accept as natural the economic imbalances between the black and white "populations." They had long lived with less—such as the hand-me-down textbooks, discarded from the white school with pages torn out. But this was the first time they had a white teacher, who represented white authority, in their school to account for these disparities and they wanted answers from the white community. This was one of the first times the children ever had a dialogue with a white person.

Leary told his students that the reason for these inequities was basically economic. The schools and black and white communities functioned within certain economic and competitive frameworks. When they asked about the football team, he told them about the relative purchasing power of the two communities. From this perspective, the inequalities apparent to both Leary and the students (more than a decade after *Brown*'s decree that the opportunity of education "must be made available to all on equal terms") were neither the result of the indifference of the greater Camden community nor that community's responsibility. Leary framed the differences as reflections of apparently fixed disparities in economic resources. Yet this economic equation was simplistic and deterministic. Moreover, it made black parents and the black community seem inherently unworthy of equal facilities.

Leary did not discuss broader institutional power imbalances within the segregated South. In his discussions with his students at that time, Leary, a celebrated athletic competitor, didn't question the unequal rewards of competition as a norm. It may be that he even saw the black and white populations in Camden as separate teams without noting that the historically winning team played by different rules.

While Leary distinguished poor blacks from wealthier whites, he ignored the complicating status of poor whites. In the logic of his oral history, he did not suggest that poor whites shouldn't be entitled to the use of the football fields. In the end, the universalizing category of "whiteness" trumped his economic analysis. A more considered economic analysis would align impoverished whites and blacks. This memory reveals that despite a common rhetoric of economic determinism employed by many white people to justify white privilege, racial lines were powerful determinants of the quality of education without consideration of intra-racial economics. The rising tide of economic and educational dominance lifted the boats of all white children. This is where the hypocrisy of "separate but equal" revealed itself. Not only did black students in Marian Anderson High School not have a football team or athletic fields, but they also had inferior facilities and hand-me-down textbooks.

A Tragic Day

Later in that school year, Leary began to feel more at home as his relationships with his students strengthened and his ability to understand them improved. Again he stood in his classroom and Witherspoon addressed the entire school over the PA system. He confirmed and remarked on the tragic assassination of Dr. Martin Luther King Jr. The school was silent. Overhearing the students' initial remarks, Leary not only saw the event through their eyes, but he empathized with them.

"I remember some of the blacks said, 'Let's kill those whites.'" Initially Leary shared his students' feelings until the literal implications of what they were saying hit him: "I got to thinking. Wait a minute. I'm a white." We both laugh. I am struck by the whiteness we shared here. Our white laughter washed over concerns for personal safety and race.

He continues: "You know, I had to tell people when I taught there, I did not see myself as white or black. And I did not see—that's going to sound like a lie—but I did not see them as black. They were kids to me. They were my students. But it did make me think I was white that day."

Leary's narrative reflects the privilege of not seeing himself "as white or black." As Ruth Frankenberg writes, "whiteness, as a set of normative cultural practices, is visible most clearly to those it definitively excludes and those to whom it does violence. Those who are securely housed within its borders usually do not examine it."[20] On that extraordinary day, when the tables turned ever so slightly, Leary reflected upon the world of whiteness within whose borders he had so comfortably resided. He began to become aware of being white when he saw the world, for a moment, through the eyes of his black students.

"I remember the principal called me and he said, 'Everything will be all right.' But by that time I'm glad it happened in April rather than the first of the year because, see, I got to know a lot of the kids and got to be friends with them and all the teachers I got to know well by that time." As a teacher and coach, he had already established personal relationships with the students and staff.

The Game

A shared love of basketball brought Leary closer to the people at Marian Anderson, forging a common bond with the black community. "I guess I fit in because I played basketball. And I brought my [adult] team to play the black high school..." While he might have seen this interracial basketball game as an informal act of integration at the time, from his story we learn that he could not have predicted the magnitude of the event. If anyone had predicted it, it probably never would have happened. The story gains what oral historian Pamela Grundy attributes to many stories of integrated athletic competitions at the time—"a near-miraculous aura."[21]

"Black against a white—we were *all* white. They were *all* black. We were all older. They were high school boys. So I told my team, 'cause I had an independent team. I said, 'We'll play y'all.' All the boys on my team they said, 'Oh, we'll go play them.' I said, 'We'll beat 'em fifteen or twenty points.'"

Leary took his white team, part of an adult league in which he had a leadership role, to compete against the black high school players of Marian Anderson. He implies his white teammates did not want to play the black team, which would not be surprising during this turbulent period of forced desegregation. But Leary assured them with confidence that they would win. His teammates wanted to maintain athletics as what Grundy calls a "symbol of white manly prowess."[22]

"You cannot believe this game. If there has ever been an outstanding game ever played in Camden County, it was that night that we played them!...Those boys were unbelievable that night. I had watched 'em play...I remember one time I think we went six minutes, nobody missed a shot. I kept on. I said, 'We're playing the best I've ever seen us play,' but I said, 'These boys are...' They wanted to beat us so bad. We won the game on almost a half-court shot at the end of the game...The score was a 150–149. Those black fans came out and just hugged us because they enjoyed the game."

Leary revives the larger-than-life athletic and cultural drama where, as Pamela Grundy points out, "communities engaged the tensions, possibilities, and contradictions of the world around them."[23] He remembers a powerful moment in which a historically divided community came together in a grand show of intimate contact: what was probably the first time some members of the white and black communities had ever hugged each other. Leary was central to making the game happen. He still takes pleasure in reliving what he appreciates as a great moment in Camden's still racially divided athletic history.

That day Leary became a bridge beyond legislated policy change in an educational institution. He initiated an unprecedented move toward interracial collaboration outside the classroom, foreshadowing the possibilities and sites of integration to come. Inspired by this collective play, all team members performed to their highest abilities. At game's end, racial boundaries dissolved as blacks and whites flooded the court and players and fans embraced each other in celebration, forming unanticipated bonds.

"The Time for Deliberate Speed Has Run Out"

By the time this mythic basketball game was played in Camden County, nationwide external pressures made it obvious that the days of continued de facto segregation were numbered. The freedom of choice plan that compelled Leary into all-black Marian Anderson school, and operated in over thirteen hundred Southern school districts, had failed to show substantive results. The dagger in the heart of this plan perpetuated by white resistance came from a tidewater, agricultural county in Virginia that was not geographically far from Camden and in many ways similar. Lessons from the vast rural areas of the South such as Camden, which are often ignored in Civil Rights histories, show why an additional Supreme Court ruling was essential to defeat resistance to desegregation.

The Green v. County School Board of New Kent County decision of May 27, 1968, has been credited as being second only to *Brown* for its impact on school desegregation. The plaintiffs argued that in effect the freedom of choice plan sustained racially dual-school systems. With freedom of choice, school boards still controlled most pupil assignments; schools remained segregated in practice; and the burden of limited desegregation fell on the shoulders of courageous black children and their families. The Court sided with the plaintiffs. As Justice William Brennan wrote: "The burden on a school board today is to come forward with a plan that promises realistically to work, and promises realistically to work now."

The Supreme Court set out substantive guidelines in *Green* that significantly affected desegregation plans. By holding local authorities accountable for the effects of the plan, *Green* explicitly recognized the critical differences between de jure and de facto desegregation. The ruling, quoting from *Griffin v. County School Board of Prince Edward County* (1964), reaffirmed that "the time for 'deliberate speed' has run out…the context in which we must interpret and apply this language [of *Brown II*] to plans for desegregation has been significantly altered." The court pointed here to the situation in which the de facto social context and practices failed to meet intended time frame of *Brown II*. The ruling charged state school authorities "with the affirmative duty to take whatever steps might be necessary to convert to a unitary school system in which racial discrimination would be eliminated, root and branch."

This Supreme Court edict, with its rural agricultural metaphor, added teeth to de jure desegregation and effectively defeated de facto rural conservative resistance. The Supreme Court's holistic metaphor effectively addressed hidden structures within the tokenist freedom of choice plan, which aimed at forestalling racial integration. *Green* required school boards throughout the nation to dismantle segregation "root and branch"—with respect to facilities, staff, faculty, extracurricular activities, and transportation.

Across the South, counties like Camden negotiated the implementation of school desegregation with social norms, community customs, and the feelings of the people. But only a year after Leary began teaching in Marian Anderson School, under freedom of choice, the *Green* ruling, along with cumulative national pressures, forced de facto desegregation. The percentage of southern black students attending integrated schools jumped from 32 in 1968–1969, the final year before complete desegregation in Camden County, to 79 in 1970–1971. With this, Marian Anderson School and the other Camden public schools changed profoundly, yet community customs and the feelings of the people did not shift as rapidly.

Before *Green* many policies allowed the roots of systemic inequality to stay hidden. The belabored implementation of *Brown* brought this persistent challenge to the surface. As J.E. Thomas has discussed, educational initiatives must focus "upon changes at the roots of the systems"[24] and as Mayo (2003) added "not on mere symptoms of what are, in effect, structurally conditioned forms of oppression."[25] The challenges of implementing de facto social change through educational law or policy remains a pressing contemporary problem.

CHAPTER 3

From Social and Cultural Capital to Social Change

Why do the refrains of progressive educational movements seem lacking in the diverse harmonies, the variegated rhythms, and the shades of tone expected in a truly heterogeneous chorus?

—Lisa Delpit

School desegregation... is hardly an educational issue. Rather, school desegregation is better understood as an issue of the political economy of this country...

—George Noblit and Thomas Collins

Wealth, often referred to as capital by economists, has many dimensions when applied to race and education even in a rural tidewater community in North Carolina. This book, in addition to weighing financial capital, looks at the important roles of social and cultural capital. The narratives of both Hughes and Leary provide insights into this expanded meaning of capital.[1]

Social capital—"the material and immaterial resources that individuals and families are able to access through their social ties"[2]—and cultural capital—"the sense of group consciousness and collective identity aimed at the advancement of an entire group"[3]—play important roles in the human ecology of Camden County.[4] These forms of capital are assets that sustained vital and often under-examined networks both in the formerly segregated and in the now integrated schools.[5] Leary's narratives involve various sources of capital and make visible white privilege and the dominant networks that controlled Camden County. Hughes' stories flesh out forms of black social and cultural capital.

Social Capital, Race, and Education

The three leading scholars of social capital—Pierre Bordieu, Robert Coleman, and Robert Putnam—share several core beliefs about the concept: human relationships matter; these relationships create social networks; individuals affiliate with the networks, invest in them, and use these networks as sources of power for mutual advantage. By bringing us into supportive groups with similar values and interests, these networks give benefits and meaning to our lives.

In the past both Leary and Hughes were part of substantial local networks. Leary's included basketball teams, the public schools, the deputy sheriffs, the slightly secretive "good old boys," and his local white church; Hughes' involved the black community, his town's Democratic committee, his barter and farmers' market customers, and his local black church. Both relied on their networks and used them successfully. But the traditions are different, and many of the networks remain racially segregated.

Social Capital in the White Community

Leary's life exemplifies dominant white social capital. From birth, Leary was a member of a politically influential, middle-class family of landowners from the oldest community in Camden County. In addition, his family's financial and social standing allowed him to enjoy the certainty of food on the table and leisure time for hunting, fishing, and exploring the countryside. These were luxuries unavailable to the Camden community's poor whites and blacks, many of whom worked long hours on farms and did other hard labor. Leary's family attended a local white church, which he still attends with his wife. By birthright, Leary belonged to Camden County and it belonged to him.

He recalls attitudes about blacks—stereotypes absorbed from white social networks: "One of the things I remember was my grandfather and this black guy worked all the time together. And I remember one time my grandfather drinking right out of this jar of water that this black guy did. I said,' "He's liable to die!' I must have been nine or ten. But I knew you weren't supposed to drink after them, see. I said, 'My grandfather is crazy! He's gambling like that.' But they were pretty close, working together all the time. And I realized that with Legette [a black coworker], when I got working with him. I would have done anything alongside Legette. It is how you are raised, grow up." As a child, with a few memorable exceptions, the networks around him reinforced a segregated mindset. Later in life, when school integration meant that he worked and played basketball together with blacks, he realized the narrowness of his childhood perspective. Integration allowed Leary to see the limitations of his inherited ideas concerning race relations, even though this social change threatened the white-dominated social networks and power structures of his childhood.

Leary attended a segregated elementary school in Old Trap. His first grade principal, Mr. Burgess, at the white elementary school, and later his high school principal at Camden High School, was the school superintendent when Leary was hired as a teacher. The same Burgess, who was one of the male figures Leary feared most as a child—along with his father and Frankenstein—helped him later to get a teaching job and avoid the military draft. This is just one example of how his childhood social networks shaped his future. Burgess also was the same superintendent who asked for a white teacher to volunteer to go to the black Marian Anderson School—a choice that dramatically changed Leary's life.

Like all children, Leary had a set of white friends at school. He did play with some black children in his neighborhood but these relationships were different: "You come home. You might play with some of the blacks, but you didn't go to school with them." Segregated schools had a powerful impact on the social networks that developed during childhood. "I try to think about my life going through school because we knew there were black kids all over the community. But we really didn't know them. Think about it. You get to know people when you go to school with them..."

Leary had an older brother who paved the way for him in school and on the playground. "That is one good thing about having a brother. Because he did defend me right much. He was probably one of the meanest kids in the area. If I got beat up, it was probably by my brother Warner... He's the farmer. And my younger brother, that I picked on, he turned out to be the policeman" (*we laugh*). His older brother's farming career was made possible by his family's capital as landowners. His younger brother's career drew the Leary family into the local law enforcement network. Through Leary his family was connected to the school network.

The segregated Camden High School was preeminent among the county schools. Unlike Marian Anderson School, Camden High had a football field. "One of the reasons they had a football field was through a lot of parent donations... They bought the poles. They put up the lights. And they put a lot of money into the uniforms." The financial and social capital of the wealthier white parents in Camden helped provide opportunities the black high school lacked.

During our discussion about the disparities between facilities for white and black athletes, Leary mentioned his surprise that so few blacks could swim—living in a rural area surrounded by water. Many of the deaths by drowning in the county were black people who couldn't swim—including one of Hughes' brothers. The response of Leary's wife, Sandra, illustrates one way the white networks of financial and social capital impacted the black community: "You look at all the white people who owned the land where the water was [the Albemarle sound]... Their access to getting to the water would probably not have been very good." Leary replied, "But they could have gone to the river any time. And we had black families that lived down by the river." To which Mrs. Leary replied, "Do you think they would go down there?" Leary responded, as he began to see the county from the perspective of black residents, "Of course, I [if I were black] probably wouldn't get in. The white people would say, 'What are y'all doing in the water?'" He continues in jest, "They would have probably shot the first black guy just because he was in the water. You don't ever know." Mrs. Leary said, "I'd never thought about it. I don't think I [if I was a black person] would have been caught out there in the water either." Mr. Leary reflected, "We've all lived through it. But you never know the other side of the story. And I've always thought about it. And really, when I taught in the black school it made me think a lot. I learned as much as they did a lot of the times." The encounter Leary related highlights the potentially exclusionary role of dominant white social capital. In this case, it prevented blacks from acquiring key survival skills for life in a tidewater community.

Leary was a well-known basketball player in high school, a sport he continued playing on local leagues into his sixties. This talent helped him get into college, where he played basketball. His athletic skills and experience later helped him to earn the position of coach at schools where he taught.

As a historian and as a hobbyist, he collected Civil War memorabilia and guns from various American and world wars. This passion involved its own social network that helped him acquire and trade historical memorabilia. The members of these networks were mainly white southerners, interested in preserving Civil War history and the glory of Dixie.

Leary has focused on the history of the Camden region: "Well, I've always loved local history and try to tell the stories." He is now the community-anointed historian for the white community. Leary inherited this job when a close friend's father, a man with a similar passion, passed away. He still visits local schools to give historical presentations. With the help of some friends and local-history buffs, Leary created the Camden Museum that is housed in the former Camden County jail. He participates in Civil War reenactments. He also volunteered at the Dismal Swamp Canal Visitors Center. In his free time, he expounds on local history to visitors and residents alike.

Leary is also tied to the network of people "from here." In other words, they were born and raised in Camden County. But as more and more people move into northern Camden County, which is becoming a bedroom community to Norfolk, Virginia, the exclusive network is weakening. Leary jokingly says, "We always talk the Civil War was a bad thing because the Yankees came here and defeated us. But at least they went home! Now this new bunch—they don't even go home!" We all laugh, but underneath this humor lies a recognition that the traditional white social networks that ruled Camden County for centuries are changing.

Leary tells stories to preserve the past, attracting people to his artifact-loaded point of view, full of military detail and heroic deeds. Compared to Hughes, he had many advantages that enabled him to roam the countryside, hunting and fishing, to compete in athletic sports, to participate in Civil War reenactments and creating a historical museum in Camden. Leary also inherited economic and cultural capital. In his working life, Leary had one vocation, teaching, and had many avocations that greatly expanded his social capital.

Social Capital in the Black Community

From birth, for Hughes to succeed, he had to grow and cultivate social capital in the segregated black community. Both black and white communities possess social capital networks, albeit in different forms. Various social and cultural groups create, sustain, and "trade" on social and cultural capital in different ways depending on their social position and broader power relations.

Hughes was a master of building and using black cultural capital as well as operating within the dominant white social capital network. He was born into the world in 1919, with a key advantage in comparison to many black families. His family owned land. He was a third-generation farmer. He was also the second son and as a result could enjoy the luxury of going to school while his older brother tended the field. His brother took on this responsibility when their father became ill.

His father's illness decreased the family's prospects substantially. At the time, the federal government had no programs to help disabled heads of household. In addition, agricultural and domestic laborers were excluded from Social Security—a policy that impacted 80 percent of black workers, a disproportionate share of the workforce.[6] Farm workers were not added to the list of Social Security recipients until the early 1950s.[7] The lack of a government safety net made informal networks and social capital vital for the survival of Hughes and his family.

When Hughes' brother abandoned the farm and his family, he tied the mules to a tree—knowing the mules were a crucial part of his family's financial capital as the mules helped work the fields. From the moment Hughes retrieved the mules, he became part of the workforce. He disconnected from an important childhood social network—school. A few years later, when his father recovered, Hughes tried to reenter the school network but was ostracized because of his social class and years of work on the farm.

Although he left school, Hughes did not abandon his education. He pursued literacy at the local black church, located a few houses away. In Sunday school he learned to read, an essential skill for his success. After school desegregation, black churches became the primary site for community business. His church was a vital part of his social capital throughout his life, as it was for many black community members. In 2005 at age eighty-six he was the deacon of his church. Caroline C. Spence, a friend he originally met when she was looking for some collards in the 1960s in Camden, was the deaconess of the church. According to the *Virginia Pilot*, "she [Ms. Spence] had missed a few Sundays because she was visiting other churches, and Hughes she said called to make sure she wasn't sick or in need of any help"[8]—an example of Hughes maintaining his social capital networks.

At a young age Hughes obtained a bank loan to help purchase his family land from his father. This introduced Hughes to the white world of capital funding, vital for farmers who need to purchase fertilizer at the beginning of the season or large equipment to work the farm. He also interacted with the white business community when he wholesaled his products through grocery stores. Although he did not have much formal education, he later recalled, "I know them boys probably thought I had a college education. Didn't have it." Yet he had developed literacy, economic savvy, and the interpersonal skills that enabled him to operate in white business networks.

Throughout his life, Hughes cultivated barter networks with other producers. These networks served him his entire life by keeping him out of unnecessary debt. When he called to check on his friend Mrs. Spence, whom he had been giving collards to at no charge for decades, she remembered with a laugh: "During that call we really started talking...He needed help in the market...I just thought I would pay him back for those greens."[9] She did this by assisting him at the market for several years. Hughes' barter relationships benefited him, even when the reciprocity was long deferred and offered voluntarily.

When a fire destroyed his sister-in-law's apartment and uprooted the family, Hughes adopted two of her children and raised them along with his eight children—a touching example of the reciprocity of social networks. He commented: "Well, we, we done it...and quite much. And uh, I think, I think that's what the Lord wants us to do is to help one another."

As his children grew, Hughes joined school networks—both segregated and later integrated. He did interact with his daughter's teacher as part of the segregated school. But mostly he left school education to the school and focused on teaching his children to work and to grow up to be productive community members. As another Camden resident J.R. Spence recalled recently, "He knew how to make a dollar...They [his children] seem to have good jobs. One of them is retired. He must have a good income because he owns a good size brick house in Shiloh (*he laughs*). All of them they have that knack for making that dollar. Nice work ethic. They are quite industrious." Hughes said of his children, "I tell you what...if you bring them up right, it's the best crop you can raise."[10]

Later as the farming industry weakened, Hughes chose to farm less land. As a garden farmer, he sold his goods at a local farmers' markets. He had long developed barter relationships and these continued throughout his life. Through the market he expanded his social network and cultivated relationships with his customers. A number of his fellow farmers who expanded their farms and relied on capital loans ended up going bankrupt. Hughes continued to make money and kept his land, his original capital advantage. For over two decades, until his death, Hughes was the lifeblood of the farmers' market.

At age seventy-two Hughes joined another social network: He went back to school at the College of the Albemarle. He was invited to speak at classes about his life experiences. The local paper interviewed him several times. He was valued throughout the black community as a storyteller and local treasure. Along with an extensive familial network, Hughes continued to enjoy his many social networks until his unexpected passing in July 2006. According to the Virginia Pilot, "Hughes had never been seriously ill and never needed to wear glasses. In a 2003 interview, he said his secret was a life of hard work and drinking lots of milk." The farmers' market closed for his memorial service. The *Virginia Pilot* wrote in a commemorative article: "Although his products brought people to the market, it was his personality that kept them around for a few minutes of conversation."[11] Hughes' sources of social capital were rich and varied, and often ones that would not be valued from the perspective of white social capital. But they brought him success and happiness in life.

Some scholars and most educators only recognize dominant white social capital as having value. But as Hughes' narrative makes clear, social and cultural capital can have substantial value in negotiating the powerful institutional and cultural forces that shape everyone's lives, especially for those who do not belong to the dominant group. Knowledge of social and cultural capital networks helps us recognize both the values of segregated black education and the strength and persistence of white resistance to school integration.

White Social and Cultural Capital and Education

The limited notion that only the dominant group possesses social and cultural capital creates a deficit worldview. As education scholar Paul Gorski explains, this view "holds that inequality is the result, not of systemic inequities in access to power, but of intellectual, moral, and spiritual deficiencies in certain groups of people."[12] In contemporary education, as sociologist Prudence Carter explains: "School authorities often ignore that students should and can possess different kinds of cultural capital."[13] From the deficit perspective, communities of color are seen as deficient and their cultural and social wealth, inconsequential. This view ignores valuable forms of social capital as well as inequitable access to it: Carter points out, "Students can occupy the same ethnic or racial groups, but their access to critical forms of social capital or resourceful connections, can vary."[14] For example, Leary had more access to social capital than poor whites in the community and Hughes maximized his social capital thorough relationships that less shrewd, less social, or less achievement-oriented blacks could not.

The deficit mindset dominated white-controlled school integration. In other words, the dominant white networks were recognized and valued and the black networks were largely treated as insignificant. Many whites, imbued with racist thinking, did not consider that the black community could add value to integrated education. Whites simply assumed that their forms of social and cultural capital would be the norm and operated integrated schools accordingly.

Integrated schools failed to bridge differences in black and white social and cultural capital. Bridging social capital, as explained by Robert Putnam, is an inclusive approach where people develop relationships outside of their groups such as across racial lines.[15] In contrast to Putnam, political scientist Barbara Arneil argues that the idea of bridging social capital in diverse communities does not imply that groups transcend cultural difference:

> In the final analysis, taking the issue of diversity seriously does not simply mean paying attention to the "distribution" of social capital via bridging mechanisms but being aware of the nature of the connection, or "bridges," that are being built. And it will probably mean, in some cases, using the metaphor of a "bridge" within bridging capital in its more literal sense; not as a transcendent mechanism to overcome difference and "bring two diverse identities together" but as a means by which people can travel between cultural places. Thus, to bridge difference is not to "bring" together two parts into one but to provide a mechanism by which those who wish to *move between* them can do so.[16]

The largely segregated communities such as those inhabited by Hughes and Leary had long operated with different forms of social and cultural capital and had little experience with bridging them. For example, in Camden those who would like to worship in an integrated church would have difficulty finding one.

During the process of desegregation, de facto segregated social capital networks continued to maintain segregation. This continued segregation occurred in formal school networks; by hiring white teachers to replace blacks, tracking white students in gifted classes and black students in special education, and employing only white administrators; and in informal networks, through the cheerleaders, social cliques, and PTAs. Social capital maintained informal segregated networks after de jure school integration—the cheerleaders remained all-white, social cliques continued to be defined by color lines, and the formerly all-white parent association ceased to meet rather than include black parents. The social capital networks help explain why de facto segregation persists in our schools today.

Many social networks resist integration. The black churches, and the black schoolmasters' club that have continued for half a century after desegregation serve important functions, particularly in a society with persistent inequality and oppression. But in order to provide equal education to meet the needs of all students, educational institutions need to also recognize and bridge nonwhite forms of social capital.

Building Bridges

Compared to many others in their respective social networks, both Hughes and Leary successfully bridged black and white forms of social capital. Their stories help answer two key questions that connect social capital and education: how does an increased knowledge of social and cultural capital inform our understanding of the social practices of others and ourselves? And how could students in integrated schools benefit from understanding diverse forms of social capital and use this knowledge in social relations?

Leary started building a fundamental bridge when he volunteered to teach at an all-black school. Billy Revelle, the first white principal of Marian Anderson, told me that he wasn't sure whether he would have had the courage to be the one white man in an all-black school as Leary did. Leary recalls: "It is a decision I'll never regret. I got to know the black community a lot. I was treated about as nice as I could possibly be... Like I tell people, 'Ain't nobody in the world could have been treated any better.'" Leary's adding, "I learned as much as they did a lot of the times," shows the mutual benefit of bridges, especially when they involve close daily contact.

Leary, as a bridgebuilder, caused ripples in his own white social networks. He remembered, "I think I got most of my criticism from the white community. Because I had one guy who said, 'We are going to erect a statue of you being the first white in a black school.'" This sarcastic comment highlights networks of white resistance to integration and the backlash against a bridgebuilder.

As Leary entered Marian Anderson, he began a relationship with one of the most renowned bridgebuilders in the area, the black principal Whittier Crockett Witherspoon. Leary remembers his encounter with him, his first black supervisor: "I remember sitting down with Mister Witherspoon. He talked to me within the first two or three days. I can remember he said, 'We are all people. And we all have got different problems.' He said, 'The only thing is...' and I remember him saying this, 'you got good and bad people in both races. The only trouble is we have a little bit more in ours.' And I agree with him on that. But it is because of poverty and the lack of family and things like that."

Leary shared a troubling memory that echoes deficit thinking. From this account, it appears Witherspoon, like Leary, internalized a social hierarchy that discriminated against those of a lower socioeconomic class, a more significant burden for blacks. Thus began their interracial working relationship, which later turned into a friendship. In this case, the process of school desegregation built a foundation for bridging social capital.

Leary recalled, "Even years later I got to know the man [Witherspoon] and I liked him. Later on I was on the Board of Elections and he was too. So on two occasions we went to different meetings and were roommates. So we got to talk to each other a lot... But listening to him, I got the perspective of how an intelligent black person must have felt in a segregated society. Because he talked about how it is bad when you can't hardly stop at a restaurant or to use a restroom. And it really made me think how wrong we were a lot of times." Through this friendship, Leary began to see the segregated world through a different lens. Leary respected Witherspoon, noted by blacks and whites for his exceptional intelligence and accomplishments, and listened in ways uncommon in many interracial relationships.

He recalls another way in which interracial bridges were built outside of formal schooling: "I tell people Elizabeth City did something right too. The schools integrated in 1969. Elizabeth City also brought in the first Parks and Recreation director then. And I remember that because not only were we playing sports, but we introduced sports where the blacks came in [the first interracial league]. And that is where we got to know a lot of the black families... We got to know these people. And playing with people is a whole lot better way of getting to know people. In our team, we had a school team [of teachers] and we had a lot of black players on our team. And we got to know the black people a lot better... You'd joke and carry on. In that environment you could do it, where you probably wouldn't have done it in other environments. I think it took us a while in Camden." When Leary organized the first interracial basketball game in his county, he brought his team of skeptical players, who found themselves in a match of equals that touched everyone—both players and the many spectators.

Leary bridged social capital through sports. He recalled, "One of the things I think that helped me a lot was that I played basketball. Sometimes I would be the only white guy in the gym. One time I just stopped. I said, 'Whoa, wait a minute.' They said, 'What's the problem?' I said, 'I think I'm the only white guy in this gym!' They said, 'Get out of here!' (*laughing*). But, you know, you joke and carry on. I was probably forty something then." Leary played basketball in local leagues into his sixties.

Hughes bridged social capital in part because of economic necessity and in part because of his dedication to a broader democratic spirit. He succeeded by establishing relationships with local white businesses through his wholesale activities. He also was acquainted with local bankers and farm equipment salesmen. This integrated social network was key to Hughes' economic welfare. He found a way to compete with the supermarkets successfully. He showed that blacks could be wily economists as well. Later when the troubled farming market would have forced him to incur more debt from lenders, he shrewdly saw the negative consequences of these networks and avoided them, unlike other farmers who lost their land.

His entrepreneurial spirit and interpersonal charm built new networks. He bartered with white merchants. He created an integrated social network at the farmers market that exists to this day. When the economy turned bad in the 1980s, he avoided relying on the lures of the white capital networks that would have piled on more debt and threatened his land holdings. Instead he became an intensive market farmer and sold his goods to retail customers at a smaller but less risky farmers' market.

Hughes also bridged social capital networks through his political activities in the Shiloh Democratic Party. He regularly attended meetings to discuss and influence local politics. At one time he was the precinct leader. Although in the minority political group in the county, his political network was an integrated network, where whites and blacks of similar political beliefs worked together to achieve political change.

These examples of bridging social capital by Leary and Hughes show the road less taken at a time in which interracial networks were unusual. Unwitting agents of change themselves, Hughes and Leary were involved with dimensions of segregation and desegregation that many school administrators rarely consider.

Cultural Capital and Deficit Thinking

Cultural capital does not begin and end at the classroom door. It involves families, social organizations, and the beliefs, values, and teachings of a group of people: "Ethnocentric bias in the conventional use of cultural capital...ignores the multiple ways in [which] the cultural resources of other groups also convert into capital."[17] Historically, because of racist ideologies, white knowledge and cultural capital have dominated the integrated school system and fostered inequality. One example of this in Camden was the practice that continued into the 1990s of allowing white children to skip school on days celebrating black history events while their black classmates attended school—supporting the white myth that black knowledge and cultural capital are insignificant.

Deficit thinking influenced the process of school desegregation. As education scholar Tara Yosso points out:

> Deficit thinking takes the position that minority students and families are at fault for poor academic performance because: (a) students enter school without the normative cultural knowledge and skills; and (b) parents neither value nor support their child's education...Educators most often assume that schools work and that students, parents and community need to change to conform to this already effective and equitable system.[18]

School desegregation in Camden was influenced by deficit thinking. In most instances the stereotype that blacks were less intelligent and inferior persisted without question when black and white children were put in the same classroom. The well-respected black principal was let go and Camden's integrated schools still have not had a black principal. Special education classrooms have been filled almost exclusively with black children. Black parents are rarely consulted about policy decisions or practices and they report being excluded intentionally from school board and PTA meetings. The deficit point of view remains an educational problem even today and can be seen in discussions of the achievement gap and the need (now decades old and still unsolved) to involve minority parents in the school system. The operating assumption is that minority parents do not want to engage in the schools, ignoring the ways historically that they were deeply involved in the black schools and excluded since school integration.

The process of deficit thinking leads to blaming educational inequality and the low achievement of some minority students on the students themselves as well as their families and communities. From this perspective, schools and their cultural norms are not responsible for ongoing inequities. Yet the innate biases of deficit thinking actually help perpetuate racial inequality in schools. As educational scholar Lisa Delpit observes:

> To provide schooling for everyone's children that reflects liberal, middle-class values and aspirations is to ensure the maintenance of the status quo, to ensure that power, the culture of power, remains in the hands of those who already have it. Some children come to school with more accouterments of the culture of power already in place—cultural capital...—some with less.[19]

This deficit thinking is based on limited understandings of the diverse dimensions of cultural capital.

In response to limited conceptions of cultural capital, two bodies of scholarship have developed—one on cultural capital and black education and the other on cultural wealth. African American educational historian V.P. Franklin defines "cultural capital" as "the sense of group consciousness and collective identity that serves as an economic resource for the financial and material support of business enterprises that are aimed at the advancement of an entire group."[20] This literature develops a specific analysis of the influence of black cultural capital, which has developed under oppressive social conditions and has often been ignored. Franklin's definition highlights the connection between racially specific social networks and economic advancement. These networks were vital to Hughes' survival, from the church doors to barter exchanges, especially after he was forced to abandon his formal education.

Carter Julian Savage, an education historian, describes the black community support for segregated education as fueled by "an African American ethos of self-determination and social advancement."[21] Although Hughes left school at age ten, he learned this cultural ethos and continued to develop informal strategies for self-determination and social advancement, whether learning to read at church, wholesaling his products, or avoiding financial pitfalls of white capital lenders.

In segregated schools, forms of black cultural capital that supported education included: "1. African Americans' zeal for education; 2. the

African American community's propensity to give to their schools; 3. the devotion of poorly paid, African American teachers; 4. the willingness of African American students to attend 'distressingly poor facilities.'"[22] Examples of these forms of cultural capital at Camden's all-black Marian Anderson school include the principal's zeal for education, the gifts of land, lumber, and labor from local families, devoted teachers, and students who dressed, behaved, and achieved their principal's dream of college attainment.

Hughes embodied a lifelong zeal for education. He had to cut short his formal education but he cultivated his natural intelligence and love of learning. His close-knit black community had its own bartering economic system that he mastered and used for the rest of his life. And the nearby church became the well for his evolving literacy and deep moral values. He also worked hard to insure that all his children received a formal education and he continued to pursue his own education at the age of seventy-two.

Black parents also contributed cultural capital: the "most explicit ways the black community used cultural capital for education was in the area of 'resource development,'" such as hosting "pie struts," "cake walks," and "queen drives."[23] In Camden, the black community sold cupcakes to raise funds for an activity bus for the black schools.

According to Savage, desegregation negatively impacted the relationship between cultural capital and black education, specifically the "loss of tradition, ownership and collapse of a school community."[24] The relationship changed permanently. Black cultural capital was not taken into account during the process of integration: "School practices were not modified to take into consideration the cultural and experiential backgrounds of African American students."[25] As both Hughes' assessment of school integration and the next chapter describe, the Camden community also experienced these losses—from loss of pride to loss of black leadership.

Some forms of cultural capital continue to be a powerful force in the lives of black students today. As Prudence Carter describes, "black cultural capital matters because it signifies in-group allegiance and preserves a sense of belonging... Black cultural capital also helps to protect boundaries around racial and ethnic identity."[26] In place of the segregated school, which had functioned as a site of belonging and source of racial identity, students today preserve these important values through the relationships and identity performances that constitute black cultural capital. In Camden, biannual reunions of the black segregated school continue this practice. While schools may not recognize black cultural capital as the vital resource, it still survives in black communities and even in educational institutions dominated by white cultural capital.

Educational scholar Tara Yosso argues that scholars should focus on the often ignored, diverse forms of cultural wealth that students of color bring into school: "Community cultural wealth is an array of knowledge, skills, abilities and contacts possessed and utilized by Communities of Color to survive and resist macro and micro-forms of oppression."[27] Yosso outlines six forms of capital that make up community wealth: aspirational ("the ability to hold onto hope in the face of structured inequality and often without the means to make such dreams a reality"), navigational ("this infers the ability to maneuver through institutions not created with Communities of Color in mind"), social ("networks of people and community resources"), linguistic ("intellectual and social skills attained through communication experiences in more than one language and/or style"), familial ["those cultural knowledges nurtured among *familia* (kin) that carry a sense of community history, memory and cultural intuition"], and resistant capital ("knowledges and skills fostered through oppositional behavior that challenges inequality").[28]

Hughes embodies resources that include diverse forms of cultural wealth—aspirational (his unfailingly positive attitude in the face of social inequality), familial (the network that supported Hughes' parents when his father was ill), social (the barter relationships and network of friends), navigational (his tactical abilities), and resistant (the variety of strategies Hughes adapted to maneuver around powerful, dominant institutions).[29]

Hughes provided his children with navigational capital—tactical and practical know-how as a critical resource to navigate the working world. He taught his children not to rely solely on education as a form of social and economic advancement. He emphasized the value of social capital—firmly grounding his life and those of his children in collaborative community relationships. This approach resembles that of a community studied by educational scholar Lisa Delpit where, "Academic education was fine and to be desired, but what really concerned them [parents] was social and moral education—the education that trains youngsters to become good people, who care about, participate in, and are proud of their communities."[30] As this example shows, Hughes approach, though special, was not unique in black communities, which needed numerous avenues to succeed despite white dominance.

Integrating Social and Cultural Capital

It would be easy to exercise the wisdom of historical hindsight and point to Leary as an example of the dangers of deficit thinking. It would be inaccurate to characterize Leary as an anachronistic educator who does not represent contemporary multicultural education. Instead it is more precise to see him as one of the first in a long line of educators that—because of their own cultural background and acceptance of dominant cultural beliefs—continue to teach in ways that fail to recognize the cultural capital of communities of color.

Educational scholars Shernaz Garcia and Patricia Guerra recognize the limitations of placing blame on educators:

> Rather than make educators the new targets of deficit thought, our work reinforces the importance of professional development that identifies elements of the school culture and the school climate that lead to institutional practices that systematically marginalize or pathologize difference. We have found that the majority of teachers are well-intentioned, caring individuals but are unaware of the deeper, hidden, or invisible dimensions of culture.[31]

Since the beginning of school desegregation, as Leary's experiences show, even white teachers that support mandated educational change were not prepared to recognize and incorporate the different forms of social and cultural capital that black students brought to school. And the education system from the school board down rarely did anything to bridge black and white forms of social and cultural capital. They continued to administer and teach from their dominant white cultural experience and thus perpetuated social inequality in education. Lisa Delpit asks a central question that is relevant to this day: "How can such complete communication blocks exist when both parties truly believe they have the same angles?"[32]

Because of a failure to translate cultural capital across the racial divide, schools have created and still sustain numerous educational problems. One reason for the communication problems is that teachers do not share a common cultural perspective with most of their students: "Many of the teachers of black children have their roots in other communities and do not have the opportunity to hear the full range of their students' voices."[33] It is not surprising that minority engagement and achievement continue to elude many schools.

Another reason for communication problems originates from "the culture of power," which is shaped by white cultural and cultural capital. This culture as explained by Delpit includes five characteristics[34]: the first aspect of power is those issues that take place in classrooms, such as a curriculum that focuses on predominantly white history and heroes. Leary's response to black students when they asked why their school did not have a football team illustrates this aspect of power. The second aspect is the codes or rules for participating in power such as "ways of talking, ways of writing, ways of dressing, and ways of interacting."[35] When Hughes was criticized for his farm attire, the students were indicating that he was outside the code of those in power at the segregated school. After desegregation, the codes or rules adopted were those of the white schools.

A third aspect is that those who have power determine the rules. So, Leary's belief in meritocracy, competition, and individualism, values he learned at home and at school along with other whites across the nation, trumped historic rules of power in black schools, which emphasized a more communitarian ethic.

Another aspect is that unless the students know the rules and codes of power, they are at a disadvantage. These implicit codes of power and education became the source of miscommunication in the integrated schools as many black students had never been taught the cultural rules nor asked themselves about their own.

Finally, "those with power are frequently least aware of—or least willing to acknowledge—its existence. Those with less power are often most aware of its existence."[36] As a result, white teachers were often less aware that the ways integrated schools were organized—from white principals to white pedagogies—were not normal or natural for black children, who had different ideas of community, culture, and education. As Prudence Carter concludes, "education is as much about being inculcated with the ways of the 'culture of power' as it is about learning to read, count, and think critically."[37]

In Camden County, the white curriculum of integrated schools excluded black ways of knowing in numerous ways: by ignoring pedagogies and practices developed in black schools, including knowledge about black history and culture; and second by continuing to operate classrooms and schools more broadly by white rules that were never explained to black students and parents. While the exclusion may not have been intentional, its effects were no less harmful.

In order to address the problem of the white-dominated culture of power in school, Delpit argues:

> The dilemma is not really in the debate over instructional methodology, but rather in communicating across cultures and in addressing the more fundamental issue of power, of whose voice gets to be heard in determining what is best for poor children and children of color. Both sides do need to be able to listen... it is those with the most power, those in the majority, who must take the greater responsibility for initiating the process.

We have yet to address this dilemma. Finding ways to bridge social and cultural capital is a necessary step toward a more equitable future in education. The bridging of social and cultural capital offers students critical opportunities to succeed. It also acknowledges that these opportunities do not have to be confined to the pedagogy and the social and cultural capital of whites. Bridging cultural capital brings about alternative modes of integration in that: what counts as social and cultural capital is reconceived; how and what students are taught is revised to account for these forms of knowledge; and these diverse forms of knowledge reshape educational institutions.

Telling Bridges

For schools to address bridging social and cultural capital would require substantive changes in education policy and practice. One way to begin to "hear the full range of their students' voices" is through narratives that highlight the diverse forms of social and cultural capital. One form of cultural capital that Hughes and Leary both possess, for their respective communities, is storytelling. Both are community-anointed and self-made storytellers.

Narrative is a significant form of cultural capital that creates and sustains a community memory and a sense of the wealth of local culture. As cultural critic Wendell Berry writes, "A human community, too, must collect leaves and stories, and turn them to account. It must build soil, and build that memory of itself—in lore and story and song—that will be its culture. These two kinds of accumulation, of local soil and local culture, are intimately related."[38] As virtuoso storytellers, both Hughes and Leary kept parts of their local communities alive. Their stories are not simply didactic narrations passed on. They are stories performed with much laughter, entertaining as they create new knowledge, particularly through dialogic exchange when these narratives extend beyond their segregated communities. Their performances hold the potential for greater cross-cultural understanding.[39]

Telling memories offers possibilities for transformation. As Pollock argues, "Insofar as narrative is a production, it is always vulnerable to variation and reinvention: it is the dynamic ground of a possible real. It charges the self and its (internalized) others with the possibilities of becoming (otherwise)."[40] Performances of memory contain potential for change as the narrator and listeners authorize new selves, alliances, and relationships.[41]

The art of storytelling also requires the courage to perform and become a mentor for the next generation. Hughes and Leary rose to the challenge and both had this inspirational quality. Leary went out planting seeds of the past and Hughes would spin tales for those who stopped by. This form of cultural capital encourages dialogue on topics from local issues that matter to the community. Barry notes the significance of story for local communities:

> The loss of local culture is, in part, a practical loss and an economic one. For one thing, such a culture contains, and conveys to succeeding generations, the history of the use of the place and the knowledge of how the place may be lived in and used. For another, the pattern of reminding implies affection for the place and respect for it, and so, finally, the local culture will carry the knowledge of how the place may be well and lovingly used, and also the implicit command to use it only well and lovingly... Lacking an authentic local culture, a place is open to exploitation, and ultimately to destruction, from the center.[42]

Both Leary and Hughes were keepers of local culture, preserving places they both loved in face of development and globalization. The challenge remains to bridge these largely segregated storied worlds.

Each set of stories contributes valuable knowledge about the complexities of school integration. Leary's stories bring us into the world of Camden's white decision makers, recalling the voices of whites in the desegregation process and the hidden transcripts of race and schooling. While Hughes' narratives come from a vernacular knowledge and experience, his stories constitute an unheralded part of our national history.[43] While people of color have been teaching beyond white pedagogy for centuries, the ways of teaching and learning resistance to the status quo and dominance that Hughes chronicles have not been integrated into the curriculum. This could be achieved (and is already being practiced in some classrooms) in numerous ways—from highlighting the significance of histories of resistance in the United States to encouraging more critical pedagogies in which students themselves identify dominant structures and ways of thinking and work to change the status quo through class activities and projects. The more we know and honor others' pasts, including these oral histories, the more likely it is that we are able to dip into the diverse well of human knowledge and thereby create truly integrated schools and education.

Figure 3 Whittier Crockett Witherspoon at work. Photo courtesy of Elizabeth City [NC] State University Archives.

CHAPTER 4

The Ghost of Whittier Crockett Witherspoon

The funeral of Whittier Crockett Witherspoon, the renowned black principal of Marian Anderson segregated school from 1954 to 1968, occurred days before my first visit to Camden County. When Witherspoon passed away, Fannie Mae Lewis, a former black cafeteria worker, noted, "that was the first time a black person was on the cover [of the newspaper] for something good." Half of the front page of the January 23, 2003, paper was dedicated to an article and photograph of his funeral. I realized at that moment that I had missed meeting one of the most important players in Camden's struggle toward school integration. But I soon found out that his ghost—what psychologist Mary Gergen calls a "social ghost"—entered my conversations in Camden everywhere.[1] He was, and still is, a mythic figure for both whites and blacks.

Witherspoon was by all accounts a remarkable North Carolinian. On July 4, 1912, Whittier Crockett Witherspoon was born in Maxton, North Carolina, to parents Estelle and the Rev. William Franklin Witherspoon, "a Methodist minister from South Carolina who spoke with a British accent."[2] According to his funeral program, "Whittier was reared in the world of sermons, prayer meetings, and church socials." His father instructed Witherspoon, "You will never think of yourself as being superior to anyone, neither are you inferior to anyone. There will always be someone you can help. There will always be someone who can help you."[3]

A Well-Educated, Well-Mannered Man

Witherspoon embodied black educational achievement and the emancipatory potential of education. Bobby "Coach" Vaughn, a friend and former colleague, recalled, "I heard him say his father and mother almost homeschooled him. They had acquired books. He read the great books and was a ferocious reader...I doubt if ten people in this town took the *New York Times* and the *Baltimore Times* and the *Washington Post*. He would get all three of them and read them on Sunday evening. So he did not have blinders on and he spoke with wisdom."[4]

Another former colleague and close friend J.R. Spence added, "Witherspoon perhaps had a unique background in that his father was a Methodist minister which meant that...he moved several places in his lifetime. He stayed with his parents so he might be in the eastern part of the state one time; the western part the other time; and another place the next time. Part of his early years was spent somewhere near Charlotte. Then his family moved around."

Several of Witherspoon's most renowned qualities reflected his minister father. He was an impeccable dresser. As the *Virginia-Pilot* reported, "He learned from his father to be a gentleman—and to dress like one." Vaughn recalls, "I've never seen him without a coat and tie...He was strictly for protocol and dress and things of that nature." Spence adds, "Yeah, he was a dresser. Sometimes you could see him with a sport shirt on but you could rest assured he was in the yard. When he got ready to go out he put on a shirt and tie." Witherspoon's dress signified his high social status and self-esteem, reflecting the social significance of attire in black communities.[5]

Witherspoon possessed a gift for oratory and a love of poetry. "He also gained a healthy respect for the spoken word from his father, who was a poet and one of the most prolific speakers in A.M.E. Zion during his time."[6] Witherspoon once said, "My father could quote poetry for an hour and a half...I can quote for one hour."[7] Spence recalls, "I have never seen anyone who could recite poetry so well...I mean anything you wanted. His poetry would suit the occasion. He would just recite it. And I noticed he would be called on to make a comment and he would say, 'It was just like...' and then he takes off with a poem. He was gifted. And he really loved Shakespeare, he could quote some Shakespeare and most anyone who wrote poetry." Witherspoon's love and mastery of canonical Western prose and poetry earned him the respect of educated whites, who were exposed to the same literature at school.

Witherspoon's knowledge of poetry and his orations at many community events contributed to his renown as a public figure in both the black and white communities. Vaughn exclaimed, "Don't even mention poetry! (*We laugh*). I guess he knew a thousand poems."[8] Spence continued, "I think it inspired his students because many of them tried to duplicate the things he did in school. Some tried to write like him [his ornate penmanship], but I don't think they can match that. And some tried to learn poetry. I don't know what his secret was but he knew it just like he was teaching it every day."

Vaughn added, "He remembered poems. Just about everywhere he went people would ask him to pray or to make a statement. And he had tremendous memory of all the fine things in life and so forth. [His father] is what probably what got him started into it...And you'd have to hear him speak. You could listen to him for hours. And he could go on and I never saw him with a note in my life."

Witherspoon's selections of poetry reflected his philosophy on life and became one of his preferred pedagogical tools. "Witherspoon...I remember one of his famous quotes was the story of the bridgebuilder. The guy who...it goes something like this. The old man comes to a cavern and he could negotiate it but he stopped and built a bridge. And someone asked him, 'Old man, why do you build this bridge?' And his reply was 'The bridge is not for me because I will not pass this way again. The bridge is for the youth that follow.' I could remember portions of it but not as well as he could tell it. He could tell it and everyone in there would be spellbound. You could hear a pin drop. And the message got to you. He was a bridgebuilder. He thrilled the audiences. He could go on with his poems and he would interlace them with practical sayings. He was one of the speakers of our time."

Witherspoon's penmanship was also renowned throughout the region. Spence exclaimed, "His calligraphy is unmatched...I haven't seen anyone who can do that. And he did it with such ease. And I remember one day I went to the bank with him and the teller looks at him and says, 'Well, I tell you one thing. No one can forge your name!' It was unique all itself." At a time when black achievement was rarely recognized because it undermined white supremacy, Witherspoon's abilities and achievements were unmatched by most blacks and whites.

Vaughn remembers, "And just about all the white churches, if they had a certificate to do, they had to find Witherspoon. He could have almost gone into business and charged fifty cents a name on a certificate and so forth like that. But he always did it willingly and people just loved it." Witherspoon's willingness to speak in public when called upon and to labor over certificates throughout the region shows that he also inherited his father's dedication to public service.

Witherspoon had a wide range of talents and interests. Spence remembers, "One thing that just looking at him you wouldn't know is that he was a concert pianist. He loved music, especially classical—Bach, Beethoven, and that company...He read music well. You could go there some days and he'd be sitting down with his stereo listening to all his classics." Well-groomed, well-read, well-spoken, and a master of penmanship, Witherspoon had learned from his childhood to be a consummate gentleman and continued to cultivate these talents throughout his life.

Witherspoon and Black Education

Witherspoon's parents dedicated themselves to edification through education: "Money was tight during the Depression, but William Witherspoon saw to it that five of his six children—one died at 19—graduated from college."[9] Witherspoon attended Johnson C. Smith College (JCSC), a Presbyterian school in Charlotte near where his family lived. He explained, "It was cheaper to stay at home and go to college."[10] The college was founded under the auspices of the Committee on Freedmen of the Presbyterian Church. Witherspoon's lifelong educational philosophies echo the contemporary mission of the University:

> Consistent with its Christian roots, the university recognizes the importance of moral and ethical values to undergird intellectual development and all endeavors. JCSU believes in the unrelenting pursuit of knowledge and in the values of cultivating the life of the mind...Further, it provides an environment in which students can fulfill their physical, social, cultural, spiritual, and other personal needs through which they can develop a compelling sense of social and civic responsibility for leadership and service in a dynamic, multicultural society. Likewise, the university embraces its responsibility to provide leadership, service, and lifelong learning to the larger community.[11]

Witherspoon graduated in 1934.

Witherspoon was working at his first teaching job when he was drafted during World War II. He served honorably in the Pacific theater. According to the *Virginia-Pilot*, "Of his time in the service, Witherspoon said he's proudest of being among three selected from 65,000 men to teach other servicemen about the G.I. Bill. Witherspoon himself used the program to get a master's degree in education from New York University...After the war, Witherspoon served as an archivist for the White House, sorting through letters to the President."[12]

Later he briefly supervised a reform school for black boys and then became principal at several segregated schools—W.C. Chance High School in Martin County, North Carolina, as well as schools in Gaston and Mecklenburg counties. When the school where he worked burned down, Witherspoon moved to Camden County in 1955 to be principal of Camden's Sawyer's Creek black school for grades one through twelve.

He worked in Camden County, but settled in neighboring Elizabeth City. Vaughn explained, "Well nobody lived in Camden but Camden (*We laugh*). If you weren't from Camden, you didn't go over there messing with their business. They've started some of that now. But then if you weren't from Camden or Currituck or Perquimans, than you better live where you're from. It just was not done...If you weren't born over there...and when Witherspoon went over there he was single and he was a nice looking young man and principal too. He couldn't afford to live in Camden." Spence confirmed, "No, not single, no."

Witherspoon wanted his new school to be a shining example of successful black education and accomplishment. Spence, a former student of the school, recalls, "When Witherspoon came in he didn't like the name. So he got rid of it and got permission to name it Marian Anderson High School [after the world famous concert singer]. [Marian Anderson School was a grade school and a high school]. I think he wanted something, as I understand it, wanted a recognized name, someone who everyone would know. He did that to sort of motivate students of what you could become...At Marian Anderson you uphold the standards that she had. There was a picture of her in the lobby."

Subsequently Witherspoon wrote the Marian Anderson High School song, which is still sung at reunions. The first two stanzas capture much of Witherspoon's philosophy: "To thee, dear Marian Anderson High, Thy praises loud we sing, To thy great precepts we strive, With hearts and minds to cling. Thy sacred walls are dear to us, Thy teachers kind and true, The mem'ry of the years spent here, We'll cherish our whole lives through."

Barbarette Davis exemplifies the sentimental attachment of many graduates to the school. The Marian Anderson class ring that Davis wears to this day, "means a lot to me. A lot of my classmates still have their class rings. I look at my kids. They don't even know where their rings are...This ring means a lot to me... It's got glass, you can't see it, but it's got glass and it looks like the Trojan [the Marian Anderson School mascot] and everything is wearing off but the Trojan head. It's been a long time ago. But I really cherish it. I love it."

Witherspoon lived by exacting standards and wanted the whole black community to do the same. He knew every teacher, student, and family connected to the school. As Vaughn explains, "He knew every child in school by first name. And he knew who is your mother and who is your brother. Everything flowed into that high school."

As Witherspoon explained to the *Virginia-Pilot*: "We must give young people back their self-esteem. They should have the feeling they are a part of the school, that they are an integral part of the school and its goings-on. We must encourage them to love the school and be proud of the school."[13]

The Power of the Black Principal

During segregation, the black high school principal was often the most powerful member of the black community. Witherspoon was no exception. As Vaughn explains, "At Camden County he was the de facto black superintendent of Camden County. During those days... the top black principal was sort of like Boss Hoggs.[14] Two different worlds... He [Witherspoon] was under the superintendent but the superintendent pretty much allowed him to run his situation. The established protocol was things flowed down from the white school to the black—the books, the school bus, the athletic uniforms. All that was something that was habit and accepted protocol and Camden County was and still is sort of blocked in and the least modern (*he chuckles*)." Vaughn explains the de facto power structure during segregation. The black principals, forced to make do with a situation that was separate and unequal, had authority over most decisions in the black school system as long as they effectively controlled the black schools.

Vaughn clarifies, "He was more, maybe Boss Hoggs isn't... In a political sense in Camden, he was not into it. In an educational sense he was the one who actually appointed the teachers of the elementary school and such like that. Technically the appointment was done by the superintendent. But he [the superintendent] came to Witherspoon and [asked him] who he [Witherspoon] recommended and the placement and the changes. And that was sort of the custom here in Eastern North Carolina. I had never seen it like that anywhere else."

Leary remembered from the time he worked at Marian Anderson: "He was a king in his own little kingdom too. I'll tell you that. And I learned a lot about black principals. A lot of black principals were, they were like their own little kingdoms. I am beginning to learn how they were so powerful. Because a lot of black schools had family units—man and his wife [both were teachers at the school].[15] And this principal had a unique control over them. I mean if you turned loose two of them, that was a whole income!...I remember him in his office and a cart going down the hall with a silver platter over there. He was treated almost like a king. He got his food special. He didn't have to go to the cafeteria...But if I was principal I probably would have done the same thing."

Because of segregation in higher education, black principals themselves went North to get degrees. Many went to top universities where they received a superior education in pedagogy and administration, which became a shared resource among black principals. Spence explains, "One of the things that was done at that time, prior to integration, there were blacks who could only attend a college of higher education and get a bachelor's degree by going out of state.[16] And I think the state sort of subsidized their tuition and they went to Columbia and NYU. Some went to Hampton which, I think, offered a master's in the late forties, early fifties. And I think North Carolina Central started a master's."[17] But by in large they went out of state and when they were out of state they picked up teaching techniques as well as testing techniques for students. They came back and formed what we call a Schoolmasters Club and this club consisted of the principals and assistant principals and they shared the ideas. And shared what they had learned with one another.

This network created a collective resource for black communities throughout Northeastern North Carolina and continues to this day. Spence goes on, "It is the sixteen-county congressional district more or less and the principals who were in this district combined and they formed this organization. And they devised their own tests, because I was in school [as a student] when they started this. And schools participated in spelling bees, groups, math tests, drama—I guess everything you have. And you were sort of tutored and challenged to do these things and taught techniques of how to take tests. Otherwise we wouldn't have known." This collective action allowed segregated schools with fewer resources to provide high-quality education to the black community and remain competitive with white schools.[18]

Spence continues, "We [students] didn't even know why we were doing it at the time. But we found the tests were simpler to do. Because we didn't understand... it taught us to time ourselves and make sure we did what we knew rather than try to do everything. That was good discipline there in and of itself because your score would be much higher than tick-tack-toe and guessing. It was very helpful."

"When he [Witherspoon] came back he was a part of this group... It is still not dissolved completely but I think the leadership got old and tired (*we laugh*). This group was not integrated, but in recent years when we were still functioning we were asked to come in and help schools and help students that were having difficulty with tests... Most students were having difficulty with that system. And we met with the superintendent here and he gave us permission to work at schools of our choosing." The Schoolmasters Club, of which Witherspoon was the president for a long time, exemplifies another enduring contribution of the black segregated system to education of blacks and whites.

Witherspoon's exceptional skills as an administrator received recognition throughout his career from blacks and whites. According to Spence, the superintendent consulted with Witherspoon on administrative matters, although this relationship was kept private. "One thing the superintendent would ask, 'How would you best do certain things?' And he would advise him based on his experience. And whatever it was I don't know, but that would be what the superintendent would implement at the normal [white] schools even though it came from him [Witherspoon]. He was truly an educator. I know the superintendent would call him in and ask for suggestions, even on integration matters. But of course you know they wouldn't discuss that publicly. That would make the superintendent look weak." This narrative reveals an interracial collaboration that few knew existed. In order not to undermine white authority, the superintendent and Witherspoon kept silent about Witherspoon's advisory role.

Educational and Disciplinary Philosophy

Witherspoon's counsel was sought both because of his administrative experience and acumen and because of his educational philosophy. Vaughn explains, "He had much of that Booker T. Washington approach [favoring a combination of classic and industrial education for blacks]. You and I and all of us know that not everyone who goes to school is going to college. And his little philosophy goes back to that little bell shaped curve. And this upper percent is going to some of the better colleges. Then you got this lower percent. But you put them together and you only have thirty percent. You got seventy percent right here in this middle."

"Even now they built a second high school but no longer do our kids take in any technical training. You are either in the college-bound group or you begin to drop out with nothing, no training. No future. And when you look at it you say we are doing a real good job with gifted and talented. And we're taking care of those with special needs. But you got a whole big group—why can't this kid learn brick masonry or carpentry or wiring if he has no intention of going on? You see he was a great advocate of that [approach] even though that is not a popular thing right now..." Witherspoon was interested in providing all students with pathways to succeed to their highest potential.

"Now this was another one of his philosophies, he said, 'Now when you plant your crop... unless you can improve the ground and the area in which your crops will grow, you are going to grow as many weeds as you are going to grow corn.' And we do this in society. We do it with animals. We breed things. But here we are trying to handle things afterwards. And we are filling up prisons... And somewhere in there, Witherspoon's philosophy is that we've got to find out why we getting all these people in the prison. We've got to stop it before it happens. Something we are doing is wrong here that is breeding a whole generation. And he said this twenty years ago." Witherspoon believed education offered the potential to diminish social ills and provide all people with avenues for success.

"And this goes back to the Booker T. Washington philosophy. You've got to educate the masses and you've got to provide them definitions and pathways to follow within the framework of their intellectual capacity. Now it is not popular to say that. 'You don't talk down to me.' All this type of thing... Witherspoon's idea is that, 'Hey, we've got a huge social problem here and we're attacking it wrong.' It's like Arthur Ash used to say, 'If the guy is beating you, then you better change your game. Because if you don't change something, he is still beating you.' Now if what you are doing is wrong, it's not working. All you can do is be worse if you don't change your tactics. And Witherspoon always thought that, and his prediction has almost come to light... We are building up the prisons. And Witherspoon predicted this. He said, "Where are we going?... We've got to be able to sow the seeds in fertile soil." In addition to working on improving education throughout his career, after his retirement Witherspoon was appointed to the State Board of Corrections by the governor.

At the Marian Anderson School, Witherspoon had his students under control. Many of the community as well as the teachers shared his philosophy of education and discipline. Spence commented, "It was a well-disciplined school. I recall he sort of turned the school around from where it was. He was responsible for the most students going to college in the history of Camden County." At one time during his tenure, more black students from Camden County went on to college than white students.

A former pioneering white teacher at Marian Anderson School, Alex Leary remembers Witherspoon: "One of the nicest men you ever knew. And I got to know him pretty well." Witherspoon also inspired fear. He walked around school with a paddle up his sleeve, ready to use it if anyone got out of line. As Rev. Ricky Banks remembered: "I saw him as a great disciplinarian and a great role model. He had his school under control. We didn't walk in the middle of the hall. We respected our elders. We took off our hats when we entered the building, and we kept our shirttails tucked in."[19]

Witherspoon used a range of strategies to discipline students. Many Camden residents at the time had strong views on his approach. Nancy and Clay Ferebee, a well-respected white farming family, commented, "It was so far as we know a very good black school, and we were very fond of the principal. He had a way of getting the boys to mind. I'll tell you, [he was] a nice fellow." Clay added, "Well, he was easy, but he also was firm when he had to be. If you were easy all the time, you're no good. He commanded respect from the children. His wife [a teacher at the school] did too." Nancy concluded, "We need more like them." Effective discipline of black children suited the desires of the white community members and the black parents.

Strict discipline in all matters was also a way to prepare black children to survive in an environment of white supremacy. One black father explained the necessity of this pedagogy:

> They [black children] had to do what a white child didn't do...A black child had to be prepared to do something in order to make a living and the other children didn't...I think that is why I was so hard on my children...And our children had to work twice as hard to get what he was getting in order to compete with the white, and he wasn't doing as much, because they do just enough to get by with a lot of other things that our children couldn't. And it is still like that now. A colored person has to learn how to give their children something of substance [at home while they're] in school.[20]

Witherspoon had support for high standards of discipline from teachers and parents. They worked together to reinforce strict discipline. Barbarette Davis, a student at Marian Anderson under Witherspoon and a current teacher at Camden Middle School recalls: "During then, teachers did, they called, well, they do it now. They call the parents. The parents seemed like then that they responded more than they do now. If the principal or teacher or anybody called our parents, we were in deep water. It was different."

Davis recalls other ways Witherspoon inspired achievement and maintained discipline, "He was really great. He walked down the hall with his head up and always said 'Good morning. How are you?' He was just different in so many ways, like I said being strict, and like I said he wanted, he really wanted them to look up and [realize that] 'Hey, you can do this! You can accomplish this in life.' He would always have that in mind, that you could do anything that you put your mind to."

"Like I say, they were really strict. There was a part of school that anything went wrong or the person found a note, he would confiscate it. He was just...it was just strict. Like one time he found a note down the hall...I was a junior or maybe a senior and he read this note. He called us in the gym...We had a program and then he read the note."

"He said, 'This child wrote a note and I would like for you all to hear it. "You may come from China. You may come from Spain. But the love I have for you would make a bulldog break his chain,"' and this girl had written it to another boy. It didn't bother her either because she kind of laughed, but it was really, really strict. But she wasn't the only one. It was like three or four [students] got up on the stage. I had to laugh because it was one of my relatives [*we laugh*]. But it didn't bother her. She just stood there. It wasn't only that note he read. He read a few others, and I guess by doing that he figured that this won't happen again."

"I think one point was that you wouldn't dare to write notes, love notes. You're there for one reason: to get your lessons, to get your work done, not to have your mind idle on other things. You're just there for your work. I mean, we had fun and we had time to do things and everything. But I guess when it came to homework, when it came to school, it was a different story. Once you were there, you were there to get that work done. That was that. He was the type of person that he wanted everything to go smoothly and it really did." These narratives dramatically describe strategies Witherspoon used to ensure students learned discipline and respect and valued education.

Others, like one of Hughes' daughters, saw things differently: "Mr. Witherspoon, he was a very strict principal. Very strict. If you were walking down the right side of the hall, you had to walk on the right. If you was walking on the left, you'd be on the left side. And I remember when he would take kids into the office. And he would turn the intercom on and he would take his paddle and he would beat you with his paddle and every classroom could hear it, you know. I thought that was cruel. You know, during that time I thought that was really cruel."

"The kids, they would be hollerin, 'Mr. Witherspoon, I ain't going to do it no more. I ain't going to do it no more.' 'You sure you ain't going to do it no more?' 'I ain't going to do it no more.' And some of those same kids, you know, they were, you know, they still do it again, you know, and he'd...do the same thing." These comments reveal the range of opinions on corporal punishments within the black community and generational differences.

Witherspoon explained his philosophy to the *Virginia-Pilot*, "Discipline is a ways and means of helping young people see the beauty, the sanity, of being an example for other young people...We had a rule that we would train the whole child...We taught them points of etiquette and hospitality and honesty. We had pleasant discussions during lunch. They were exceedingly interested in all that...We must tell them, 'You can be anything you want if you want to be it bad enough.'"

Spence summarizes the way Witherspoon ran Marian Anderson: "I don't think there was anything corrupt about him. He played it straight but his ideas he sort of rigidly enforced. I don't know anyone that worked under him that was dissatisfied with the way he was running the school or his philosophy of education. I don't think anyone was dissatisfied with that. He was a good administrator."

"He just sort of had some rigid ideas that he upheld. He ran a school that was regimented. It was like a military school...When classes changed in high school if you were on this side of the hall you go down to the end of the hall, turn around, and go down the other side of the hall. You didn't walk in the middle of the hall. You didn't walk all over the hall. If you come into class and your class was on your right you'd be on the right hand side of the hall; on the left, on the left hand side. You didn't cross over the hallway when you got to class. You would go down to the end of the hall and make a circle. That was part of his regimentation."

"And if he saw you doing otherwise, you would get called in...And when you walked down the hall, you weren't making noise. That was the kind of school he ran. And he didn't have to be there to enforce it. At study hall you could find someone goofing off, but they didn't goof off and make noise. And he would apply the paddle, I understand. He would apply the paddle and no one wanted to go into there so therefore they acted right. But if he did it on the PA system, that was something he didn't have to do often. You didn't want to go in there."

"He ran a rigid institution. I mean he would explain what he wanted done. People understood what he wanted done. And he would call assembly… When he got up to speak it was quiet—nobody was whispering, nobody was wiggling. If he caught you doing that he would call you up there. No one wanted to go up there because he'd keep you up there, and when he was done he'd take you down to the shop (*we laugh*). I used to tease him about it, 'From so and so and so and so, I heard…' And he'd say, 'Awwww, I'm just letting them know who is in charge' (*more laughter*). But I don't think he had to do it often because they understood. From day one when he got there he told him what was and what was not going to be." Despite dramatic stories of strict discipline, Witherspoon does not appear to be a capricious disciplinarian. He clearly established and enforced his rules and used dramatic moments to punish disobedience.

Describing a later point in Witherspoon's career, when he worked at Elizabeth City State University (Witherspoon's supervised disciplinary cases, rarely expelling students), Vaughn explained, "His philosophy was if he can save a mind or train a mind he has done well…" In contrast to some of the more dramatic memories of discipline in Camden, Vaughn remembers Witherspoon as an educator committed to finding ways to correct misbehavior to save a student.

Whites as well as blacks respected him. The *Camden County Press* noted, "According to local residents, it is obvious Mr. Witherspoon was the right man for the right job at the right time; this was the era that ushered consolidation into Camden's schools. Mr. Witherspoon demonstrated patience and understanding as he served as ombudsman and peacemaker during this difficult time in our county."[21] Many people, black and white, credit his leadership at Marian Anderson School as the reason school integration went smoothly.

Witherspoon's excellence as principal, including strict discipline and high standards for achievement, smoothed the road for school desegregation. Black parents who worked closely with Witherspoon to educate and discipline their children also helped ensure that integration in Camden would be a relatively uneventful process.

Witherspoon's Departure

Witherspoon left his job in Camden in 1969, the year before mandatory desegregation. He crossed the bridge to Elizabeth City to work at the historically black Elizabeth City State University (ECSU). From across this narrow river, he continued to be an iconic example of successful black education.

The reasons for his departure from his beloved Marian Anderson School and a decade of excellent leadership are not part of the public record. When Witherspoon moved on, few knew the specifics of his departure. Articles about Witherspoon say he had retired from the North Carolina Public School system. His friend Vaughn explained, "He came here [ESCU]. He was a former principal retired at Camden County. When he retired there, he came here. And when he came to the University he was the Director of Student Affairs... Now it would be Vice Chancellor of Student Affairs or whatever like that. And they had a Dean of Men and a Dean of Women and he was, I think, one of the first to have that title at the university."

"He was enticed to come here. Well, he was a little bit disillusioned with the progress of racial integration there in Camden County. It's a small county and they did things the way they did them... It is a combination of him being kind of forced and opportunity. He looked for the opportunity because he was principal of Marian Anderson. And the superintendent of the new integrated high school wanted him to stay on as principal. But the board did not."

Witherspoon's friend Spence adds, "Well mine is part speculation, part what was implied. He was there and had run a school that the superintendent was very satisfied with. However, when the time came for full integration, the superintendent was reluctant to put him there although he was the best principal they had. But he wanted him to go over there [Camden High School]—and this was not official—but they wanted him to go over there and be the assistant principal and he refused. I mean he just moved on instead of going over there and taking that job at the high school. And then with the reduction in the size of the school he also chose to move on and he got this job over here [ECSU] as the Director of Student Affairs. They wouldn't say that openly anyway because that would be against what the whole process was all about. They didn't know what kind of repercussion they would get from the other community. So I am sure that is why they simply made him that offer. So he left." After he left, Marian Anderson school, the only black school still used for integration, was renamed Camden Middle School. Witherspoon's departure signaled the beginning of school integration and closed the door on a period of great success in black segregated education in Camden.

Desegregation Begins

Many changes followed at Marian Anderson School and in black education more broadly. Spence comments, "I think perhaps the reason some of it was lost was because integration came and they had white principals...They have all been white ever since that time. That meaning [of Marian Anderson's name] meant nothing to them and most of the black teachers went other places. So the intent of the naming perhaps was lost then."

"They went in and renovated, and added on, and changed the front, and tore down the wooden structure, and added a new structure. And I still thought everything was there and then someone said, 'They've taken down the pictures and all this other material during the renovation of the building. That is not the name of the school anymore.' That happened quietly."

After Witherspoon's departure, the school changed quickly. "But since the school became a [integrated] middle school, as I understand it her picture [Marian Anderson] as well as Witherspoon's [have been taken down]. I have no idea [who removed it]. No one wants to take blame for it. I was told at one time they were just stored and it was just a matter of getting them. But no one seems to know who stored them or where..."

Nancy Ferebee recalls: "They named it Marian Anderson School to give them some pride of accomplishment in what she had done. Then when they integrated, they had a little argument about that. They just called it the Camden Middle School." It remains unclear who changed the name. No one I have asked in Camden has told me. Billy Revelle, Witherspoons' successor, doesn't recall what happened to the name of the school or the photographs. But Leary explains the rationale of a decision probably executed by the school board: "Well, most of the white people didn't want to be known as Marian Anderson. I can tell you that. The School Board [made the decision]."

According to Hughes' daughter, the role of discipline changed in schools after integration: "Yeah, the discipline did change. Because when I was in school, you stood in fear of a teacher. You know, a teacher was an adult, a teacher. And I know when my kids were in the school system, I'd go into the school and they'd be all hanging around the teacher's neck and you didn't know who the teachers were. But we didn't do that. Yeah, this was in Camden High School when my kids came through in the 1980s. My daughter started school in 1980 and that was the difference, you know."

"And, um, so integration has been good in one way. Uuhh, well in many ways it has been good. And in some ways it has not. Because you know, we just, the school systems has just lost their standards. The kids, they just... Now speaking from the point of the black school, the teachers they were just strict. And like I say, when they integrated I think some of that strictness let up."

Joyce Gallup, another student at the time and subsequent teacher at Camden High School, explains the changes ranging from discipline to pedagogy: "We had a lot, we knew a lot more about black history... When we got to high school, we didn't really hear it. The discipline was quite different because... you didn't act up because you knew if you did, then you were going to get the same thing when you got home, and they kept in close contact with the parents."

"So I think it made us good people, good students and good adults. But that didn't have anything to do with color. I think it should be done now. I think the discipline system is not good at all. We can't spank them anymore. Something needs to be done quite differently than what's being done because kids are really getting out of hand. But we didn't, because we knew what was going to happen. They were really strict on us. It was like a family relationship pretty much. A lot of them [the teachers], they knew our parents."

Gallup describes her experience as a student in the integrated school: "We were pretty much on our own. Over there [at Marian Anderson School] we felt like a big family and everybody knew everybody. If they saw you in the hall and if you were doing something, whether it was their room or not, they got on you. But when you went there [to the integrated school], it was like you were on your own. They threw us out on our own. It was quite different that way because like I said, we had to accept more responsibility because they didn't call home like they did over there. And you were expected to be, I guess, more grown up when you were in high school... But it was quite different at the [integrated] high school."

New Position, Same Philosophy

Across the river, Witherspoon continued his dedication to black education with great acclaim as director of student personnel from 1969 to 1974 at Elizabeth City State University. He brought with him many of the same educational values and practices. Vaughn recalls, "All the freshman was taught social graces. And he got all of us including myself (*we laugh*). Well, he pushed me. He said if I could get the athletes to do certain things, that the rest of the students would follow. He said, 'If the athletes start holding doors for ladies...' and we started a dress day on Friday. Friday was a sit-down dress day dinner. If I could get the athletes and the band, he said half of the student body knows them and admires them and says, 'If those old crazy football players can do this, I can do this.'"

"The social graces—which obviously come last to the poor and those who have not been in the environment—they don't even know and they reject them. It worked on them. He worked on that. He thought by doing so he could develop character and there would be fewer problems that we would have to deal with. It was part of their training. It was part of their education."

"That was Witherspoon's saying that, 'Hey, you all think this is foolish. What [difference] does being able to eat your soup [make]? You don't bring your head down to your soup, you bring your spoon up to your head'—and so forth. It could be the difference between getting a job [or not]. And he talked about dress and appearance. And he would push us. We had little workshops. 'Athletes, I don't want to see you go in that building with a young lady and you go in first. I want you to hold that door.' And they would say, 'Coach, are you crazy?!' And after a while they would do it and get in the habit of it." Witherspoon taught all students the same social graces that had enabled his father and himself to achieve great success in life.

The Bridgebuilder

Although he was an outstanding educator in the segregated school, Witherspoon dedicated his life to actively promoting interracial relations. This prompted him to join with Cader Harris, a local white merchant, to found the Hope Group after the riots in Los Angeles to ease racial tensions in the community. The group focuses on helping the races get to know each other better by such activities as speaking at local civic groups, visiting churches, helping renovate homeless shelters and low-income housing. Witherspoon was committed to the spirit of integration. Spence explains, "That was the thing behind the Hope group. Because Cader Harris at that time owned the clothing store downtown. Of course that was one of the few stores that blacks could go and get an account... Cause his daddy did that and so Cader simple carried on the same thing..." In 2002 Cader Harris was one of three people in the state to receive the Nancy Susan Reynolds award for contributions to race relations.

Vaughn elaborates, "The Hope Group was formed by Cader Harris and Witherspoon to bring whites and blacks together. They never had an agenda, didn't have a budget. Cader was named Tar Heel of the year by the Duke Foundation. Born and bred here. That was a passion after the riots in L.A. 'Burn baby burn and so forth.' And you had a new generation coming up. 'Destroy this' and so forth like that. That's when this got started. Let's just bring these people together. Let's just sit down and talk about things. Informal, it was not appointed by any city organization. But it did, still does [have influence]. It still meets. I belong to it. We go visit black churches, white churches, Jewish churches. A representative group will go to just about every church around. The agenda is just to help people, and be there, and be involved." Witherspoon and Harris felt that of all their Hope Group work, their friendship was their most important accomplishment.[22]

Spence continues, "He was a man that always had ideas. And of course he wasn't satisfied with the relations between blacks and whites in this community. They started the Hope Group. I remember when they started and that purpose and that group was a force around here. They started aging. Those who were in it are dying, aging, or in the rest home... So they aren't as large as they used to be. But that was one of his brainchilds. Many people don't understand exactly what it is all about. They should, because they visit one or two churches a month. There are no young people in the Hope Group. The ones I saw are retired. I don't know they [the younger generation] may not agree with the philosophy."

Witherspoon explained his philosophy to the *Virginia-Pilot*, "I am tired of hearing about African American or Jewish American, and all these kinds of things... Many of us of color have never been to Africa. We know little about it. We are not African Americans. We are Americans. This is the way I feel about it... When a race sees that they have as good a chance as any other race does in this democracy, that they can put their training to use, you're not going to have much trouble with race relations... Prejudice is taught. Hate is taught. The child is the imitator."[23] Through education and friendship, Witherspoon dedicated his life to intervening on this process of inculcating racism.

Political Power

Witherspoon's success in politics later in life provides further insights into his philosophy. Many accounts of Witherspoon report that he was able to get along with anybody. In 1996 one reporter wrote, "His career in education over, Witherspoon turned to politics. He served with H. Rick Gardner, now mayor of Elizabeth City, on the Pasquotank County Board of Elections. Even with a Republican majority on the board some of those years, Witherspoon, a devoted Democrat, was repeatedly named chairman."

According to North Carolina representative W.C. "Bill" Owens Jr. who first encouraged Witherspoon to run the Pasquotank County Commission in 1987: "The day I asked him to run was the best day's work of my life... He adds stability to anything he does. Time and time again when tempers flared, Witherspoon would come in and calm the waters. Largely because of his influence, that board got along very well. We felt like it was our second family."[24] Witherspoon was elected to the Pasquotank County Board of Commissioners, the first black member in the three-hundred-year history of the county. According to Vaughn, "Witherspoon was a guy that when he ran for County Commissioner the first time, the shocking thing was how large the white vote was that he got." Later Witherspoon became chair of the County Commissioners.

His political success was likely aided by the advice of his brother-in-law. Spence explains, "Did you ever hear of Buster Wilkins? That was his brother-in-law. Buster Wilkins was Mr. Democrat for blacks and whites. If you wanted to get elected to a state office, nobody would run for governor or senate without contacting Buster Wilkins. He had more influence... I think he was pro-integration. But if you are just going to integrate for the sake of integrating, then leave it like it is. Don't do a token thing. If you are going to integrate, integrate. I think that was his philosophy. He was tough. If you are a Democrat and governor, you don't come down here without contacting Buster Wilkins. He was Witherspoon's brother-in-law... So Witherspoon I am sure picked up a lot of things from him. They were good friends as well."

Once in office, his lifelong love of reading and pursuit of knowledge distinguished him on the board. "When he got on the County Commissioners, they leaned on him a lot. Because when they had a meeting and they were talking about some place that was on the agenda, Witherspoon would visit it, do his homework, and read up on it. If it was John's Lane and they wanted to put something on it, he'd been out there and saw it. The old county commissioners didn't do that. They were Boss Hoggs... They were in awe of his mind and his intelligence."

"Many whites in this area... had never had the opportunity [to meet a black man with] the real advantage of a quality education and they almost feared him because he was almost never wrong and he was a great researcher. One of his famous sayings was, 'Wellllllll, I've got to think about that.' What he meant was, 'Hey, I've got to find out some more information and check into it. Give me to tomorrow and I'll get back with you.' In the mean time, he's gone and researched and he was one that wouldn't just give you a [snap] answer like that."

Spence adds, "They [the white community] respected him...His approach may have been unlike something they would prefer to do. But he got what he wanted one way or another. And yet he was firm about getting it...Because he got what he wanted, even as a County Commissioner. He would introduce something and of course another member of the Board would say, 'I think that is a good idea.' He couldn't really introduce because he was the Chair of the Board at that time, but he got it through...I am sure there were some who disliked him. But they probably wouldn't do it openly.

"He knew how to get what he wanted. If he'd think it wouldn't fly he would mention it to somebody, 'What do you think about' so and so? And that is how he would get a lot of things done at the County Commissioners without introducing it himself. Or he may introduce it and he'd say, 'I think this is a good idea. What do you think?' And by that time he'd get about three of them [to support him]. And most of the time they'd probably vote unanimously..."

Vaughn recalls Witherspoon was criticized by some blacks. But in response, "He puts his blinders on and keeps on going." He also used these disagreements as educational experiences in politics for other black community members, "Because,...several of us went to talk to him and I learned a lot from him. We were talking about going along with the power structure of the County Commissioners on land development and things of this nature." Witherspoon's support of progress and willingness to compromise meant he was sometimes at odds with parts of the black community.

Witherspoon favored political pragmatism over taking a politically unfeasible principled position. "His philosophy was this—in fact I told it to one of the young councilmen who was always fussing—I said I learned this from Witherspoon. I'm a past president of the North Carolina Hall of Fame, the first black that they ever had in there...I got there I guess because of Witherspoon's influence on negotiating. If I had a candidate I wanted to push, then I needed to push for someone else's candidate who could vote for me when I get to my candidate."

"Witherspoon said, 'If you want them to pave Southern Avenue, which is down here, and they want to pave Church Street first. Church is predominantly white and Southern is predominantly black, even though Southern may need it first. If you don't have the votes, then you vote for Church. And then you call in those favors. And you get Southern paved.' His philosophy is that you can find two or three people who want that and need your vote who will in turn give you their vote. On the other hand you can fight them and not get Church Street paved or Southern Avenue paved (*he laughs*). And this fight just goes on. And there are still some who say, 'No, no, no, no. Why can't we do this first? Why must we always be second?' His philosophy was, 'Well, second isn't bad. It's next to first' (*he laughs again*). And he meant by that, last could be next to twentieth. But second is next to first. You look at it and you sit down and you think about it and you say, 'Wellllll, yeah...' [but I am not sure I agree completely]. But he would explain things like that."

"He was against confrontations, at least in public. He thought that eyeball-to-eyeball you can negotiate. You can go though all the records of the County Commission. Now he had some 'no' votes. He wasn't always a 'yes' voter. But his 'no' votes were on a 6–4, 5–3. It wasn't like an 8–1. Even though he didn't like particularly what he was doing, if he could build a bridge to use later, he preferred to build that bridge, particularly if the item he was going along with was not offensive to him. If it was offensive to him, and usually he had somebody else it was offensive to, he wasn't afraid to take a minority stance. And he wasn't afraid of taking a solo stance except he thought that it did no good. It didn't change anything. What you are there for is to make progress. And you do something that does no good, and actually sets you back, then you have not helped meet the needs of the changing time and progress."

When the County Commission considered naming the new library posthumously after Witherspoon: the minutes reported, "Rev. Melvin Tate said there are only two kinds of people in the world, those who build bridges and those who don't. He stated that bridge builders are considerate people who do their very best to encourage and support others, who understand the power of a kind word and the importance of sincere praise. He said bridge builders make outstanding mentors because they are eager to share their talent and experience; they are team players and lead by example; they unselfishly invest their time and energy helping others reach their full potential; and they help people without concern for personal gain or credit. Reverend Tate stated that W.C. Witherspoon was a bridge builder who believed that lives ought to have purpose and communities could always be better. He asked that the Board carry on the legacy of W.C. Witherspoon."[25] After debate, the council decided the name—the W.C. Witherspoon Memorial library.

Witherspoon continued to mediate and negotiate when others would take a different approach. Vaughn remembers, "Witherspoon was never one who would march with Martin Luther King and all that stuff. He was a mediator—meeting on common grounds... There were differences in opinion as in all things. Those who want it now. 'Burn, baby, burn,' whatever, and so forth. But he had a calming effect."

"I do know he was very diplomatic and one of his famous sayings was, 'You can be anything you want to be.' And he would always inspire [people] that in the most difficult situations you could be a better person. And a better person will make you a better family member and a better life... That was his whole philosophy: mediate, negotiate. He just thought that there were two things: looks and knowledge. You can acquire knowledge and look good."

"Well, he was trying to be the mediator. And elements on both sides didn't like it. There were blacks who thought he was an Uncle Tom, who was selling them out because he wouldn't march and he wouldn't call them a 'cracker' and things of that nature. On the other hand there were whites who were intimidated by his intellectual ability and just thought, 'He ain't from here. He is one of those uppity niggers.' And all this type of thing." By choosing to mediate rather than acceding to white power or taking the confrontational approach advocated by some members of the black community, Witherspoon was criticized by both sides.

"He really would entertain a meeting with Martin Luther King and things of that nature. But he would not go down and march on the street with them. He sort of liked to stay out of the limelight and he was getting pushed. People were saying, 'You got to choose one or the other.' And his thing was, 'The only way I choose is the right way.' You know. And he had some difficulty selling the blacks as well as whites."

Uncle Toms and Social Change

Vaughn's comment about the accusation of Witherspoon being an Uncle Tom by some critics prompted an extended discussion of what that term meant, revealing the multifaceted and sometimes contradictory uses of the term. Spence explained, "It carries the connotation that you will tell a white person what he wants to hear to get what you want. That's how I describe it." Uncle Toms often put personal advancement ahead of community interests. Vaughn clarified, "Or you're their message boy... Uncle Tom provided the white masters with all the information about what was going on. That is the whole connotation of that. And there were a few Uncle Toms in this group here (*He points to the photograph of the School Masters Club. We all laugh.*) Like I told you yesterday, many of these guys were the Boss Hoggs of their county... But even here this was the president of the college [Dr. Sidney David Williams] (*pointing to the photograph*) and you could not buy a house, buy a car, or go to the bank without them asking you, 'Did Professor Williams approve?' 'If he says you can do it, you can do it'...But again, that wasn't all bad. They had ways of getting things..." Uncle Toms, for better and worse, functioned as bridges between the white and black communities.

"Just to give you an example on Williams. There were two dormitories behind Williams Hall. The legislature was thinking about closing Elizabeth City State Teachers College because we got enrollment problems. Down as low as 375 when I went to the army. And no buildings and nothing until after World War II. And I remember because I was his driver that time at the legislature. And they had to set up a special session over the Negro presidents. And I remember him saying, 'I think you are right, we ought to close it. We can send all our colored children down to Eastern Carolina [a predominantly white institution]. Yeah I guess we could get these little colored children and get them down...' And he used the word 'colored' to them and they liked that you know. And we got all sorts of things right away (*we all laugh*). And they would be walking out of there hand and hand and the next thing you know he had a gymnasium. But that is the way many of them had to operate in those days." Uncle Tom's were savvy operators in white communities. Vaughn points out that some "Uncle Toms," despite the pejorative connotations of the word, did use their position strategically for the betterment of black communities.

Historically an Uncle Tom was known as a betrayer of his community. "So coming out of slavery the Uncle Tom was a guy who told everything that was going on to the white master. Though the slaves—such as my grandfather who was a descendant of a slave—he told me that he was a child they also used the Uncle Tom for some things that they wanted. And they would plant things with him not telling them if they really were going to do it. But the uprisings, they [the whites] knew about it. Because it is hard to imagine how a few people could control five hundred slaves. Because the runaways were a big problem. Especially if they had early word of who was going to leave tonight...But the Uncle Tom, it still goes even now, a lot of people knew how to feed them things." Vaughn points out that savvy black community members knew how to effectively manipulate Uncle Toms. The meaning of Uncle Tom changed, but the term has persisted and continues to function as a way to stigmatize powerful blacks who are disloyal to the community.

In the late 1960s, the growing militancy of many civil rights advocates increased criticism of Witherspoon's approach. Vaughn explains, "At that time the new breed of [black youth]...like a kid asked me sometime...I said something about crowding on the back of the bus. He said, 'What the hell you doing riding in the back of the bus? You get up right in front.' But that's his philosophy. 'Don't tell me about it. It's your fault.' What it [that approach] does is build confrontation. And so one group comes up with a confrontation. And so he [Witherspoon] had some difficulties. That middle lane is not always the easiest lane and the safest lane."

"That is the way he stood. He would not take sides for the sake of taking sides. Whatever you ask him to do, if he felt it wasn't in the best interest of where he stood or the best interest of all, he'd probably wouldn't lean in that direction. I guess in his position it was best that he didn't take sides in many of those instances." Despite some criticisms of his approach, Witherspoon continued to be a bridgebuilder and receive acclaim from many blacks and whites.

Public Acclaim

In 1987 Governor James Martin awarded Witherspoon membership in the Order of the Long Leaf Pine, the highest honor the North Carolina governor can bestow upon a civilian (one shared by such luminaries as Maya Angelou and Rev. Billy Graham). Elizabeth City named a street after him and, posthumously, the new W.C. Witherspoon Library.

The County Commission minutes reflect that Judge Small said, "Mr. Witherspoon was also a great man in many respects and probably made the greater contributions to the community. He explained that Mr. Witherspoon was one of the most honorable men he has ever known, was color-blind, and contributed more toward racial harmony than anyone in the community...He added that Mr. Witherspoon is as worthy of honoring as any man he has ever had association with."[26] Raymond Rivers, president of the Pasquotank County Branch of the National Association for the Advancement of Colored People (NAACP), said, "He knew Mr. Witherspoon for 40 years and was his neighbor for 30 years. He said he has not heard anyone say anything derogatory about Mr. Witherspoon and he leaves a legacy that is impeccable."[27]

On the opening day of the 2003 state legislature, Senator Marc Basnight, president pro tempore, expressed his feelings by saying, "Mr. Witherspoon was a radiant example of how we all need to work together for the betterment of North Carolina and its people. He was honorable, merciful, trustworthy...there is no limit to the adjectives that describe this special Samaritan."

Throughout my conversations in Camden and Pasquotank Counties, the Shakespeare-quoting, elegantly dressed ghost of W.C. Witherspoon's appears with remarkable frequency in both black and white memories. Despite the efforts by the white leaders of integration to erase all traces of black educational success, Witherspoon remains an iconic symbol of the heights of achievement that anyone can aspire to achieve through education in its broadest sense. But even more powerful is his indelible presence in the stories and memories of the many people who honored and revered him.

Figure 4 Billy Revelle at home. Photo by Alan Ternes.

CHAPTER 5

The Gentle Rebel

For more than a decade after the Supreme Court ruled in 1955 that school integration should proceed "with all deliberate speed," North Carolina's leaders showed how slow deliberate speed could be, as segregated education in the state continued largely undisturbed. But by the end of 1968, federal regulation threatened to dismantle North Carolina's powerful and persistent resistance to integration. This de facto[1] resistance had successfully forestalled de jure desegregation for fifteen years under the strategic code of civility that put a premium on peaceful race relations and managed, incremental change—a policy skeptics called the "progressive mystique."[2]

A decade after *Brown*, the overall impact of integration was low throughout the South: only one in a hundred black children attended an integrated school. The integration rate of North Carolina schools was even lower than in the diehard segregationist states of Alabama, Mississippi, and Arkansas.[3] In fact, North Carolina lagged behind the rest of the South: in the Tar Heel state only one out of every two hundred black children attended an integrated school, and in some counties like Camden, none did.[4]

North Carolina was well-known for its successful low-key resistance to integration—a fact that drew the interest and praise of Southern neighbors, who were experiencing unwanted federal government intervention, conflict, and even violence. In the state most of the white population opposed school desegregation. However, Tar Heel politicians and businessmen deliberately avoided the inflammatory rhetoric and open resistance adopted in some southern states. Such resistance could "harm the state's reputation for racial moderation, forestall new economic development, and invite judicial intervention in the operation of the schools."[5] Consequently, North Carolina took a "moderate" approach to race relations and education.

Unavoidable Desegregation

When large-scale educational and social change arrived in North Carolina, it was out of financial and legal necessity and was not based on the desire of the community. In 1965, the Department of Health, Education and Welfare (HEW) began investigating the process of desegregation in historically segregated states, including North Carolina. HEW was responsible for enforcing the Civil Rights Act of 1964, including Title VI, that banned racial discrimination in "any program of activity receiving federal assistance."[6] Title VI of the same Act focused on two key areas of desegregation by: (1) calling on HEW to supply technical assistance to schools in the process of desegregation; and (2) enabling the U.S. Justice Department to file lawsuits against resistant districts, based on parental complaint.[7] Passed in 1965, the $1.3 billion Elementary and Secondary Education Act—which offered desperately needed funding to southern schools—provided the carrot for compliance with the Civil Rights Act.[8] That year, in order to comply with HEW's enforcement, schools were required merely to sign a form stating they offered Freedom of Choice, to demonstrate a "good faith start" toward desegregation in four grades, and to aim for full desegregation by the fall of 1967.[9] Camden schools stalled until 1965 to initiate a freedom of choice policy.

This pro-forma acceptance of HEW's guidelines concerning "freedom of choice" and "good faith" did not, however, substantively alter the racial makeup of Camden's classrooms. As historian Kotlowski has noted, this obstructionist tactic was widely adopted:

> In countless school districts across the South, freedom-of-choice desegregation plans became the preferred method of satisfying the law. The plans left segregated patterns of schooling all but untouched, and the reasons had little to do with either freedom or choice...The success of freedom-of-choice plans for segregationists depended not only on white intimidation but also on a vigorous legal defense that attempted to take advantage of the *de jure–de facto* distinction in Title IV.[10]

De facto resistance to integration continued in many parts of North Carolina, highlighting the limitations of de jure desegregation. Finally, North Carolina's state attorney general, responding to attempts by the state's educational superintendent to further delay integration, penned a decisive blow to continued resistance. Citing the congressional Civil Rights Act of 1964, the state attorney general stated firmly that if a county or city board of education in North Carolina accepted any federal funds, then "the conditions must be complied with and administered in good faith and this means total and complete desegregation of all schools in the county or city school system." Even if the school system refused federal funds, "the Attorney General of the United States under Title IV of the Civil Rights Act of 1964 can institute legal proceedings to force the desegregation of any school or school system." To insure compliance, the letter continued:

> Neither the State Board of Education nor the county and city boards of education asked for this situation, but they must live with it and they will have to work with such clay as it is handed to them. No form of token compliance, clever schemes, chicanery or subtle or sophisticated plans of avoidance—no matter how crafty or cunning—will in the end prevail. No devices or plans whether ingenious or ingenuous will constitute any legal defense to the mandates of this Federal statute.[11]

The state attorney general's acceptance of complete desegregation foreshadowed subsequent changes in HEW enforcement. As freedom of choice failed to integrate schools, HEW tightened its guidelines in 1966, requiring "substantial compliance" in the 1966–1967 school year—the year before Leary taught at Marian Anderson School as part of teacher integration.[12] In 1968, HEW continued to permit freedom of choice plans until the 1968 *Greene* decision unequivocally ended freedom of choice.[13] In the meantime, HEW set a deadline of 1969–1970 for full desegregation. Camden County complied at the last possible moment.[14] Fifteen years after *Brown*, the combination of HEW enforcement and legal rulings resulted in the rapid decline of the percentage of black children in small Southern segregated schools from 68 percent in 1968 to 18.5 in 1970.[15]

Brown and the subsequent legal decisions, including *Green* (1968) and *Alexander v. Holmes* (1969), had finally succeeded in dismantling de jure school segregation. Despite this legal progress, white resistance to substantive integration persisted, and even strengthened as it took new forms.[16] The implementation of desegregation was on white terms. In effect, integration meant tolerance of black students in white schools with white pedagogies. Integrated schools included little black educational history, black pedagogy, or black school-community relationships. The persistent belief in white superiority—that had long rationalized inferior funding and facilities in black schools—undermined the radical possibility of integrating black and white approaches to education. Desegregation slowly lurched ahead, unwelcomed by many of both races. The day-to-day steps toward integration fell to students, teachers, and parents who responded with little acts of heroism and many acts of cowardice. But most of the criticism for executing this unpopular mandate fell on the shoulders of school principals, whose substantial efforts received no appreciation.

When Camden school superintendent Dempsey Burgess conducted a difficult search for a principal to replace Witherspoon and to change Marian Anderson into an integrated middle school, he selected Billy Revelle. Revelle knew he was walking into a challenging job when he accepted the position. His background as principal at a freedom of choice school in nearby Elizabeth City, his experiences with the Office of Economic Opportunity, and his non-confrontational approach made him a choice that blacks and whites could accept.

A Family Legacy of Good Deeds

Revelle's early life experiences prepared him for what, in retrospect, was perhaps an impossible job. As he explained: unlike Camden County, Northampton County, where he was born and raised, had "lots of black people, the largest percentage of blacks in the state."[17] Because of his background, Revelle grew up with the experience of integration in everyday life. In contrast to whites in counties with smaller black populations, Revelle and his family were not strangers to black people: "So black people did not scare me or mystify me or something like that."

Many of the values and beliefs that inspired Revelle to work for economic and racial equality were nurtured in his childhood. Born to parents Claire and James Revelle in 1928, Revelle grew up with a family tradition of commitment to the good of the community, informed by a strong Christian ethic. Like his parents and grandparents, Revelle and his wife Earlene have lived lives of quiet dedication and are unusually modest in their retellings. He recalls: "We all come from different perspectives. I think one thing would be the influence of my mother and my grandfather, my paternal grandfather. They used to say, 'You've got to take care of everybody.' I think maybe that's where it [his commitment to issues of poverty and racial equality] came from."

Revelle's generous spirit, which I originally attributed to his religious affiliation, was in fact deeply grounded in the generations of practices and stories of his family. He recalls with pride: "I remember my brother telling me later on that a black man told him that the first time he ever ate cornflakes was at my house. My mama kept cornflakes and just things like that. My mother graduated from high school. I didn't know this until after she was dead. She taught one year in school where she lived. My grandfather and grandmother both were always looking out for everyone. I kind of think that's what caused it [his ethical philosophy]." Revelle's family legacy of helping less fortunate blacks and whites through a personal act of generosity as opposed to institutionalized charity inspired him to continue in the same spirit.

Economic Justice

Before moving to Camden County, Revelle had long supported movements toward economic justice and racial equality. While his personal attitudes were radical for a white person at the time, Revelle took a nonconfrontational approach, waiting patiently for social change while working individually "to take care of everybody."

Throughout his higher education, Revelle studied the connections between education and social change. He began studying history and social change as a college student at East Carolina University. He went on to earn his master's degree in education, minoring in history. His master's thesis addressed the effect of school consolidation, forced by financial necessity, on education. At the University of North Carolina, Revelle obtained an advanced principal certificate. After graduating, he began teaching in high schools in the area near his home and later met his wife Earline, who was teaching eighth grade in Ahoskie.

When they married, Billy and Earlene Revelle moved to her hometown, Elizabeth City, which borders Camden County. Revelle "taught two years at the high school and then I was principal of Sawyer School six years. Up until the last year schools were completely segregated." His last year in 1965 was the first year of freedom of choice in Elizabeth City: "I remember we had eleven black children come in."

Before moving to Marian Anderson School in Camden, Revelle took a break from teaching to direct the Economic Improvement Council (EIC) in the impoverished sixteen-county Albemarle Region, which includes Pasquotank and Camden Counties. The EIC grew out of Lyndon Johnson's War on Poverty, announced in his 1964 State of the Union address. A series of laws were soon passed by Congress, designed to reduce the high national poverty rate. It included the Economic Opportunity Act, which established the Office of Economic Opportunity (OEO) to administer the local distribution of federal funds in projects targeting poverty. The rural tidewater region of Albemarle, North Carolina was one of the regions that benefited from the EIC.

The EIC partly grew out of the North Carolina Initiative, a local program created to address poverty in the state. Poverty had grown in the region during the 1950s and 1960s particularly due to the decline of the textile industry, which had been a major source of jobs in North Carolina. The problem was so serious that it had led to two decades of significant migration from the state.[18] In response, Governor Terry Sanford and liberal Democrats created the North Carolina Fund to "awaken the state to the human and social costs of poverty and racial inequality."[19] Reflecting on this initiative, Sanford said, "The Fund's first effect was to disrupt existing power structures within communities so that change in the status quo could occur. In most cases, this amounted to radical changes in community relations and activities—but this we did knowingly, realizing that positive results would occur when existing structures were challenged by the new."[20] As the regional administrator, Revelle supervised a number of VISTA volunteers and worked with communities on issues of poverty and racial conflict across ten counties.

Like these volunteers, when Revelle went into the community for the EIC, he found himself in what has been described as "a tangle of connections that tied racism and poverty to political power, class interests, and the privileges of whiteness."[21] While at the EIC he met with the Ku Klux Klan because he saw racist oppression as closely tied to issues of poverty: "One time when I was head of the EIC, I called and asked the leader of the Klan to come meet me and we talked and we just disagreed, but we didn't have any shouting matches. Just trying to see if there was any way we could kind of quiet things down a little bit." According to Friar Moses Anderson, at the time, the Klan presence included "a big sign on the bypass, 'The Klan welcomes you to Elizabeth City.'"[22] Working for economic and social justice was a lonely endeavor in Elizabeth City, one of the principal sites of Ku Klux Klan activity in the region.²³ When I complimented him for his courageous confrontation with the Klan, Revelle replied, with characteristic modesty, "That was really no big problem."

As a person committed to economic equity for all races, Revelle became an object of, in his words, "fussing" by parts of the white community. Verbal intimidation was a way whites kept their own in line, maintaining white power. Revelle was criticized by some for his work with the EIC and the black community. He recalled an exchange that exemplifies attempts by white people in positions of power to squelch interracial efforts to reduce poverty. "Well, I remember one County Commissioner over in Perquimans County really fussed with me about taking this job, doing that job, and I don't know whether he used the word 'nigger' or not, but he was the kind [a racist]. Well, I was helping the niggers out (*he mocks the commissioner's racist point of view*) ... He also mentioned I have a second cousin who was a county commissioner. He couldn't understand our county commissioner with a cousin [Revelle] who would do something like that."

He recalled, "Well, any time you do anything for black people, you were called a nigger lover. This again was a big change for people. I could relate to these people because most of my kinfolks—not my parents or my grandparents—had the same problem [racism]." While the views of his relatives on race relations were different from his own, Revelle recognized and tolerated racism in his "kinfolk" and many whites in the community.

Revelle shrugged off his social change activities. He admits, "I usually don't respond too much. I just let people fuss and get it over with. I'm not a fussing person myself." He played an active role in confronting structures of oppression but did not engage in interpersonal conflict about race or defend himself. While Revelle did not claim his calm response to challenges was a strategy for dealing with racism, the pattern of refusing to respond to fussing worked as a protective armor against extreme white supremacist backlash.

Revelle's greatest challenge, however, was not the racist Klansman or name-calling community members: "I was trying to think of other things like that, but I remember the county commissioner. I've forgotten his name now, and a few other people fussed, but not too much." He continued, taking a deep breath, "I think the main thing was, during the EIC period there was very few times people said, 'I think you're doing a good job.' That kind of support would've helped. I feel like I was all alone with no help." As Korstad and Leloudis write about initiatives by the North Carolina Fund, these stories at their best "underscore the role of inter-racial, cross-class alliances in nurturing an inclusive, democratic society."²⁴ In remote areas, far from Raleigh and

Chapel Hill where such ideas were fostered, pioneers such as Revelle engaged in the struggle for social justice found few allies.

White Resistance

At the time of his transition from one controversial position to another, from EIC director to principal of a previously all-black school, Revelle had expected a more positive reception from the black community. The superintendent had told him the black community would support his hire.[25] But Revelle knew the reactions of the whites, including his neighbors, who "were very violently opposed" to school integration, and by extension to him as a prominent symbol of change. As a bridge between the white and black worlds and a traveler between his white neighborhood and an all-black school, he was subjected to stigmatization and exclusion, albeit often in subtle ways. For example, one day when Revelle went out to get his mail, he found his neighbor cleaning off the nameplate on his mailbox. He joked with Revelle, "I wouldn't want to be mistaken for you." He recalls, "I got fussed with several times but never threatened physically or anything like that during EIC or at Camden."

Despite my repeated attempts to laud his efforts for integration, he persisted in being self-effacing, downplaying the significance of his actions. This humility served Revelle well in his efforts to work as a bridge between the black and white communities. He did not try, and still does not, to portray himself as a hero, a powerful leader, or a community icon. Rather he sees himself simply as an educator.

Full of positive visions for school integration and increased social and economic equity, Revelle failed to foresee the reaction of the black community to his position as Witherspoon's successor and the first white principal of the segregated Marian Anderson School.[26] "Well, I wanted to get back in education. I had had six successful years at the Sawyer School. One time when he was hiring me, Mr. Burgess did say something about that people in the black community would accept me." He did not realize all the obstacles of community sentiment and racism he would face as a principal walking into the quagmire of implementing de facto desegregation.

Revelle was as an integrationist. Concerning the rationale for desegregation, he claimed that is it was "time to make things right." Revelle was pro-everybody, believing that neither race nor class should limit the opportunities and the rights of anyone. As a principal of Marian Anderson School, he was integral to school desegregation in Camden. For the school year 1969–1970, his first at the school, Revelle oversaw an all-black student body, and was part of the integration of administrators and teachers.

The First White Principal of Marian Anderson School

For the 1970–1971 school year, Revelle became the first principal in the newly integrated middle school. While the integrated elementary and high schools were originally white schools, Marian Anderson was the only black school that was chosen to host an integrated student body. The changes at Marian Anderson, which Revelle oversaw, were significant: a quiet white outsider took over the role of principal from a renowned black leader; the name of the all-black Marian Anderson School was changed, upon integration, to the Camden Middle School; the school colors went from crimson and gold to blue and white; and photographs of black class graduations (which had been displayed in the corridors)—a visual history of black educational achievement—were removed. Revelle said he did not make any of these decisions, nor was he consulted. He speculated that they were made by superintendent or the all-white school board.

Revelle's memories of his first year at Marian Anderson stand in stark contrast to his second year, when full integration began. When he began at Marian Anderson, it was a school of all-black children from grades one through eight. The next year the school became fourth through eighth grades and was integrated "about sixty percent white, forty percent black." On his arrival, a complicated set of tasks awaited him. One was to administer the then all-black school. The other part of his job the first year was to prepare the black school to meet white expectations the following year. He found the school facilities and supplies were inferior to the white schools where he had taught. Revelle affirms what many had long known: the facilities and resources of the black schools were not equal to those of white schools despite *Plessy*'s mandate.

Looking back on the implications of being the first white principal in a historically black school, Revelle remembers that he had been led to expect a relatively calm reception: "I don't know how much there was some resentment that a white person would come in and take over. But the superintendent at that time told me later on that he had talked with right many people in the black community and that I would probably be pretty well received." This expectation was perhaps not logical given the fact that the arrival of a white principal foreshadowed a massive loss of power of the black community to shape the education of black children. In addition, Revelle's arrival highlighted the loss of their beloved Witherspoon, a self-made model of black male authority.

Despite assurances from the superintendent, Revelle's kinfolk were concerned about his safety as a white authority figure walking into a black school, and in the face of significant social resistance to integration by both black and white communities: "I think I told you before that my aunt was afraid I was going to get cut up. This is a thing that we felt that blacks always used knives. There were people that were afraid for me, I think... But I really did not feel a great deal of fear." These comments bring to life the rampant white fear of black violence, which shaped desegregation, even when whites had full authority over the formal process.

Discipline in Black and White

Despite his calm demeanor, Revelle, after some reflection, recognized his own concerns in his new role as the only white principal in a black school in the county. "Like I said, the first year I did not sweat it out too much. I was a little apprehensive, to be honest. I really was going over there alone. But they had had white teachers before." Instead, he was most concerned by the storied difference between the strict disciplinary practices of Witherspoon and some teachers in contrast to his own: "It was something I don't know if I told you or not, but Mr. Witherspoon used to spank boys over the PA system. And I remember one teacher allegedly—and I just heard this—when she would punish a child, sometimes she'd pour alcohol up their nose. Cat of nine tails[27] would probably have been better." In contrast, he characterized his own attitude to discipline as being less confrontational: "I am easy to get along with. I don't like to paddle or stuff like that, not real hard-boiled... Passive... Sure, it was just a personality difference."

When Revelle arrived, the sound of Witherspoon's paddlings still echoed through the school. So did the memories of the strict discipline, respect, and order demonstrated by all students as they walked single-file through the school halls, shirts tucked in. Discipline, as many Marian Anderson students remembered, took such everyday forms as students never wearing hats in the school and always demonstrating social graces.

The more lenient discipline introduced by Revelle created a sense of loss of an important value for black teachers and parents alike. Not all teachers welcomed this change: "I think in a way the teachers under me adapted to that pretty well. Some of them fussed about it. I remember I would give a light tap, tap that's all. She [one teacher] wanted real discipline. I admit I'm too far the other way." Strict discipline was a vital aspect of black pedagogy at Marian Anderson School, and both parents and educators upheld its value in their community-oriented approach to raising children.

Revelle's nonconfrontational approach clashed with that of many of those in the community, whose philosophy more closely resembled "Spare the rod, spoil the child." Revelle brought to Marian Anderson School his strong beliefs in equality and justice. He was not prepared by his education or previous experiences to use the disciplinary approach of the black school community, born out of centuries of inequality and injustice and a desire to succeed despite the restrictions of white supremacy.

Challenging Times

As our conversations continued, forgotten memories arose out of a sea of forgetting, tender moments when black and white experiences and cultural values conflicted. Some black teachers did not share the priorities Revelle brought to Marian Anderson School. One such memory involved Revelle's desire to make school pictures inexpensive enough for most children to buy. This goal conflicted with the desire of some teachers to raise money for their school.

"I remember I had done something about school pictures, so the school would not make a lot of money but the pictures would be cheaper for more children to buy. That is what I was trying to do. One day I was explaining that to the teachers and one [Mrs. Witherspoon, Principal Witherspoon's wife] said, 'that's the craziest thing I've ever heard in my life.' At first it kind of hurt, but then everybody kind of laughed. But I could see her point. This was money we could use to buy stuff for the school. But I wanted more kids to be able to buy pictures. Things like that, just snapshots, come back and forth."

Revelle, familiar with economic hardship and inequality, wanted all students to have a photograph. The black teachers, long familiar with insufficient school funding, wanted to increase the financial support for a good education. Revelle, who also had to balance the budget, was working to straddle both the needs of the school and financial difficulties of poor families.

Even though the change in leadership and resistance to desegregation caused some strains, Revelle considers his first year as the easiest time of desegregation. He does recall, however, a few occasions that reflect the volatility of the situation and the black resentment: "I probably told you before that one black bus driver I thought one day was going to run over me. But she was very angry about me. You could tell by the expression that she was very angry about integration. Plus the fact that the black community was losing their school, so much of their social power to a large extent." This observation is typical of Revelle's empathy toward others, his ability to interpret the emotions behind the facial expressions of others. He could understand her anger. Even at times when he felt threatened and could have responded with authority, he instead paused, reflected, felt empathy, and moved on without invoking authority or engaging in conflict.

Only after extended conversations did Revelle revisit my questions about concerns for his personal safety. "There were a couple of times I was a little scared. I remember one time I had to get in the gym. One evening I went down there to do something and saw the lights on. But I went on in and called them, and they all came and just as nice. They liked to play basketball, and that was the only place they could play basketball. They had found out how to get in the back door. I remember talking to the superintendent about it, but I forgot what we decided, whether to let them keep on. There were a couple of the high school boys there. They said, 'we take care of it so we don't cause any problems. If anyone gets out of line, we take care of it.' As far as I know they have. But it was a little scary to go in there because, see, I had been indoctrinated with this idea that blacks were this, that and the other. It takes you a little while to get past it. But the young boys were very nice about it. Other than that I didn't have any scary moments."

In retelling this moment, Revelle remembered his own attitudes toward race from his upbringing, attitudes that shaped his initial perceptions. Unlike some relatives and community members, Revelle did not confront or escalate delicate situations. He tried to understand the perspectives of the blacks he encountered—such as the simple need for children to play basketball in the only space available to them.

Revelle then recalled other incidences of conflict: "Maybe a couple of times. It could've gone that way [violence]. Not really a physical danger. I don't remember. Now the last day of school...some black boys came over from the high school. There was an old house over in front of the school, and they were over there kind of doing a little mouthing but nothing too bad. Just they were angry because their school had been taken over."

He clarifies that he was not the object of their mouthing but an audience: "I think they were just talking out loud. One of them came over on the campus, and he mouthed off a little bit, but I don't remember too much.

I could kind of understand where he was coming from. I don't think most of them were angry with me." An essential quality of his successful handling of potential conflicts is that he does not take them personally. Instead he listens and continues to be a bridge, however tenuous, between black and white community members.

Unlike many white and black community members at the time, Revelle believed integration was the right policy: "Well, as you probably have gathered, I have been pro-black for a right long time now. Basically I would say I'm an integrationist rather than pro-black. Yes. It was time to make things right." In this turn of a phrase, Revelle undermined the twisted racist mindset that would call him a "nigger-lover." Revelle was pro-everybody, not letting race or class limit a person's potential. Yet he was not color-blind. He knew that race and racism powerfully influenced daily life.

Despite Revelle's dedication to what he felt was just, his attempts to bridge the racial divide exacted a strong toll on his spirit and body. He recalls, "Well I am, I'm kind of a scary person. I mean I'm not real brave and outgoing. Things just bother me...I had an ulcer one time from the stress like this. That was my problem. I think it was more of a fear that you have two groups of people who are coming together and they don't like each other. You don't know whether it's going to blow up or not." In this uncharacteristically bold choice of words, Revelle remembered the volatility of the situation he faced in the early years of integration. In the face of this potential crisis, he found solutions to the fundamental challenge that sociologist Kenneth Plummer raises: "How can we create bridges, find connections, make links across divides?"[28]

White Students in a Formerly Black School

Revelle crossed multiple thresholds, bridging them in ways others did not. While at the EIC, he met with the Klan to request that they discontinue their activities. When principal of Marian Anderson School, he stood at the threshold of the school as white children first entered into the newly integrated Camden Middle School (the name of Marian Anderson School after desegregation). This scene of racial desegregation, unimaginable to many, unleashed further white opposition to integration. The white community was awash with derogatory depictions of this unknown school.

Revelle describes one incident: "To give you one example, before [integrated] school started, they had a meeting...a big rally...at the courthouse. This was an open meeting, opposing integration. OK, and basically all of them were white. I'm not sure whether any blacks were in the group or not. I was not there. Now who got that meeting together, I don't know. I've got an idea it was probably a county commissioner, but I'm not sure about that." Many whites felt federally mandated school desegregation was an unwanted governmental intervention in their community. This anti-integration rally at the courthouse demonstrated white public power to challenge laws of the land in favor of long-standing racial formations.

Revelle, true to the notion of a *public* school, invited the white community members to tour the historically black school. "I let it be known if they wanted to come over [from the rally] and go through the school, they could do that...A lot of people came by and walked through the building and everything. There were some angry looking folks there. That [his opening the school] is one of the things that made the superintendent really angry...I probably should not have done that."

By inviting people to see the actual school, Revelle saw this as an opportunity to reduce racist ignorance and fear and decrease opposition: "Well, I kind of felt like the schools are the people's property and they had a right to look." Revelle's interpretation bespeaks a more fundamental philosophy of education. He did not let himself be limited by past traditions.

He explains why he believed opening the school might reduce white resistance: "See, most of them had never been in Marian Anderson School, which it was still at that time. Most of them had heard it was a pigpen. For example, one day before school started, two or three white young men, boys, came by, and I heard one of them say, 'I wouldn't let my hogs live in something like this.' Just a typical racist attitude." Revelle surmises that much of the resistance arose from long-standing racist stereotypes, demonstrated as a performance of backlash by some in the white community.

Revelle was a rebel in his own way, wanting to bring about profound social change quietly. He did what in his judgment made sense and was the right thing to do, despite potential consequences. As principal, he had to contend with vehement white resistance at the beginning of forced integration. Although he knew Marian Anderson School was an inferior facility, he also recognized that in a poor, rural community none of the school facilities were ideal: "I think that was part racism. Like I say there really wasn't that much difference between Marian Anderson Middle School and the high school. Both of them were kind of run down. Both of them were kind of crummy looking. But it was just anything, that, 'I don't want to do this [integration].' A lot of it was just griping about something I have to do that I don't want to do. I'm just going to gripe and raise Cain about it."

Many whites, unable to find legal recourse to continue segregation and unwilling to welcome de facto integration, channeled their resistance into anything relating to Marian Anderson School as the lone remnant of black education in Camden County. Prior to mandatory desegregation, no white voices had publicly addressed concerns about the condition of black facilities.

According to Revelle, fears about the implications of integration underlay white public resistance. He explained the white parent perspective: "I think one thing, it was children that they wanted to protect from 'second-class' citizens [blacks]. We were pretty well totally segregated. After we lost this battle, we were going to integration. The next big thing was intermarriage. Our children are going to be in school where I can't protect them and things [could] happen to them." For some white parents, desegregation meant a dilution of the caliber of students and teachers in the schools and a weakening of their parental ability to control the educational and social environment of their children.

Revelle suggested that parents from both races had their own struggles: "Basically I would say a majority of it [resistance to desegregation] was parents. If you take the two groups, black and white, about twenty percent integrated pretty well; maybe thirty or forty percent of each group had a little trouble; and then you have about twenty percent who just had been taught racism on both sides." Among the many concerns of black parents were fears that their young children would be further subjected to racism and retribution by students and teachers.

While Revelle understood the feelings of opposition, he worked to reduce them. He gently promoted integration in the playground and the classroom, despite some resistance and apprehension. Remembering the values of his mother who had helped poor people regardless of the color line, he insisted his school was a public school for all the public—black and white.

Given his record of taking controversial positions that lacked community support, Revelle was not overly daunted by the challenges of the first year: "Yeah, there were difficulties, which were not insurmountable. I know a couple of remarks about some of the white teachers saying something about the black children that were a put down—and once in a while you still get that. Then there was a lot of reluctance on the part of black teachers to accept whites. There was a lot of reluctance to accept a white principal. Well, I think reluctance all the way around. This was a big change for us, of course." He realized that changes of this magnitude would not occur overnight without the complications of mistrust and racism, but he felt that with persistence and patience change would prevail.

Compared to parents, teachers presented fewer challenges to Principal Revelle: "Teachers again, I think, went through the motions of getting along pretty well. There were some snide remarks every now and then from one teacher. But I don't remember any teachers fussing at each other because of black and white. There were very few that were very loudly racist. It's kind of hard to tell because sometimes you don't know how people really feel. I know one lady who lived down here who is now dead, but she said something about talking about black children that was a little bit of a racist. But a comical racist remark."

Because Revelle was an outspoken advocate of integration, he often was not included in circles where vocal white resistance was expressed. He recalls, "I did not hear most of them [white comments]. To some extent I kind of stayed by myself. I'm not with people all the time. That's still true." Revelle recognized that de facto integration would take a long time and that segregation and supremacy were seeded deeply in the minds of racists. "My granddaddy said one time, a few heads are going to have to die before racial equality will work." This philosophy encouraged Revelle to continue his antiracist activities, rather than abandon them in the face of social pressure and ostracism, and ultimately led to his termination as principal.

Let Go from Camden Middle School

Mr. and Mrs. Revelle and I had a frank conversation about him being terminated after the first year of integration. What follows is an extended conversation between the three of us, which is perhaps most telling in dialogue. Mrs. Revelle began, "I told him one day that all I did was small talk. He's not good at small talk." Revelle responded in agreement, "I'm not really that much of a people person." She continued, "I also told him the reason that, in forty-six years we have been married, I don't think he has ever stood up for himself. I mean he's always been..." He finished her sentence, "passive. A walk over." Mrs. Revelle continued with an incensed tone, "I just feel that there have been times when you have been taken advantage of. Just like that losing the job over there [as principal]. Now he never had an opportunity to defend himself. He never demanded an opportunity to go before the school board. I think I would have. I would like to know what, tell me what, I could have done differently."

I recognized myself in Revelle's inaction, and commented, "I probably wouldn't have gone to the school board either. I think about my little sister sometimes. She kind of has a more fiery personality and the things that she would say, they kind of make me chuckle, but she stands up for herself much more than I would do myself." Mrs. Revelle continued, acknowledging the benefits of this approach, "Well, I know that Billy doesn't argue and fight and that sort of thing. I don't like that either."

Revelle chimed in, "One of the nicest comments I ever got was from Mrs. Forbes. She was a fourth grade teacher over there, now dead. She says something to the effect that, 'most things don't bother you and you don't really raise a fuss or anything like that. But when you think something is important, then you stand up. And that's what matters.'"

Revelle, who consistently stood up for equality without making a fuss, used this strategy perhaps as much because of his disposition as because of its effectiveness. He chose to only make a fuss when he felt the issue was of utmost importance. In his eyes, the termination of his job was not worth the fuss.

He recounted some of the details: "Well, Burgess had already told me I was gone" (*we laugh at his frank discussion*). Mrs. Revelle interjected, "Maybe he didn't know at the time he was gone too." Revelle laughed and continued, "There was a lot of politicking going on. I did not participate. I was no party to that." Revelle's refusal to engage in self-serving internal politics distanced him from the school board.

Revelle explained, "I don't know if the school board was probably trying to avoid taking blame for integration. I really don't know. They had a three-member white school board. Then Mr. Burgess, who was superintendent, kind of ran things. They went along with him, I think, most of the time. Whether they got together and decided that he could not continue, I really don't know what the story was there." While Revelle did not know how or why he and the superintendent lost their jobs, he understood that their dismissal was a result of ongoing resistance to the implementation of integration: "I think everybody saw it [integration] happen all around. There was no way out of it except you just had to go along with it…" While the school board could no longer postpone federally mandated integration, it could not fire the agents of this unwelcome change. As usual, the principal took the heat.

Memory and Forgetting

In finishing this touchy topic, I ask: "Is there anything else you remember about that period?" After a long pause and an awkward laugh, Revelle replies,

"Largely it's something I kind of want to forget." Although he is a historian, is pro-integrationist, and believed, "It's time to make things right," he wants to forget, revealing the powerful ambivalence of memory. To understand this ambivalence, historians Roy Rosenzweig and David Thelan's book, *The Presence of The Past* (1998), raises the question: "To which pasts did they feel most connected?"[29] Revelle had two, somewhat conflicting, sets of memories: one of himself as a white man who felt alone in his fight for social justice, and the other as a man who bridged white and black educational contexts.

His warm memories of his first year overshadow the tensions of that time at Marian Anderson School: "I don't remember it being stressful as much as the following year when we had integration... Generally, as I said, I have pretty fond memories of the first segregated year. The three girls I was talking about a while ago just brought it back. There was another girl, Ms. Lee and this is right funny. Sometimes when we're out here at Belcross I'll show you where she lives. She has this son who is a colonel or a general in the Army. But one day her daughter was working I think as a maid at one of the schools and as I went by she said, 'I'll never forget you' or something like that. It just makes you feel good." Living in Camden, Revelle often crosses paths with former students. These chance encounters stir up fond memories.

When Revelle encountered a student who he remembered from a fight at school, the passage of time allowed him to see the episode in a new light: "One of the black boys got in a fight. I saw him a couple of years ago. I was delivering Meals-on-Wheels to his father. He was kind of glad to see me. He was such a big strong boy. I don't know whether I could've taken him down or not [when he was in the fight]. Right now he probably weighs three hundred pounds. I'm five-nine. Things change. People forgive."

Here Revelle remembers two contrasting experiences concerning the same student: the school fight and his concerns about whether he could stop it and the more recent interaction when Revelle, as a volunteer for Meals-on-Wheels, encountered the grown-up student in his home. The encounter mixes past memory in which Revelle the principal gauges whether he can physically intervene in a fight, with the present situation in which an elderly Revelle delivers food to the father of a former student. These two community members, at one time in antithetical positions because of a schoolyard fight, encounter each other with warmth. Despite the tensions of those moments during desegregation, Revelle's perseverance in antiracist work points to the possibilities of reconciliation aided by time, patience, and grace.

Revelle was a gentle rebel, but did his approach work? It certainly was different: He was a gentle administrator, not a domineering figure of white authority. He avoided strict discipline, reluctant to impose painful punishment on black bodies, corporal punishment that could have invoked specters of slavery and exacerbated interracial animosities. He made great efforts to understand the feelings and motives of others, always reaching for understanding by dialogue rather than reaffirming a hardened position. He chose his words carefully, not jumping to vocal racism like the boys who "wouldn't let their hogs live in a place like this." He firmly believed that equal opportunity within an integrated public school was an inalienable right. He rejected a divided system that sustained white power. Revelle respected the human dignity of all, rather than paternalistically thinking he knew what was best for others. While he approached change with patience, he was persistent and stood firmly when "it was time for a change," rather than defer to the foot-dragging of "all deliberate speed." He refused hate, although he was surrounded by a world of racism and social strife. He is a kind-hearted timid person, who demonstrated bravery. He overcame his fears through his convictions of what was right; he was not a white supremacist hiding inside white sheets while creating terror. He refuses accolades, displaying an unrelenting modesty about his untiring efforts for a more just world, rather than being a self-promoting, image-conscious power seeker, who crumbles when his façade is revealed. And, with a self-deprecating sense of humor, he would probably deny all of these traits.

Revelle offers a road less taken that has garnered him, in the fullness of time, a deep respect in both the black and white communities of Camden—a respect that is rare. His approach demonstrated that he could listen to all parties, take the best intentions of education seriously, and carry out an enduring commitment to social justice. This uncommon approach, especially by many whites in positions of authority, offers a fruitful alternative for addressing issues of race, education, and equity today—a road that if walked in the company of other ordinary people can pave a path toward a dream fulfilled.

CHAPTER 6

Pedagogy and Social Change

> What will happen to the children?... Would the new academic environment still encourage black students to learn?
>
> —Vanessa Siddle Walker

White resistance long delayed the educational changes that *Brown v. Board of Education* (1954) promised. Many blacks did not welcome this change either. As Judge Loren Miller wrote, "The harsh truth is that the first *Brown* decision was a great decision; the second *Brown* decision was a great mistake."[1]

The ambiguity of *Brown II* (1955) created two basic problems. First, as scholars Charles and Sarah Willie argue, "Failing to define operationally the concepts of public interest, private consideration, all deliberate speed, good faith compliance, and reasonable start, the Supreme Court effectively slowed the desegregation process, in Robert Dentler's words, to something less than a snail's pace."[2] Second, those given the ultimate power to implement school desegregation—the white school boards—often opposed integration. Willie and Willie point out, "To devolve authority upon local school boards to solve the problem of public school segregation that they were responsible for creating and maintaining is like asking the fox who was caught stealing from the hen house to act as its security guard."[3]

At a time when imminent legal sanction left no other option, Witherspoon and Revelle were the appointed leaders of this unpopular transition. It is easy to look back on history and choose the right path. It is a far greater challenge to be in the midst of the storm called progress and choose a righteous path. Both Witherspoon and Revelle embarked on this often-lonely endeavor, especially during the early days of school desegregation.[4] As Witherspoon's friend Coach Vaughn said, "That middle lane is not always the easiest lane and the safest lane." Many people wanted Witherspoon and Revelle to pick a side. Both of these educators preferred to mediate and negotiate in polarized communities. On the few occasions where a position or an action was against their moral values, they refused to compromise. Generally, however, they realized there were a variety of goals and strategies for bringing about change. They both favored a moderate approach to bring about change quietly.

Witherspoon and Revelle bridged racially divided communities. As they learned, interracial bridgebuilding was not a safe occupation in the late 1960s and early 1970s. It remains challenging today. One of the first conversations I ever had when I arrived in Elizabeth City captured the depth of enduring racism. I suggested in partial jest that the bridge between Elizabeth City and Camden be named after Martin Luther King Jr. to represent the spirit of integration. One of my friends from the Museum of the Albemarle replied, "Heavens no! Then people would have to swim across!" This satirical remark captured a reality of the region that I had yet to understand—many interracial bridges are still not welcome or well traveled. Witherspoon and Revelle had both labored to build critical foundations to these bridges, decades earlier. They weathered the racial and political turmoil differently: Witherspoon just put on blinders and went right down the middle, riding on his beliefs. Revelle, unused to navigating the storm of racial conflict, internalized the strife.

Witherspoon, famous for his knowledge of poetry, often used the Edwin Markham poem "Outwitted" in his public presentations. This poem captures Witherspoon's approach to the racially exclusive politics he encountered:

> He drew a circle that shut me out—
> Heretic, a rebel, a thing to flout.
> But Love and I had the wit to win:
> We drew a circle that took him in!

Time and again when Witherspoon faced potential confrontations, he moved away from direct conflict and found the wit to win by his political savvy in building interracial alliances and expanding his circle of influence. After a decade of leadership in the segregated black school system, when he faced the option of being demoted and working in a smaller school, he did not publicly fight the demotion. Instead he found another position where he could continue to advance black education. Later he and a like-minded white businessman started their own interracial effort to bridge the white and black communities through the Hope Group.

Witherspoon, Washington, and Du Bois

Witherspoon was a high-profile leader, as a principal in Camden, a dean of students at Elizabeth City State University, and later as a long-time county commissioner. He was a public figure, respected by both the black and white communities, who admired his leadership. Some criticized him as an "Uncle Tom," others as "uppity." The barbs Witherspoon brushed aside resemble the criticism leveled against two famous black educators—Booker T. Washington for being an assimilationist, and W.E.B. Du Bois for being a radical.

Education scholar Derrick Alridge argues that Washington and Du Bois shared a similar perspective on success for blacks: "It is important to mention that their goals of racial uplift through economic means and hard work were similar, in that both men were ultimately concerned with Negroes gaining economic stability and becoming self-sufficient. The difference lay in their means of accomplishing these goals."[5] Washington and Du Bois are often positioned as polarized figures in black thought, but Witherspoon's approach to education showed a subtle and complex understanding of their convergence. Like Washington, Witherspoon saw value in vocational education for some black students. He felt that providing every student an avenue for success was an important function of education. As his friend Coach Vaughn explained, Witherspoon supported various pedagogies that led toward racial uplift and away from dropouts or prison.

Like Du Bois, Witherspoon supported the value of segregated education. As educational scholar Jerome Morris writes, Du Bois "concluded that the cultural sustenance of Black schools and teachers, for Black children, should not be ignored in the overall effort to eradicate legalized segregation in U.S. society."[6] Witherspoon dedicated decades of his life to this cultural sustenance. He understood both the strengths and weaknesses of segregated and "mixed" schools as described by Du Bois:

> The Negro needs neither segregated nor mixed schools. What he needs is education. What he must remember is that there is no magic, either in mixed schools or in segregated schools. A mixed school with poor and unsympathetic teachers, with hostile public opinion, and no teaching of truth concerning Black folk is bad. A segregated school with ignorant

> placeholders, inadequate equipment, poor salaries, and wretched housing is equally bad. Other things being equal, the mixed school is the broader, more natural basis for the education of all youths. It gives wider contacts; it inspires greater self-confidence; and suppresses the inferiority complex. But other things seldom are equal, and in that case, Sympathy, Knowledge, and Truth outweigh all that the mixed school can offer.[7]

Witherspoon knew the merits of segregated schools, the dedication of black teachers, and the important bond between the segregated school and the black community. But he did not fight against integration or for continued black control over their segregated schools, as some blacks would have preferred.

Witherspoon did not confront racism directly. Aldridge argues, "By engaging race and racism and providing viable strategies for ameliorating the conditions of Negro life, Du Bois placed racism at the center of American life and educational philosophy and included race as an integral component of his Negro emancipatory educational strategy."[8] Witherspoon led a segregated school that helped the black community succeed in a racist society, but he did not publicly oppose racism. Instead, he worked with whites, a position that some critics felt was too accommodating. But despite his moderate stance, Witherspoon ran his school in line with Du Bois' hopes for black education: "The community must be able to take hold of its individuals and give them such a social heritage, such present social teachings and such compelling social customs as will force them along the lines of progress, and not into the great forests of death."[9] Witherspoon achieved this, at one point sending more black students to college than the white school of Camden did.

Witherspoon's philosophies of education for both segregated and integrated school emphasized progress. By pragmatically embracing the ideas from both black educational leaders, Witherspoon bravely walked down the middle of the long, rocky road toward the bright but distant future of an uplifting education for all.

Responding to White Resistance

Revelle measured his success at the black Marian Anderson School in part by his ability to avoid racial conflict. When asked what he was most proud of from his time at the school, he replied: "Getting though the year! As one retired teacher told me, 'As long as you didn't burn down the school, you did all right!' (*he laughs*)...At any time during those two years that I was there, things could have blown up a lot worse than they did." He had employed the same nonconfrontational style when he worked at the Economic Improvement Council.

He recalled a community conflict where his approach prompted resentment. "There was an idealist young man [a VISTA volunteer] who was living in Hertford. And if you want racism, you went to Hertford (*we laugh*). That was the worst place. And I forgot what happened, but they were about ready to have a riot and so we [the EIC that Revelle ran] pulled him out." Revelle stepped in here to avoid racial conflict.

"And there were a group of fifteen to twenty black women and one black man who called me over to come talk with them. And I met with this group of people and they were about as mad as anybody could be. And I think if it hadn't been for the black man, I might have been run out of town (*he laughs*). I don't know. But I explained to them that rather than have a riot we needed to cool this. And the principal of the black school came to our defense also. He was a pretty big guy. He said that 'We're not going to tear Hertford up.' He was a calming influence. He'd kind of rebut some of their arguments."

"They were angry at me for pulling him out. He [the VISTA volunteer] had started a black Boy Scouts troop and he was out marching them up and down the road. In the sixties, that would scare most people to death. At that time this was a big deal." While Revelle worked for social change, he would not fuel conflict and confrontations.

In a similar but less public pattern to the late Witherspoon, Revelle continues to work on interracial initiatives—from county social services committees to Meals-on-Wheels. Revelle kept his head down and went about working for social change. Fannie Mae Lewis, a former black cafeteria worker who saved a pro-integration letter that Revelle sent to the paper in 2005, said, "Mr. Revelle is Mr. Revelle! He is just a good man."

Both Witherspoon and Revelle remained committed integrationists. Forces external to Revelle and Witherspoon limited their respective abilities to bring about school desegregation. The school board, white resistance, a racist society, persistent de facto segregation, and time, all limited their ability to achieve full meaningful school integration in the short term.

Brown (1954) and impending school desegregation prompted massive white resistance. The white boys who passed Revelle at the all-black school and said, "I wouldn't let my hogs live here" are one example of this resistance. Their use of animal terms and the performance of disdain worked as way to rearticulate white supremacy in the face of inevitable desegregation. The trope of blacks as animals (grounded both in a history of white representations of blacks as well as in agricultural terms local to Camden) is employed to degrade a historic black educational and community institution. Prejudice is an embodied practice. Judicial rulings and abstract concepts of equality and opportunity are not. As Linda Moore argues: "Prejudices are organized on bodies...cannot be disorganized by appealing to abstract claims of freedom and equality of a tradition which regards the body as its chief enemy. If prejudice is organized on bodies, it must be disorganized on bodies."[10] Bringing black and white children together in school did not guarantee that blacks would gain freedom, equality, or more power. In fact, it prompted a white backlash based on deeply engrained prejudices. Revelle, as the white principal, had to navigate a path through such backlash toward integration. He recalled, "At that time, I don't remember that there would be five percent of white people who were in favor of integration."

Revelle's memories illustrate the limitations of *Brown*, specifically, and the law, more generally, to integrate a segregated society. His experiences are an example of what Noblit and Collins point out is the misplaced burden of school desegregation on education. Desegregation of education facilities could be legislated. School systems could be charged with implementing this change. But, while law opens critical spaces for change, law alone cannot be expected to end the historically sanctioned prejudice and racism. Philosopher and cultural theorist Luce Irigaray writes, "The symbolic order is an imaginary order, which becomes law. Therefore it is very important to question again the foundations of our symbolic order in mythology and in tragedy, because they deal with a landscape, which installs itself in the imagination and then, all of a sudden, becomes the law."[11] In other words, the symbolic order as it "becomes law" is a powerful force in shaping social change. Integration has been delayed far more because of limits of imagination, the constraints of our symbolic order, and interests in what Du Bois called the "psychological wage" of being white (in other words, as Segrest writes, "a modicum of economic privilege and a dollop of racial superiority"[12]), which exceeds the reaches of any judicial decision.

White Power

These same forces of white resistance did not maintain Witherspoon as the black principal of an integrated school, nor did it preserve the name of famous black opera singer Marian Anderson in the integrated middle school.

As educational scholar Gloria Ladson-Billings points out, racism and white resistance undercut *Brown*: "What the decision and its supporters could not account for was the degree to which White supremacy and racism were instantiated in the U.S. cultural model."[13] In Camden, the school board was a significant force in institutionalizing white resistance in the process of school desegregation. Both Witherspoon and Revelle were subject to the decisions of the all, white school board that did not welcome school integration. They both served at the Boards' pleasure. Revelle commented on Witherspoon's situation as a black principal: "If he were radical, he would have lost his job. And it is as simple as that. In a group that wants things certain ways, it is good to know how far to push and when to back off." Sociologist of education Robert Crain noted, "The more positive the attitudes toward the civil rights movement on the part of the school board members, the greater the extent to which the school system will move to integrate (desegregate) the schools."[14] The Camden school board did not welcome the Civil Rights Movement. Instead they sought to deny it.

Blacks and many whites saw desegregation as a change implemented primarily by the whites. And in Camden it was. White leaders maintained control of the process. One of the unresolved questions of this research is: exactly who were these people who made the decisions about desegregation? The answer to this question lies hidden under a veil of whiteness over Camden County and continues to enshroud the disproportionate white authority, including the school system.

According to theologian Reinhold Neibuhr, "equal rights before the law" (in this case, the opportunity for white and black children to attend the same school) is "minimal justice."[15] "Justice is not just about 'Who gets how much of the pie? But also, what kind of pie is it and, who is to decide?'"[16] In Camden, the all-white leadership made all the decisions for the process of school desegregation and the future of integrated education.

Like other white school boards throughout the South, Camden's board members had "a highly developed sense of responsibility for the preservation of the economic power and prestige interests of... the classes with which they were affiliated."[17] As educational scholar Donna Davis echoed, "The school boards often resisted the mandates of *Brown*, and when compelled to comply they did so in a way that protected the interests of Whites."[18] As a result, school desegregation arrived in Camden on terms dictated by a white school board—without integration of white and black interests or pedagogies or power sharing.

Persistent De Facto Segregation

Another ongoing obstacle to school integration was the entrenched de facto segregation throughout the Camden community and beyond. Schools desegregated to a degree but much in the broader community remained segregated—from neighborhoods to churches. As Davis argues: "Until we confront deeply held beliefs about race in this country, our schools will reflect the patterns and ideologies of a racist society."[19]

As a principal of a segregated school, Witherspoon ran a successful school surrounded by racist society. Revelle led a school during the precarious first steps of integration and, despite his efforts to avoid and reduce confrontation, found himself a lightning rod for racist antagonism.

As leaders at a time of unpopular but mandated social change, both Witherspoon and Revelle faced a daunting challenge. Both principals were committed to school desegregation. Both wanted to lift up people through education. Their motivations for helping to bring about this change were shaped by their experience. Revelle learned his ethics from the values and good works of his Christian mother; Witherspoon's model for his outstanding accomplishments was his father, the preacher.

Witherspoon modeled racial uplift in the black community through his own performance and through strict discipline and exacting standards. Revelle's goal was to lift up the poor—which included whites as well as blacks—in Camden because the fluctuations of its agricultural economy hit the poor of all races. "Generally I have always been for the underdog, which would be part of it. And again, that it is right to treat people without regard to color." He conceived of the school as a public good, responsible to and belonging to everyone.

Yet Revelle's ethics and philosophy also contain elements of white assumptions that limited the potential of integration. His conception of public education as a public good, while itself radical, did not preserve the rich role the school had in the black community. For blacks, the Marian Anderson School was a vital source of community power—where the child, family, community and education connected, and where black people went to vote. These core values got scuttled during the first year of integration and have not been revived.

Revelle felt that it was time for integration to happen. But as a pro-integrationist, he was too far ahead of his time for many in Camden, particularly the white school board. Witherspoon was behind the times in some ways, dedicated to formalities and social graces that the younger generation rejected in favor of social activism and black power. Witherspoon was so formal that racists couldn't stereotype him. His formality served as an effective shell. Although almost outdated, his performance allowed him to lead in a racist society. Witherspoon was ahead of his times in other ways—actively trying to bridge black and white communities and working as a community leader to improve race relations while others preferred confrontation and living in segregated worlds.

Both Witherspoon and Revelle were patient change agents but they offer different lessons about leading social change. Revelle was the everyman change agent—an average citizen doing his part to improve the community; not everyone will be a Witherspoon—an outstanding member of his community and a consummate public figure. Revelle was a trained historian and yet unwilling to show the historical importance of his position. Witherspoon was not a trained historian, yet he was aware of the historical importance of the time and his position in it. Witherspoon's success was more widely recognized even though he was black. Revelle as an ethical, thinking person did not gain the same respect as Witherspoon, nor did he seek it.

Their stories draw attention to the challenges of bringing about equality and justice, particularly in the context of education. The oral histories bring home the entrenched nature of prejudice—especially by those who benefit from structures of white power. The struggles of Witherspoon and Revelle reveal the dehumanizing effects of racism both on blacks and whites. Their stories address the possibilities and limits of education as a vehicle for social change.

Costs of Desegregation

Desegregation in Camden County resulted in a sense of loss for both white and black communities. Whites feared the loss of control of the school system and the mandated association of their children with black people. School desegregation was subtle but potentially undermined the traditional racist system that upheld white power. Both communities bemoaned the loss of discipline and respect by students in the integrated schools, a change they attributed to desegregation.

Desegregation introduced cultural difference into the classroom for which administrators and teachers were ill equipped. Elizabeth City State University ran a Desegregation Institute in 1970 to help teachers from the region prepare for this change but Camden sent only one black teacher and no white teachers to it. The losses endured by the black community when coupled with enduring racism and the dominance of white pedagogy proved especially costly. As educational scholars Yosso et al. write, "many Black communities experienced desegregation as a disruptive and often violent process."[20]

On a fundamental level, as education scholars Dempsey and Noblit argue, "School desegregation in many ways ignored that there could be desirable elements of African American culture worthy of maintenance and celebration."[21] Specifically, the close relationship between the black community and the schools,[22] a curricular focus on "racial uplift,"[23] and the powerful role of black teachers and educational leadership were missing from desegregated schools.[24]

When black students and families entered the desegregated school, their tradition of social and cultural capital in support of black education had no place. Instead, white administrators assumed that exposure to white social and cultural capital would lead to a better education for blacks. As education scholar Jerome Morris argues,

> In many ways, desegregation policies fractured this relationship [between the black community and school]. The policies were grounded in the notion that Black students would receive equalized education and have greater access to resources and information networks (social capital) if they attended middle-class, predominantly White schools. Unfortunately, many Black students who attend predominantly White schools do not benefit from the social capital in these schools.[25]

In Camden, black students predominantly populated special education classes; white children received the lion's share of academic awards; the social networks black parents possessed in segregated school greatly diminished with white control of schools; black teachers that left were routinely replaced with white teachers; and Camden has never hired a black principal.

Black teachers, already viewed as less qualified by many whites, could no longer employ the pedagogies that had long nurtured and successfully educated black children.

There are other losses that often get erased in the trauma of desegregation. A disproportionate number of black teachers and administrators lost their jobs.[26] Revelle frankly explained the rationale for these decisions. "Racial discrimination basically. As a white southerner now I used to think, most whites thought, blacks were inferior. That was a given fact here, and their degrees, in many cases, they thought were from not good schools and so forth. You kind of rationalize all this stuff. Some of the teachers I had at Marion Anderson Middle School were, there were some blacks that were not qualified. Of course, there were some whites that were not qualified. But the funny thing about it was that year [after the first year of integration] there were two people that lost their jobs, myself and one other white lady." I asked, "Was there any outcry from the black community when you were let go?" He replied, "Not that I know of. And then I wonder if there had been any outcry, would it have been listened to?"

Revelle's responses, unlike many other white people I spoke with, frankly and unequivocally implicate a racist logic, even as he acknowledged his own complicity. He names racism as it continued to be the basis of decisions in desegregated schools. While there were many decisions made by the school board and superintendent that even as a white principal he was not party to, including his own termination, which he jokes about, his comments offer valuable insight into how decisions were made and how logics of white supremacy continued to inform de facto decisions about the process of integration.

Integration: Past and Present

These racist-type decisions continue to haunt education today. As Morris argues, "In today's post-*Brown v. Board of Education* (1954) era, stronger communal bonds among schools, African American families, and communities are greatly needed...Too often these relationships are characterized by the failure of schools to involve African American families and communities in the affairs of the school."[27] Since desegregation, from PTA meetings to parent-teacher conferences, black parents have often been left out of dialogue on what is best for their children. This exclusion is a fallout of the white control of process and the underlying assumption that white education is the best education.

By pointing this out, blacks are not simply mourning the losses of segregated education or waxing nostalgic. They are signaling out the practices that have been abandoned in which black parents were consulted on how best to rear their children and black teachers designed culturally appropriate curriculum. The stories of black educational success involving Witherspoon and recounted by Vivian Jones (in the next chapter) provide a vital resource to contemporary educators. As Morris argues,

Lessons can be learned from the historical documentation of how some all-Black schools before *Brown* successfully bonded with families and communities. These lessons are relevant today because a majority of African American students in urban areas attend predominantly African American schools. These schools have to successfully create communal bonds with African American families and communities.[28]

Yet during desegregation in Camden County and most other communities in the South, this aspect was not considered as a part of integrated education. As Yosso et al. explain, "Without listening to these lived histories, the Supreme Court could not foresee that the onus of eliminating racism in schools would subsequently be placed on those who experienced its subordination."[29] This lack of communication, of listening to vital black experiences nurtured by segregated education, perpetuates ignorance that continues to shape integrated public education.

The narratives of black educational success embodied in Witherspoon, as well as the challenges and sense of failure Revelle endured during desegregation, raise questions about whether the road taken was the best way to implement *Brown*. "Could *Brown* have been implemented in a way that respected the social, cultural, and historical value of predominantly Black schools to their communities and the families of the children who attended these schools?"[30] "What if *Brown* had asked what disadvantage do Whites experience as a result of attending racially isolated, White monocultural schools?"[31] While these retrospective questions cannot change the past, they point to roads not taken and versions not heard. They also expose the often-ignored memories of those who actually lived through desegregation.

Revelle's judgment on the process is ambivalent: "I was trying to think to put the two years together and say what I thought about it. It is kind of hard. There are some things I think that went very well. The next year I felt kind of like this was a sacrifice that somebody had to make, to get through that first year [of full integration]. Maybe if I had been tougher and stronger I could have stayed on. I don't know. Maybe I could have stood some of the storms that came along."

The still-pressing question for contemporary educators and policy makers remains how the promises of *Brown* can be realized more than a half century after the Supreme Court decision. From the lessons of success and failure offered by Witherspoon and Revelle, as well as similar studies, one message resounds loudly and clearly[32]:

It is also important to place the issues of social support and cultural affirmation within the national debates on school reform. Whereas there is a national preoccupation with standardized measures of student outcomes, it is equally important to consider how the relationships among individuals and institutions (e.g., schools, communities, educators, families, and children) can also lead to effective schooling.[33]

This is a point that Camden's stories of school segregation and desegregation make repeatedly.

Revelle, the largest supporter of this book in word and deed, shared his hope for uncovering the stories of this time, "Well, I think, I'm hoping it will give both black and white a little insight to the other side's story. When we understand where another person is coming from, we can quite often do better at getting along."

CHAPTER 7

"You Forget This Is a Democracy"

Before desegregation, blacks and whites were committed to their own schools—raising money, supporting the schools and teachers, and cheering on the sports teams. White parents paid for a football field and lights that still shine every Friday night in the fall, visible from neighboring counties. Black parents worked together to purchase the school's first activity bus through local efforts such as selling baked goods on Friday evenings. In both communities, the schools were tremendous sources of pride and centers of activity.

Because most whites assumed blacks were inferior, segregated schools were normal and desirable. In the black community, segregated schools functioned importantly as what bell hooks calls a "homeplace"—a site of care, nurturance, and humanization in the midst of "an oppressive and dominating social reality."[1] Integration transformed schools, once comfortable segregated spaces into discomfiting places. The possibility of social change, which occurred as historically segregated spaces opened and increased interracial contact, changed the nature of the schools as homeplace and white power, respectively.

In Camden County, the change of Marian Anderson School from an all-black segregated school to an integrated middle school transformed both communities' relations to public schools and to each other. The changes to the now-shared public schools occurred on many interconnected levels—from students occupying the same space and integrating teachers to influencing pedagogy and discipline. School integration reverberated at the levels of home, family, and turf. Because it was intimately connected to cultural issues of space, identity, power, and politics, integration unsettled the community in ways that extended far beyond formal education. As communication studies scholar Raka Shome argues, "Spatialities of power constitute and reconstitute our identities... we need to think of space and spatial relations not as inert backdrops against which the struggles of identity occur. Rather, these relations themselves must be seen as active components in the unequal and heterogeneous production and distribution of identities, politics, and actions."[2] While desegregation forced everyone in Camden to reconceive their identities at schools, the black students and teachers had to change their pedagogies and practices to a much greater degree because of white dominance of education—from curriculum to administrators to school mascots.

What black communities and their schools lost in the process of integration was, as Shome describes, a "means of self-representation, autonomous signification, and cultural (and thus social and political) practice." No longer was the black or white community fully able to represent itself on its own terms, in ways that reflected long-standing cultural traditions and values. These early losses in the desegregation process are not fully captured in most discussions of integration, which focus more on the inequalities of segregated black schools, the mechanics of desegregation, or its broad effects.[3] Yet the losses Shome references are arguably the greatest. When schools integrated, they lost their symbolic values as centers of raced communities. This resulted in a sense of estrangement from schools for both blacks and whites. Blacks lost their "homeplace" and whites could no longer feel at home in their own schools. The presence of black students and teachers meant that whites could no longer operate without considering black students. In recalling desegregation, blacks and whites tell markedly different tales. The common white version considers the process as a historical accomplishment. These memories contain an inherent timeline that indicates continued progress in race relations. In this narrative, desegregation is done and belongs in the past. For most blacks (and some whites), it is far from complete. Such memories understand desegregation as a constant struggle for equality and justice. In this narrative, the dream of integration remains in the future. These racially distinct memories reveal deep fissures in our understanding of race, education, and equity. They complicate and yet may facilitate ongoing movements toward full integration.

Forgotten Stories of Black Education and Integration

The Camden County Office building, a typical drab government building, is not where you would expect to find a civil rights advocate. But Vivian Jones is not a typical civil servant. Working there for forty years has not diminished the fire that has motivated her since childhood. She was born on March 5, 1932, in Camden County to Luther and Carrie Bogues, the tenth of eleven children. She attended Camden's segregated black school system, the Ivy Neck Primary and Sawyer's Creek High School.[4] Jones married George Jones in 1951 and raised four children, two of whom went through school integration. In the early 1960s her home served as a licensed day care for migrants and seasonal farm workers—where Jones cared for children ages three–six as well as her own. Subsequently, she obtained a civil service job, working for the Economic Improvement Council for thirty-nine years.

Her job within the county government gave her insights and a systemic view of local racial politics. Her role as a parent provided an intimate understanding of integration's effects. As Jones says herself, "If I were good at words, I would write a book." What she does possess are profound local answers to questions like those posed by educational historian Vanessa Siddle Walker about civil rights, including the process of integration of the schools: "In what ways were parents involved in the school? How did the school interact with the community? What kinds of educational activities did teachers and principals view as important for the successful education of black children?"[5] Jones' memories paint a clear picture of what, in her words, "was lost in the translation of integration" of the schools.

The typical narrative description of desegregation emphasizes its benefits to underfunded black schools. For example, in 1951, North Carolina blacks made up 30 percent of the state's population but only possessed 14.2 percent of the school facilities.[6] The many strengths of black segregated education—from active parental and community support to race conscious pedagogy—often get obscured by these memories of inequality. As Siddle Walker writes: "To remember segregated schools largely by recalling only their poor resources presents a historically incomplete picture... Some evidence suggests that the environment of the segregated school had affective traits, institutional policies, and community support that helped black children learn in spite of the neglect the schools received from the white school boards."[7] Through her narratives, Jones recalls the positive qualities of segregated black education.

Jones remembered: "I asked the principal why is it that there is nothing that tells the students about [the black contributions to school] integration?" This question reflects a widely held belief by many in the black community that all of the positive contributions and symbols of black school were erased during the process of desegregation. In fact, Marian Anderson School was built near a black neighborhood, with the help of I.M. Trafton, a black farmer who sold the land to the school because of his commitment to black education.

As Jones asks: "What happened to the name Trafton? The name Trafton, T-R-A-F-T-O-N. All the land surrounding Marian Anderson School was owned by the Traftons. You hear no mention of it. You don't hear no mention of it. And I said to one of the superintendents, 'I'm sure the amount of money that they paid Mr. I.M. Trafton for that property was nothing like what it was due.' But he was just so involved in education, and that the school needed to be enlarged and everything, that he almost gave it to them. I said, 'Now the county doesn't even have the guts, or whatever it is, to even use his name!' You don't see his name anywhere. And why not?" Prior to integration, a portrait of Trafton hung in the school to recognize his contributions.

Jones' comments highlight the symbolic significance of Trafton's name that is particular to the black experience. The disappearance of Trafton's portrait represents the larger phenomenon of forgetting black control of their education and its achievements. This symbolic degrading of the memory of the Marian Anderson School also discounts what scholars of black segregated schools, Irvine and Irvine, call the community's "collective stake in the educational progress of youth."[8]

Jones provided another example of this collective effort that resulted in the first school bus in Camden County for black children. Jones situates this event toward the end of her own education. "When I went to school, there was no integration. I went to an all-black school... The school that I went to, there were, there were only two teachers in the school; two teachers taught the whole one through seventh grade; Then high school, eighth through twelfth. There were only three teachers in the school. So I tell these kids now-a-days 'you don't know what a privilege you had. You're just sitting here nonchalant...' But I'm here. I missed all that. That was the schools at that time. And I never rode to school but one year. There was no bus. There were buses here in Camden, but not for black students."

Jones notes the past inequality of white and black school transportation and the ways in which black youth today take for granted the advantages they have over the past inequalities their parents fought to redress. "I think the regular school buses were donated [hand-me-downs from the white school]. They were taking kids to and from [school], but the first activity bus was parent purchased. I remember walking down the road selling cookies and cupcakes. My parents were very active in the PTA. My mother and Mrs. Annie Banks, they put up like a prize for the one that raised the highest over one hundred dollars would get a trip and they won because they were good cooks and there were a lot of us [children]...So they bought the first activity bus that Camden black students had. They [Jones' mother and her friend] never got to ride on it because both of them had passed away before it came into being."

Jones' stories of school segregation in Camden focus on what the black parents, principal, and teachers accomplished with few resources (as compared to the white schools). Her memories are not stories of black deficit. Instead she speaks of black cultural and material capital devoted to education and the advancement of the younger generation.

Today all Camden County students benefit from Trafton's support for education as they attend Camden Middle School, but this black contribution to education is neither recognized nor recorded in the history of the integrated school. As Jones notes, an important remaining question for the schools of Camden is: How can the black educational experience be remembered in integrated schools that are dominated by white pedagogies and practices and controlled by white school boards?

Because of white domination of the process of desegregation, the formerly all-black schools such as Marian Anderson that were included in integration sustained the most change. Marian Anderson School was stripped materially (through the removal of pictures and trophies, and changes in curriculum, tradition, and even its name) and lost its symbolic status as the institutional seat of black power in Camden County. Yet through memory, shared stories, and continued reunions, black alumni of Marian Anderson School maintained this important source of black pride. Jones' memories create an alternative version of black accomplishment and dedication to education. These acts of remembering are an important counterpoint to the biased contemporary educational discourse that too often emphasizes a deficit narrative about the black student, the "minority achievement gap," and the disengaged black parent.[9] By resurrecting these underknown histories, Jones opens up the problems of whiteness inherent in most educational institutions. Such counter-stories speak to her desire that integrated schools act like a center for an integrated community.

Parental Perspectives on Desegregation

In 1969, when school desegregation became an unavoidable eventuality in Camden County, some black parents remembered feeling apprehensive about this change primarily implemented by whites: Why now? Why integrate schools? Why go where the whites don't want us? This kind of questioning grew out of an inherited caution essential to black survival in a white regime, as well as opposition to losing the powerful black educational institution.[10] Some residents wanted to maintain the Marian Anderson School, a central part of Camden's black community, which served as a site for such diverse events as funerals, elections, and even a recreation center for basketball.

Other parents responded with ambivalence. These parents sensed the uncertainty of a future filled with benefits and risks in either system. Spatial integration would make it harder for black parents to protect their children from the brutality of racial discrimination. Black parents also feared that white teachers and administrators would continue unequal education in the integrated classroom.

Both blacks and whites shared uncertainty about what this process would mean for Camden. Jones recalled, "Camden County didn't accept integration (*pause*) freely. But they really didn't think that it would work. They really, I don't know, there have never been bad people. You know, there has never been no confrontations like in some areas, you know. But I guess it came from the leadership. Everybody looked up to the leadership and whatever the leadership said. You know, 'We don't need to do that.' And that was it." The latent racism based on the educational practices of the leaders perpetuated segregation.

As Jones' comment reflects, blacks and whites saw desegregation as a change implemented primarily by the whites. The decades of gradualism that followed *Brown,* along with the county's all-white school board and informal power structure, communicated that the de facto process of integration was controlled by white officials. And in Camden it was. These local, mixed memories of blacks and whites complicate the national collective memory of school desegregation.

Looking back at the tumultuous time of desegregation and the ongoing struggles toward integration, Jones said: "I think the number one problem really was parents. Even today the number one problem is parents because the students don't seem to mind. Sometimes I see now in the high school a lot of the students rebel against parents. This is what I tell them. I say, 'You're rebelling against your parents. You are trying to force this integration issue against your parents because you know your parents object to your association.' They [white students] say, 'This is another day and my parents grew up not liking black people, but not me. I don't see any difference.' But when they go back home, it's a different thing. Even some of the families I work with, they're saying that the problems they have with integration, they were taught that whites are supposed to be separated from blacks and that you all are different." Color-blind youth return home to parents who still favor racial separation, especially in romantic relations. These generational differences result in the interpretation that children in interracial relationships are simply rebelling against their parents.

Jones does not separate problems parents created at the time of desegregation from ongoing problems of integration based on their continued purposeful racism based on skin color difference. To Jones, the generational conflicts over race relations in the present are a continuation of racial problems rooted in assumptions of white supremacy and the merits of racial segregation. Jones remembers a particular encounter she had with a white mother and her child that demonstrates how individuals persist in racist thinking despite social and policy changes. "The most exciting thing was, I was working with a family and I had to take the mother to help the father over in Elizabeth City. And when you're going in for services, they tell them to bring a baby-sitter or what not. She said, 'Do you mind keeping her?' I said 'No, if she doesn't mind staying with me.' So she asked the little girl. She's maybe two, two and a half. She could talk. So when the little girl came to me and she said, 'Can I touch you?' I said, 'Of course you can.'"

"So she just touched. You know how blind people do. She just felt me all over. Everywhere she could touch. She said, 'You're soft.' I said, 'Yes, I'm just like you.' She said, 'You have ears like me. Your hands look like my hands. They're larger, but they're the same.' I said, 'Yeah. Same person made you, made me too.' When her mother came out, she had her head on my shoulder. She said, 'Did you have any problem?' I said, 'No, not at all.' I said, 'She kept me busy.' So the girl said, 'Ma, Mrs. Jones is like me, but she's brown.' I could see the expression on the mother's face. I was just waiting for her to say whatever she thought. She said, 'Yes, Mrs. Jones is like you. She has skin...' The mother didn't know what to say. It sort of embarrassed her...the expression on her face...she didn't know how to react." For Jones, this exchange highlighted the ability of children to adapt to interracial contact and in fact to push parents to relate racially in new ways. But the mother's response also captures the parental unease with integration and her latent racism.

As a parent herself, Jones experienced challenges with integration that she remembers when she looks at Camden High School in the present. "There is some of that [unequal treatment of whites and blacks] right now because you go to the high school and you see the students that are chosen for cheerleaders and are chosen for the different prestigious things. It's always those that the teachers say, 'It's grades, because of their grades and all that they excel so much over the other students.' I don't know. I'm not there but when my students were there, it went on [special treatment of white children]. But I knew my students, and if there was a position or something that came up that they didn't consider my daughter or son, I was there. 'Why is this? Why is this grade level so low and all of their grades prior to this were—what did you do here?' By that time they said, 'Sorry, it was a mistake.' I'm sure it was." As a parent she committed herself to advocating for her children. Jones came from a family that expected her to pursue her rights, such as the right to vote. Her narrative reveals practices of institutional racism within the school.

"Now my daughter's third year in high school, she went to Camden High School, and the school integrated. She was good at typing. She wanted to excel in typing. I said, 'You're going to get into typing.' We bought this old typewriter from Grants. We brought it back so that she could practice at home. She couldn't get into typing class. 'I'm going to remedy that the next year,' I said." Jones supported her daughter's aspirations, recognizing them as important for her career advancement.

Jones went to Camden High School before the start of the following year. "The teachers are at the school one week prior to school opening and the students go, and I went to that school and talked to every teacher and talked to the guidance counselor about what I would like for my students."

"Going through what the students were going to take, my daughter loved to cook and she was cooking. She was in the home economics class at first. So they had her signed up for the home economics... I said, 'I'm sorry, but she's not going to be in that class.' They said, 'Well, she's a good student, blah, blah, blah.' I said, 'I know.' I said, 'But she cooks at home for her two brothers, her father and me, and I know she's good at home economics. She's good, but she's not going to be in that class. She wants to excel in typing. Her goal is to become a business administrator or typing, shorthand and all that. I don't see any of that here on your list.' They said, 'Well, it's filled up.'"[11]

"You can imagine how I felt. Now this is the week prior to school and the class is filled up. I said, 'How can a class be filled up when the students haven't even gotten here?' So I said to that teacher, 'Is the principal here? Thank you for your time. I need to speak with the principal.' I went to that principal's office. I said, 'My daughter is not going to be in that class. She's not going to take home economics. I'm not going to allow her to waste another year in home economics.' They had to change it."

"There were other parents that didn't do it soon enough. That didn't get their students in. But she would probably be cooking now, I guess, because she's still loves to cook and eat. But I saw that she got into the typing and shorthand, the whole bit, and excelled in it and came out with honors. But if I hadn't gone... and see there are a lot of parents that didn't do it because they told me, 'The class was full.' They told me, 'That's not for my student.' See, the guidance counselors a lot of times would be looking at the background of parents and say, 'You're good at whatever.'"

While Jones' story ends with a sense of personal success, she notes that many black parents did not push back on the school system when they were told the classes were full and they would accept the profiling that schools did based on the reputation of the parent. This encounter is an example of what Jones claims got lost in the translation to integration. At Marian Anderson School students were expected to achieve to their highest potential, but at the integrated school in subtle ways they were denied opportunities to reach that potential. The narrative reveals how racism operated within the practices of an integrated school. The loss of parental voice in school captured in Jones' story relates to what Delpit calls the "silenced dialogue" in which blacks are alienated from the educational process and frequently experience miscommunication.[12] This communication breakdown was not simply unintended or innocuous but stems from what Delpit calls "the culture of power."

Jones was more aware than most of the rules of the "culture of power" as she worked in a government office that operated under its own culture of power. Many blacks knew the rules of the culture of power in segregated schools under administrators such as Witherspoon. They lost the ability to play largely by their own cultural rules when integration occurred: Many black schools experienced what education scholar Carter Julian Savage described as "loss of tradition, ownership and the collapse of a school community."[13] After desegregation, the white culture of power pervaded the schools.

What Was Lost

In the desegregation of Marian Anderson School, black students and parents lost their close relationship with the teachers. "The positive effects that I see and this might be [still the case]... if there were more black teachers in the school. But the black students don't get that mother/father [figure]. See many come from one-parent households and when they go to school they don't get any... you know... that home [that the segregated school provided]." Jones notes the loss of school as homeplace—where teachers and administrators served as parental figures.

"They can leave home angry and they go to school angry and they stay angry. When the schools were not integrated, those teachers when that student came into that school with anger, the teacher used to say, 'Why do you have this chip on your shoulder?' They [black teachers] had a way of talking to them [black students]. You know, making them talk about it. And the teachers called their parents after school and said: 'There's a problem. We don't mean to be into your family business, but there's a problem with your child.' You know, that's no more. I don't see it anymore."

This way of talking to students, of "making" the students speak about their problems, and the subsequent parent-teacher interactions were all critical modes of pedagogy and communication in the black community. Jones' memories mark the all-black school as a place that connected the student body to "family business." Black teachers recognized that these issues could not be separated from education or simply relegated to disciplinary action. As Nathan Wright Jr. explains, "some of the leading black educators [were]...striving for...the greatest good of complete human liberation and fulfillment."[14] After integration, as black families and teachers faced a new culture of power, this practice of intimate parent, teacher, and school contact disappeared.

"That's no more. I don't see it anymore. But now there's integration, students are so busy trying to imitate each other. I don't think students are focusing enough on teacher and some of them tell me 'it's the teacher, she can't teach or he can't teach. They're just in the classroom making time. We can go here and we can do that.' But you're supposed to be focusing on the teacher. See the teachers, before integration, were interested in teaching students. They say they are now. I'm not there that much. But when my children were in school, if I thought it was a problem, here I go. I'm going to the school this morning. I didn't have problems with teachers. If my children were not excelling, they came home with no books. That interests me because they had book bags. 'Why would you come home with an empty book bag?' 'I don't have any homework.' 'What did you do in school that you don't have homework?'"

"But kids now get on the bus with no books and get off the bus with no books. I know it's a parent thing too. Teachers can't do it all because of home problems." Jones highlights how integration weakened the teacher-student relationship. With integration, white teachers rarely extended themselves beyond the classroom. In other words, their pedagogy and approach to parent-teacher relations continued as they had with white children and families in the past. But this was an unfamiliar culture of power to black children and families alike. Despite cultural norms, certain black and white teachers did care for their students' welfare in ways that went well beyond the classroom (e.g., driving them home or buying them shoes). However, because of school segregation and limited interaction between whites and blacks, many teachers were reluctant to treat the newly integrated children as they would the students in their respective segregated schools. In retrospect, desegregation inhibited the dialogic relationship between the community, home, and school that existed in the black system. The white culture of power invoked new rules of individualism in education and alienated many black parents.

To resist the white dominance of education, many blacks continue to tell oral histories recalling the glories of Marian Anderson School before integration, remembering a tight-knit educational community and a curriculum that emphasized black role models, parables, and history. Graduates still wear their class rings, carry laminated copies of their diplomas with Witherspoon's ornate signature in their wallet, and meet biannually for the school reunion—a gathering of hundreds of past students and teachers from around the country.

Jones describes the reunions: "They go to big hotels and convention centers because so many attend. They have a good time. See the amazing thing is because they just, you know how you can hear this sound, whoa, when there are two or three hundred people or more. Last year the committee called each, they had a table set for each class area. Like 1945, '46, '47, '48, '49 and on. So in the '40s we all could almost use one table because my graduation class was two. The class coming behind me was three. But one was killed so that leaves two. The class ahead of me was three. One was ill."

"So when they called those classes to stand up and we stood. 'Is that the graduating class?' They were saying, 'the percentage, what is the percentage?' The spokesman was saying, 'What's the percentage of students present?' Of course I was the spokesman for my class. I said, 'We are here one hundred percent.' You could just hear [a gasp] because there were only two of us that graduated [this was at a smaller local school prior to the creation of the consolidated Marian Anderson School]. This was it. Can you imagine only two graduating from a high school? We had the pomp and circumstance. The two of us, we just walked up on the stage." These reunions reminded younger generations of the significance of the school for the black community—of the dignity and success of their own indigenous culture of power and the possibility of reclaiming it through such memories.

"But none of the frills and all this for graduation that the kids take for granted now. You all should be proud. You are graduating. People used to come from far and near to attend Marian Anderson's graduation. The principals, Mr. McMurray and then Mr. Witherspoon, they had a well-organized graduation. It was a serious thing for those two principals. Education was it!"

"The teachers had on gowns according to their degrees and all... When the organist, pianist or whatever the music started, nobody moved. The auditorium would be just jam-packed wherever, but they would march in. You know how you would be in the military. You would only see this. Then the students as well—there was no giggling. There was no... the kids were proud to be graduating, and the parents and family members would come from far and near just to be in the presence of that graduation exercise. I mean, it was really something to see."

"Here because Mr. Witherspoon said, he taught that you should be proud that you made it this far. You didn't play. You didn't come through this school playing while he was principal. So don't be walking down that aisle. And now I see them [students today], the organist playing 'Pomp and Circumstance' or whatever it is that they're marching in, waving and giggling at folk. Some of them are 'hee hee hee.' There was none of that." Jones contrasts the Marian Anderson graduation as a performance of respect, dedication, and achievement that reaffirmed the significance of education with today's integrated graduation, which is more like a party than a milestone in the community.

"If they said the processional would start at four o'clock [during Witherspoon's administration at Marian Anderson School], at four o'clock the ushers at the door and everything, they would seal up the doors... There were fifty, seventy-five, eighty, whatever number of students graduating. There would be all the teachers leading the procession. Everybody would be just... people would leave home early to make sure they got in there and got a seat because it was so impressive. But there is no history of it. There was no movie cameras. So only those that participated and were there know that this is what happened." These unrecorded memories of black educational excellence and community achievement continue to shape black community celebrations to this day. Through such actions of remembrance and community celebration, blacks continue to resist the historical whitewashing of their educational history.

The ongoing significance of the Marian Anderson School to the black community is illustrated by an exchange she had with the white superintendent: "They [the white superintendent's office] always ask, 'Why do you let black parents have church activities or birthdays... family birthdays or something at the school?' I said, 'Because that school is part of us.' I said, 'Because I know my father owned woodland, and people in the community owned woodland,

and they extended that school from a two-room school to a three- or four-room school. They've been in the woods and cut that timber and they took it to the school.' I said, 'And that's, that's part of us. You know, we feel that that's home school.'" Jones continues emphatically, "Even now Marian Anderson is seen as the home school...And it was just the ideal school for a community of people."

Apparently unaware of this history, the superintendent imposes white norms about the separation of public school from religious or community celebrations. In contrast to the superintendent, many blacks still view the now integrated Marian Anderson as an appropriate center for black community activities, including religious events, funerals, and celebrations. Jones' response that the Marian Anderson School is "part of us" draws on a deep community tradition of support and engagement with the school. As Siddle Walker documents: "The segregated school is most often compared with a 'family' where teachers and principal, with parentlike authority, exercised almost complete autonomy in shaping student learning and insuring student discipline. Parents played an active role also."[15]

Jones also remembered how the black community celebrated the history of the Marian Anderson School by displaying pictures of every graduating class on the school walls. "Marian Anderson had a very energetic principal, the late principal Mr. Witherspoon...he was really into history and seeing that things were documented and kept...Each year after he became principal of that school...they would take pictures of the graduating class and they would start yearbooks and all this. They encouraged parents and students to buy them that they would have some history to pass down to their children..."

"Each year they put them on the wall and any students, any parent or anybody could come from far and near to see that their pictures. And just as soon as integration those pictures disappeared." After Witherspoon's departure, the pictures of the students, of Marian Anderson, and I.M. Trafton vanished, an often-noted indignity by many in the black community. Revelle has no memory of the pictures. This begs the question: What disappeared and what remains of the history of segregated Camden schools? The desegregated Marian Anderson School, stripped of its name and its black history, became a politically charged space where struggles for identity occurred, especially in the form of who had the authority to decide what symbols of the black community were present.

The white school (Camden High School) also changed their mascot, a Rebel (a Confederate soldier) at the time of integration, to a bruin (bear). While a mascot change is not of the same magnitude as a school name change, the mascot also caused community consternation—whites resented having to abandon their original mascot. Marian Anderson also changed their mascot from the Trojans to the Bruins and changed the school colors from maroon and gold to Camden High School's blue and white. Leary remembers, "I'll tell you what. It wouldn't have been Bruins if I'd been in the school. But a friend of mine, he was a schoolteacher. I think he had a lot of persuasion. And he wanted to go with the Bruins. Somehow the committee at that time changed to the Bruins. I had just left. I hate the UCLA Bruins. You know, that was not my favorite name. And we had a lot of people, 'Bruins?! That's a sorry name.'"

While mascots and school colors may not influence the school system as much as who is selected to serve on the school board, they remain fifty years later in the memories—the mattering maps—of people who lived through that time. Such stories show that the initial school desegregation briefly destabilized the white culture of power. They also show the importance of Shome's focus on space and the way it shows "the unequal and heterogeneous production and distribution of identities, politics, and actions." Integration, the desegregation of white and black spaces, disrupted the spaces, their politics, and the identities of students and teachers—but the effects were uneven. Together these threads impact the strength and quality of public education and the greater community.

In another such example, Jones reveals the fate of the photographs: "They came to light—somebody had put them in somewhere. I don't know, but there are a few of them that had gotten kind of moldy and what not. But maybe five or six years ago, maybe a little bit longer than that, some of the former students said, 'We want those pictures'... Those pictures came to light. They had been thrown in something and some of them were faded away."

"You should see the numbers that attend, and then look at those pictures and say, 'That's me and that's...' and invite the teachers, the former teachers." Jones celebrates the reclamation of the symbols of black educational achievement. "But see, that's all they have now, is the pictures. What happened in the course of integration?" From Jones' perspective, the graduation pictures are an important but inadequate historical representation and memory touchstone. The larger remaining question on which Jones finally charges all Camden residents to reflect embodies many concerns that continue to shape integrated education today: a sense of not knowing all that happened to blacks and whites in this process; blacks not being a part of decision making nor knowing who were the decision makers; as well as a sense of loss of rich black educational practices, history and traditions. School desegregation challenged the Camden educational system and the community. Efforts at integration provoke memories ambivalent in their judgment of this process. As Jones commented: "Integration has been good...and then it has some flaws...Something was lost in the translation of integration...I can't explain it, but it was lost." The phrase, "lost in the translation," speaks to the problems at the heart of integration: the loss of the black culture of power and its familiar rules—a significant loss for the black community.

De Facto Segregation Continues

One example of the failure of de facto integration relates to black history month and Dr. Martin Luther King Jr. celebrations in the present. Jones speaks with passion: "Now this has really been disturbing to me since my children have been out of school. They set aside maybe a week—they have a black history program. The [white] students that didn't choose to stay to listen to it, they were allowed to leave that school campus. Yes, they were allowed to leave the school campus. This was high school. Can you imagine the principal and students agreeing to this?"

"It's been a few years back because I moved to this campus here [she is referring to the government offices where she works] in '89. It was in the '80s and even today, even now, when they have black history, I'm told. When they have black history programs, parents that don't want their children to sit, be a part of it or be in the midst of it, they will send a note to the school that their child will be dismissed. And this is 2003. And it happened in 2002 (pause). I think February, black history month. So, you know, how do you consider the thinking of people now in this year of 2003?" Jones' narratives highlight the persistence of institutional racism in integrated schools and the continued resistance to black cultural icons, pedagogy, and achievement.

She challenges claims that desegregation is achieved when schools privilege white history and leadership. Despite the ongoing resistance, the march toward integration goes on in Camden. "Dr. Martin Luther King's birthday this year was the third [annual celebration]. It happened here in Camden County, the first time they honored this as a county activity. We have as many as seventy-five or a hundred or more people marching from Grandy Primary School to the courthouse...This year it was held at Camden High School. It grows every year. Out of that number of people, there are such a few whites. We pass them on the road and we see the curtains, looking through the curtains but yet, 'I'm not going to be a part of that.'"

Thirty-four years after Leary stood in segregated Marian Anderson school and heard about Martin Luther King Jr.'s assassination, and sixteen years after Dr. Martin Luther King Jr. Day was declared a national holiday, the county government began to celebrate the holiday. And still the celebration of the prominent national figure and his dream of integration has been largely a segregated event that heightened awareness of residual segregation. Jones concludes, "Segregation is very much alive here in Camden County (*long pause*). Sometimes, my philosophy is (*pause*) if you have been segregated mind, soul and body for 2,003 years, you cannot change it (*long pause*) in thirty days" (*she laughs*).

Jones gives an everyday example from her own work of how segregation persists in people's minds. "They [her EIC clients] come in here talking to me because sometimes if they are referred—I'm talking about whites. Sometimes they receive a referral slip from another agency. 'You go and see Mrs. Jones. That's who you need to talk to, especially if it's housing,' certain assistance programs that we operate here. And they'll come and knock on the door and they'll come in. They'll say, 'Oh I must be in the wrong place. I know I'm in the wrong place.' I'll say, 'Who did you come to see or who referred you?' They'll hand me the referral slip. I'll say, 'You're in the right place. I'm the Mrs. Jones that you have on here. How may I help you?' They're just so...sometimes they can't really get themselves together. If they have time then they'll get into the issue. I'll say, 'Why did you think that you were in the wrong place?' I'll bring up the issue: 'You did not expect to see a black person?'"

"Sometimes they'll say, 'I really didn't because you don't see many black people here in Camden. How long have you been working here?' So Camden County as a general rule didn't hire black people. It hasn't been too many years that these offices have become integrated. I was born and raised here and I know it's a big change for Camden. But we still have a long, long way to go." For black Camden residents who were well acquainted with segregation, the reality half a century later reminds them that much work remains to achieve de facto integration. Even in governmental positions the lack of representation of black people sets an example of racial inequality. As a result, Jones, who has been working in her job for over three decades, has to explain her position to disbelieving white people. These are the same people she has dedicated years of her life serving.

The experience Jones recounts exemplifies everyday racial power relations that James Scott writes about: "The practices of domination and exploitation typically generate the insults and slights to human dignity that in turn foster a hidden transcript of indignation. Perhaps one vital distinction to draw between forms of domination lies in the kinds of indignities the experience of power routinely produces."[16] Jones, a black professional, endures slights by white community members as they question her position of authority, based on her race. While this kind of indignity may be mild in comparison to the violent history of race relations, these encounters reveal racist thinking that continues in the present. She still does her job, but she takes the opportunity and time to gently question their mindset.

These encounters were all too familiar to Jones, who had spent most of her life in community organizing and service—both as a vocation and avocation. "That was my job the first two years when I worked with the health department as the aide. And then the next phase of EIC program was community organizing, and we did. We had to go knock on doors and petition."

"And I said, 'If I were good at words, I'd write a book about the reaction of [white] people': 'What are you doing that for?' 'Why didn't you think?' 'You are in the wrong place. I know you're trying to start trouble.' 'We don't need that here in Camden.' This was from different households. You wouldn't skip a household. The dog was barking and all this. You didn't go up. 'We're just trying to petition the county commissioners and the board of education to consider…' 'No, I'm not interested,' hang up. Then we'd go on to the next."

Democratic Change

Both blacks and whites recall the absence of outspoken black resistance to racial inequality, even when protests were breaking out across the nation and across the bridge in Elizabeth City. But the organizing Jones speaks of, for which she is accused of "starting trouble," was simply the work of the EIC.

"But then I, of course, was working because of a survey for SSI and I did the survey before the program came into the area. We did a survey for a housing program. In the white neighborhoods that didn't accept me, I always knew one person in there. I would get to know one person. I'd spend time and explain to them that 'this is not for black people. This is for all people. Will you help me? If I get these to you, will you help me get them filled?' They would do it in their white neighborhood, but they wouldn't do it in the black neighborhood, which didn't bother me. I said, 'That's not a thing. The thing about it is we want to get it done. You want Camden County to be counted in this program.'" Jones describes ways she learned to work around de facto segregation.

"Because they thought I was trying to start something. You know, 'We aren't interested in that government stuff.' I said, 'You forget this is a democracy. You're looking at the government. You're the government and I'm the government. So what are you talking about?' See, a lot of people don't understand it that way. They think when you're trying to organize something or get them to attend a meeting to voice their opinion, you're trying to start trouble. You know, 'They're going to do what they want to do anyway. Ain't no need of us going up there.'" Jones captures a long-standing resistance to any federal intervention in Camden County and the broader white resistance based on "local rights." Jones, in contrast, sees participation and voting as key responsibilities of a democratic citizen.

"This is what they thought when we started organizing communities and everything. I said, 'Look, you elected these folks. Let's go to the Board of County Commissioners meeting on Monday night and you voice your opinion.' Because they didn't, when I say they, not all of the Board of County Commissioners and the Social Service Boards and all this, they didn't accept the way that I did things. But then I told them, I said, 'If I do not give these people the right information as it's given to me from the State Department, I'll be drawing my paycheck falsely. I'm not about to be doing that because I believe in it. They're not here just by themselves. I believe in it. So we are here tonight to request you to consider their...' whatever it was... Sometimes they [the people who joined Jones] wouldn't be just blacks. There would be some whites too." Jones describes encounters with white authority structures and their efforts to resist Jones' organizing practices. But as she points out to the board, she is just doing her job.

"The county commissioners and the precinct meetings and all this, there were all kinds of ways to keep people of color out of office. The meetings wouldn't last but two to three minutes and they'd come in with a slate. One of them motions and the other one seconds, then meeting dismissed... Certain people have governed, been elected or gotten themselves elected and appointed into positions that their way of thinking and their way of doing things has trickled on down. I guess people are just getting tired of letting them go. 'I'll just pay my taxes, and they'd better not be messing on my property.' But now the county boards of commissioners, the state said, 'You have to have this plan and all this stuff. Then sometimes people get angry. They'll come to the Board of County Commissioners meeting, and it's already enacted into law and they make some noise sometimes [but too late to make a change]." Like the PTA meetings or school board meetings, Jones describes the strategies white power holders used to maintain control of the county (making changes without openly inviting public comment). Her job acquainted her with the intricacies of these efforts.

Her commitment to democracy stemmed from her family's belief in democratic participation and her own struggles to gain the right to vote. "My parents were community people. They were church people. They were all-around people. Every one of us, there were ten of us in the family, and when every one of us became old enough it was a must that you register so that you can vote. 'As long as you stay in this house you're going to school. You're going to get an education. Along with that education comes work. You're going to work. Don't think that you're going to come back, just like these kids do now.' That wasn't my parents."

"So when it was time for me to go and register it was right here where this building sits... So it was five of us [going to register]... Saturday morning was the only time you could come up here and register. We came up and the registrar says, 'You've got to know the preamble [of the U.S. Constitution].' 'Uh uh. What does that have to do with register to vote?' 'You must have it.' So we went back home. 'Can't register you today.'"

"We... studied that preamble, studied that preamble and came back the next week, Saturday... We had to be able to write it and punctuate it, just as it was printed. Next Saturday we missed it. I said, 'Well, I'm coming back one more time.'"

"But we had, in the county we had the NAACP. We were members of the NAACP, and they said, 'You don't have to do all that. You do not have to do all that.' The state NAACP representative Mr. Charles said, 'When are you all going again?' We said, 'We're going back Saturday.' He said, 'Well, I'll be down to go with you, with your president and with your officers from the NAACP.' Now I knew without a shadow of a doubt because I had really studied that [preamble] and I had sat down and written it and punctuated it and capitalized it and all this stuff. But that was a hard thing to do. A whole lot of time just to get registered."

"I'm sure they [whites] didn't but all black people [had to]. That was a thing for the black people during that time... Mr. Charles and Mr. Charles H. Barker who was the president of the Camden County branch of the NAACP walked into this building and said, 'I understand that these young students have been coming down here trying to register. What's the problem?'"

Jones shifts to contemporary concerns: "If these kids [today's children] [could] see if they would show some of these movies of actually things that happened, they would understand why things are the way they are. I think they would get a new perspective on why it's necessary for us to register to vote.

We, our people, and what other folks went through to get to this point." Jones' story slips from struggles for the civil rights in the 1950s to the present.

"Here we are standing on the outside of the door, and they've got to go in and tell the man that this is unlawful. Then guess what he did. 'Bring them on in.' All we did was sign our name. That's all we were supposed to have done the first time. So then he [the registrar] continues to try that. But then the Camden County branch of the NAACP kept monitoring until... they finally just let people go to register. So if the Camden County branch of the NAACP had not really stayed up on it I don't know how long it would have been before people of color could have registered. This is little old Camden County. I know the people right now." Her experience with the NAACP underscores the role of social organization for resisting oppression—a lesson she utilized in her own career.

"If the truth was printed so that each generation could see, it would change some things. Because if I would go to the family members and to the persons that were running the elections boards and all this now and tell them, 'This is what you did,' I'm sure they would deny it. But it was me they did it to. Mr. Barker, Mr. Charles and many of those people that were involved in the struggle of getting the change have passed off the scene. But I know, it was me. 'It was your father. It was your mother. It was your [she doesn't specify] that was sitting behind the desk.' And I'm sure the grandchildren wouldn't believe that it happened but it did happen."

Jones story of disenfranchisement and her times at the EIC reveal the persistence of white efforts to oppress blacks in Camden County... through employment discrimination, voter suppression, white-controlled integrated schools, and control of property. Jones provided another example of covert attempts by white authorities to exploit blacks. "It all came out that if you don't pay your taxes or however they do it, your land gets sold. And you're too young to think about how they manipulated it and your, your property. I would just take a walk through the [courthouse] lobby and see those property reports. Some of them I would know and I would call them and say, 'Do you know your property is going to be sold, your parents' property is going to be sold?' They'd say, 'What?' I'd say, 'It's going to be sold at the Camden Courthouse, date.' I said, 'You'll need to come down here and see about it.' Maybe a family member usually pays the taxes and just missed and the other member's thinking it was being paid. They would come down here and pay it. See, they didn't know it." Because she worked in a government office, Jones saw the property reports and knew how to interpret them. She made the effort to inform people so they would not lose their land unknowingly.

"You want to know how I know they do this, how they manipulate that? Because my parents, my parents' family was about to lose property. My father's younger brother used to pay the tax, but then when he passed on, his wife didn't know anything about it—paying taxes and doing business and all this stuff. They just thought it was being paid. The late registrar of deeds called me and said, 'Mrs. Jones... do you know [your parents'] property is going to be sold?' I said, 'What property?' He told me about it. I went over and talked to him. He said, 'It's already in the lawyer's hands.' I called my father and said, 'Do you know your property is being sold?' He said, 'No.' I said, 'Then we need to go and see the lawyer.' We went up and talked to the lawyer and he said, 'If you can pay what you owe and everything y'all can still retain it.' That's what we did.'"

"My father called his other sisters, his two sisters, one in Virginia and one in Baltimore, a brother in Massachusetts and they said, 'Pay it.' They'll reimburse you. When they sold that, there was cypress timber. So you know they got two or three times what they had invested just saving it. Then they sold it because none of them were ever going to do anything with it. There was somebody getting ready to get that property and to do the same thing they did, have timber cut off and sold." A near victim of losing her family land for someone else's profit, Jones knew to pay attention to the covert exploitation of unsuspecting blacks.

"I could go on and tell [more stories]... There are some properties being turned over right now. Integration doesn't tell people that you need to let your family know that your taxes aren't paid. So as I said, if I were good at words, I would write a book." From voting rights, to property ownership, to course enrollment, Jones' memories highlight how much blacks stood to lose at the hands of whites, unless they remained vigilant and knew how to protect the rights all people were supposed to possess. Her stories also provide detailed examples of ways in which institutional and covert discrimination perpetuate inequality.

Costs and Benefits of Integration

Jones continues, returning to education: "So this county has come a long way. I can't understand the thinking of some people. You know, why is it so difficult to accept other people now? (*pause*). There are still some people who think that there shouldn't be integration. They still think that 'My student, my child is supposed to have first preference.' You know, and I say, 'Why do you think that?' 'Because that's the way it's always been.' This is 2003, 2003! What's wrong with the change? Change of attitude, change of mind might help all of us."

Jones points out that integration is not simply a black issue. As bell hooks argues, "Mutual recognition of racism, its impact both on those who are dominated and those who dominate, is the only standpoint that makes possible an encounter between races that is not based on denial and fantasy."[17] Jones' stories illustrate that racism implicates and impacts all of us. Mab Segrest points out, "exploitative relationships have cost us personally, familially, and socially."[18] More directly, Segrest (speaks to the heart of what we all might gain from a more meaningful integration:

> What, then, is the cost to white people of racism? . .
> Racism costs us intimacy.
> Racism costs us our affective lives.
> Racism costs us authenticity.
> Racism costs us our sense of connection to other humans and the natural world.[19]

Toni Morrison writes about her concern of "how to convert a racist house into a race-specific yet nonracist home." This task remains salient in ongoing efforts toward de facto school integration. Morrison's call to domesticate the racial project resonates with the memories of this racially divided county. The deep-seated differences between black and white memories of public education continue to shape understandings of integration today.

Sociologist Howard Winant claims, "race and racial identity, are not merely produced by racism, as neoconservatives (as well as some on the left) might claim. They are also means of self-representation, autonomous signification, and cultural (and thus social and political) practice."[20] Jones' shared memories of Marian Anderson School are forms of racial identity. As Jones makes clear, this form of racial identification is not defined in terms of racism but instead in terms of self-representation. It is about remembering the black community in spite of challenges of living in a "racist house." Her memories work to transform segregated schools, long familiar as sites of racism, into spaces of recognition and belonging defined by the local black community itself.[21]

The oral histories reveal persistent, valuable social practices and memories of the black educational experience. They resist a half-century of integration dominated by white pedagogy and cultural values. They give value to black graduates and to the under-recognized black educational system.

By resurrecting these lesser known stories and histories, Jones exposes the whiteness inherent in educational institutions. According to a 1970 report, "What is happening... is not integration; rather it is disintegration—the near total disintegration of black authority in every area of the system of public education."[22] In practice, de jure integration has come to mean white dominance of education—an integration of all students into dominant (white) ways of seeing, thinking, and knowing. But Jones, who passed on in 2006, never accepted white domination—during her lifetime and in her immortal memories.

CHAPTER 8

Working toward Integration: White-School Cafeteria Worker by Day, a Black Mom for Integration by Night

Fannie Mae Lewis' home symbolizes her values and commitments. A sparkling, freshly cleaned white Lincoln that her husband Harry carefully maintains stands in the driveway. He also tends the colorful flowers in the well-landscaped yard that communicates pride of place. Inside, her spotless white carpet and meticulously arranged living room show the care she takes in presenting her home. Lewis wears slippers to protect the carpet from the ubiquitous Camden spring mud. Upon entering her home, I feel impelled to remove my shoes as well.

A throw blanket with a portrait of the Rev. Martin Luther King lies on her white leather chair. From any angle, King's eyes seem to be looking at you. The blanket once created a problem in her house: "They [her children] had it hanging in the hall. My husband was scared. He said his [King's] eyes were looking right into his eyes." Like the relentless gaze of Dr. King, the home reflects the continuous dedication to faith, education, and family. Lewis, whose six children went through the Camden schools, worked for the school system for many years as a bus driver and a cafeteria employee. Above the television console hang large photographs of her six children in academic regalia proudly displayed on the wall. This home serves as a strong base for her unyielding determination to achieve racial equality for herself, her family, and the black community.

Narrative Inheritance

Lewis explains one motivation for her dedication to racial justice: "My granddaddy...his ancestors—I'm going to say his mama and daddy—were left property in Old Trap. You might have heard tell of Old Trap. He said, after dark, black people couldn't be caught in Old Trap. So when they left my granddaddy the land...my granddaddy said it was so mean down there he didn't want no land, didn't want any part of it. Because in the first place he said his daddy told him they cut off two of his toes so he couldn't go [leave the family he served as a slave]."

"Anyway, to make a long story short, I think by him telling me all these stories, it's me. And I brought my children up telling them, 'You treat everybody right because when you do wrong, then the wrong comes to you.' That's what I always think. I said, 'If you treat everybody right, then everything will just be smooth sailing. But you put your heart and soul in whatever, whatever you say you're going to do...' One thing, I wanted to see all my kids graduate because I didn't get to do it...All of them got some college education."

Lewis' response highlights the extent to which narrative inheritances become our own. She reveals the enduring currents of memories that flowed from her great grandfather whose toes were cut of to ensure his enslavement; to a "granddaddy" who spurned his material inheritance of land while carefully passing on a determination to defy oppression; skipping a generation to Lewis; and now continuing in the stories she tells her children and grandchildren.

Camden's First Kindergarten

As a parent, Lewis fought against community pressures to keep her children segregated. Twenty-five years after *Brown v. Board of Education* (1954), Camden County had no kindergarten—for blacks or whites. As she said, "The reason they didn't have the school [kindergarten] is they didn't want little white kids going with the little black kids. That was the problem." Although the other grades had integrated a decade earlier, the youngest of Camden's children remained segregated—reflecting some of the community's ongoing emotional resistance to integration. Lewis fought to establish the first kindergarten, one to which she was proud to send her son.

"Do you know a bunch of us got together because during that time we wanted to start a kindergarten? The kids wanted kindergarten. Only over here in Camden County we didn't have a lot of the kindergarten schools. In Elizabeth City they had their Protestant kindergarten, which was the Roanoke Institute. This was for the black school. Then they had the Catholic school. They would take either, black or white. You could go there, mix together at four or five years old. Over here in Camden County we didn't have that."

Lewis worked with her friend Jones, whom she called "Sister Jones," because they were in the same black women's social organization, the Order of the Eastern Star. Together, Jones as an EIC organizer, and Lewis as a concerned parent, they collaborated with community members and Volunteers In Students To America (VISTA) volunteers to organize a letter-writing campaign.

"I was involved in it, and we got so many letters and wrote to Governor Hunt. You know, he'd been in there forever. Up there [Raleigh] they didn't know what was going on down here. But you know the reason they didn't have the school is they didn't want the little white kids going with the little black kids. That was the problem. And believe it or not, the next year they [Camden children] could either go [to the new kindergarten] or send them somewhere else. He [Gov. Hunt] opened it up so they could have kindergarten."

"If it's anything you can do right, then you do it. But don't let nobody tell you you can't do anything. You set a goal and you go for it. That's what I told all my children... We just keep right on trying. We don't ever give up... We always said, whatever you do, or whatever you put your mind to do, you can do it! You can always do anything that you want to do. You say, 'I'm going to do it!' And you can do it!" By fighting for her children's educational opportunities and showing them that they could control their advancement, Lewis believed her children would have an advanced education and a better future.

Part of the story of school desegregation in Camden County relates to continuing efforts of the black community to gain educational equality. Another challenge was to get whites to accept integration. Some whites continued to resist the integrated kindergarten by sending their children to "segregation academies"—private all-white schools created to avoid integration.[1] "The ones that kept them out didn't send them [their children] over here [to Camden schools]. They would send them to Elizabeth City or something. They always had a place that they could go. It's just, it's like a lot of things they didn't know about us. They always would talk worse about us."

On the buses, in the cafeteria, and as a parent, Lewis witnessed everyday life from the beginning of Camden's school integration. In these spaces, micro-performances of residual segregation and racism continued. Lewis remembers, "There were so many that took their kids to school, didn't want to ride the school bus. They didn't want them besides us. We didn't smell good and we this and that. They just had a whole lot of stuff about us... But, see, they didn't know. They are going by what they were taught. Because I even had one girl tell me—she said, 'You're not at all like...' I said, 'Not at all like you were taught.' I said, 'See, you had to work around us and know us and know how we are.'"

Family Pedagogy

Lewis emphasizes the role of family in passing on prejudice and ignorance to the next generation. As a parent herself, despite her own and her family's experiences of oppression, Lewis taught her children to avoid simplistic racial stereotypes. "I always told my children this. Regardless of whatever, there's always the one good person. I said there's always the one good person because even during when Harriet Tubman was doing the Underground Railroad... I said, 'How do you think she got that far? She had to have some white people helping her... Not all people are hateful... You have good blacks and good whites...'"

Lewis passed on this hopeful pedagogy to her children. She recognizes that racial prejudice is still practiced by all. "It's both sides. Now we've got black people that are prejudiced, that don't like white people. I hear them say that and I said, 'But how do you think you're going to make it from there?' I said, 'You can't.' I said, 'Because you've got to go to the white people to get your money.' I said, 'That's where you're getting your checks from.' I said, 'You've got to treat everybody right. You've got to like them.' I said, 'Now the ones that don't like them, look where they are. Right out there on the street.'"

Lewis portrays a reality for many rural blacks. They were economically interdependent with whites. Some blacks could be independent in black enclaves in urban areas. "I've seen younger people say that before [anti-white comments], young black people. Where are they? Doing nothing. It's nothing that they can do if they don't have anything. If you go out here and you own a business, you can talk that. But then you can't talk that because you still have got to live with white people."

"We never had that problem. That's why I say (*jokingly*) that maybe might be a bunch of junkers in our family. But I don't know any family on this road that y'all couldn't go in and have a conversation with. But I'm not going to say that everybody would be as friendly as I am. See, that's life. You might have some that would say something bad about me, but very few, I'm thinking."

Lewis told her children how to relate to whites and counseled them to choose their words carefully. "But they would call me, 'Well, what do you think?' I said, 'You say it unto yourself and see how it sounds to you.' If you're going to say something or do something, first say it over and over. Wait and then see how it sounds to you. I got my oldest daughter, now she has been working with white people, working together since 1976. She has many white friends. Then when you work together so long, you feel like family."

Lewis also lived this philosophy. "I worked as the school cafeteria manager for about nine years. I was the first black to work at Camden High School. Worked with a bunch of sweet ladies and they just, we got along real good, and they were older than me. We got along real, real, real good. One of them had a big birthday party that she wanted me to come to the birthday party... She had recommended that I be manager."

Lewis' success depended on knowing how to get along with whites. But she still faced institutional obstacles and individual prejudice. "You know how that worked. The white ones didn't want to work under me. They did everything they could. They would steal stuff, and they would do this, and they would do that, and they would talk about me or whatever. It happened that one, they caught her really taking something, but they didn't fire her. That's another thing. See they don't fire them [whites] or anything. Just transferred her to another school."

Jones highlights the career challenges she experienced based on her race. Some white coworkers resisted having a black woman as their supervisor. Unlike blacks, white workers who broke organizational rules were not fired. This discrepancy in treatment mirrored some of the black parents' concerns that their children were facing the same unequal treatment in their school.

"I don't know because we didn't get in the classroom that much. Back then we had PTA meetings [at the integrated school], and it wasn't like when we had PTA meetings [at the segregated school]. By the time when we [black parents] got to the PTA meetings, they had had their little meeting before. Like they tell us to come at eight o'clock. They'd be there at seven, I guess. And they'd have done all the plans and did everything. I said to them [the white-controlled PTA] one night, 'If y'all are going to do this, there's no need of us coming.' So then they changed it [the PTA]. They had us going and visiting the teachers instead of having the whole big meeting. Well, it wasn't any need of us coming. We're going to get there [to the meeting], then they're going to tell us all what to do."

"That's right. We just stopped. The PTA stopped then. I don't know how many years that's been. We all [black parents] used to have the PTA.... We discussed things and what they were having and what they're doing or whatever. They [white PTA leadership] didn't like that. It didn't work with them. They didn't want us to have any part of anything. Sometimes you think [as a black person], 'Are you in this society? Are you an American? Are you a citizen of Camden County?'"

Lewis describes how informal sites of participative democracy—such as the PTA—were unable to operate as an integrated community. While participatory democracy may not thrive in the political institutions of the United States, the "resources of participatory democracy" live in the "places people occupy as they go about their daily lives,"[2] including, for example, neighborhoods, some school associated organizations, churches, and volunteer groups.

Instead of integrating the PTA and creating space for the black parental voice, the PTA—a major liaison between home and school—ceased to operate. Educators Michael Apple and James Beane argue that schools "create democratic structures and processes by which life in the school is carried out and create curricula that will give young people democratic experiences."[3] In this Camden school, democratic structures were compromised in favor of maintaining white authority. As educator Donna Davis argues, democratic schools provide "all stakeholders in the school—students, community members, staff, teachers, and leaders—with a voice in how decisions in the school are made."[4] Lewis' story exemplifies a phenomenon widely experienced in integration: "Families of color have regularly been excluded from the decision-making mechanisms that should ensure that their children receive quality education. The parent-teacher organizations, school site councils, and other possibilities for democratic participation have not been available for many of these families."[5] In Camden, many blacks experienced school desegregation as limiting the democratic participation that was central to Marian Anderson School. They were not welcome at the PTA. The school board was a tightly guarded source of white power. Black parents felt their voices were rarely heard and even less understood by white administrators.

Legacies of Violence

While some forms of institutional racism were difficult to challenge directly, Lewis resisted racist acts in indirect ways. She recounts a story of when she worked at Albemarle Hospital in Elizabeth City. Whites were trying to prevent blacks from moving into previously all-white neighborhoods. "They were talking about crosses. I worked out there...part-time. One of the waitresses came in...and she said they were going to burn some crosses in a couple of yards. She said somebody was going to burn a cross because somebody was just gotten permission to build. It was a county commissioner. I can't remember exactly who it was."

"But anyway, I just scared them. I said, 'You know what...' I said, 'When they start burning those crosses...don't you know that we're going to be sitting out with a gun.' I said, 'We're going to be sitting out there with guns.' I said, 'Do you know that?' She said, 'Oh, my God, let me go out there and tell them.' I said, 'You go tell them because I know my husband has got his gun ready.' He didn't even have one. He doesn't even have a gun. I said, 'If they want to start that, they'll start something now.' She went out there and told them...I didn't ever hear any more about any more crosses."

Lewis' story of the crosses connects back to her own career. In the case of the county commissioner moving into a white neighborhood, racists tried to prevent residential desegregation despite his professional and class stature. Lewis experienced whites limiting her professional advancement at the school. Black high-status professionals experienced whites trying to avoid residential integration. In both cases, long after de jure school desegregation, some whites lived their everyday lives perpetuating de facto segregation. These narratives illustrate a broader argument made by Ladson-Billings: "Desegregating schools is a limited way of dealing with segregation as an institution. We need to think about ways to desegregate the society."[6]

This continued dissonance between de jure school desegregation, supported by the rule of law, and de facto community segregation and racism supported by white community power holders, helps to explain the tensions in Lewis' next story. In particular, given the violent history of race relations and continued oppression, Lewis holds on to historic fears of the black community while still continuing to fight for equality. Her story was prompted by a conversation we were having about a black high school student—one of the first black children to choose a white school during the freedom of choice period. While walking home from school, he was struck in the head by a bottle allegedly thrown from a pickup truck by white male students. The victim sustained a disabling brain injury—a chilling memory of the violence against the trailblazers of desegregation. Lewis remembers the boy ended up "in some type of mental place." The perpetrators were never brought to justice.

She discussed another close encounter with racial intimidation—cross burnings in Camden County. "They were burning 'em [crosses] in South Mills [the northern area of Camden] a lot (*serious tone*). But it's so funny they burned 'em in South Mills (*bemused tone*) because we say the light skinned people [blacks], most of them live in South Mills and Ahoskie and places like that. And that's where they were burning them, up there in that area."

Lewis' tone in the first sentence acknowledges the serious nature of these hate crimes. Then she notes with acute awareness the gradations and hierarchies of blackness as it is distributed geographically in Camden. She immediately moves on to how these acts of violence and intimidation have, and have not, touched her life.

"I didn't ever have any burnt. We didn't ever have any burned in our yard, thank goodness. But if our son [who dated white girls] was growin' up back then—(*she interrupts herself.*) You know, this is funny. But you can laugh about it now. But it's not funny because—I was telling my son that the iceman…" (*she interrupts herself again*).

She told her son, who is in an interracial marriage. "I said, 'Daddy can tell you more about him than I can.' There was this white lady who was married. And back then in the fifties we got ice. There was this man taking ice around and putting it in your icebox. Okay, there was this black guy was going with her (*lowered voice*), sexualwise. And the iceman came in and caught 'em. And she hollered rape. And they first got my husband's brother, picked him up. He was on his way from work. And he said they picked him up and made him get in the truck and carried him down there."

"He was talking about that the other night, matter of fact. He told Harry [her husband], he said, 'You know, Lord was with me, because they could've killed me.' Said they carried him somewhere and they told 'em 'No, no, no!' Said 'He's not the one. That's Lewis' son. So I know that's not him.' That was one of my husband's older brothers. I think he's about, well he might be, about seventy-seven or so. But anyway, they stayed up all night long looking for the guy. I think his name might have been Richard, but they called him Big Lee." This family story reminds all listeners how close racial violence came to the Lewis family and the inadequacy of the justice system to protect black people.

"And for a long time this other man used to tell me, 'You know they hung my cousin [Big Lee] down on this tree on the courthouse lawn.' I said, 'What tree was it?' 'Next time I catch you I'll take you and show you what tree it was.' And he did. That's, gosh, that was back in the late sixties when he showed me that was the tree back there at the courthouse. I think it's probably down now... Said they hung him. And he was really going with the lady. And that's why I think about [my son], but I guess if it was back in those days, you wouldn't have ever gotten that close."

Memory's Multiple Meanings

This story tells two tales. First, it teaches that despite the seemingly immutable segregation of races, whites and blacks have always been in intimate relations. And yet the story also reinforces the taboo (as well as the real dangers) of interracial mixing—especially in the case of white women and black men.

The narrative illustrates the contradictions and complexities within Lewis' own experience. She fought passionately for an integrated kindergarten, committing time and energy as well as emotional support to the cause. She also worked against ongoing racism in informal contexts. Lewis tells stories about change, inflected with incredulity. Yet she was still influenced by fears concerning a black man (indeed her son who was in that first integrated classroom) engaged in an interracial marriage—another form of integration. While her son's marriage to his college sweetheart is sanctioned legally, the social sanctions remain tenuous. Interracial couples in Camden County continue to face strong prejudices, even though his own family supports the relationship. These powerful and persistent emotions about racial segregation and integration in Camden County are also powerful reminders of the community's covert resistance to integration.

Lewis' frequent narratives of upward mobility communicate a sense that blacks should have every opportunity available—"don't ever let anybody tell you that you can't do something." Yet the story of the iceman constrains that opportunity by warning against racial mixing. Such an emotional legacy is a powerful lesson that a black man can do what he wants in certain contexts, but not in others. Lewis' narrative shows that deeply engrained prejudices influence race relations as much, if not more than legal prescriptions.

Lewis' story presents different interpretations. The narrative can be empowering or disempowering. For instance, what is the meaning of the lover's betrayal? The moral of the story is not simply that bad things can happen when you cross the color line. It is also about the white woman who betrays her lover for her own selfish purposes. When she is forced to choose, she sides with her own race. This is not the tale of Romeo and Juliet but a cautionary tale concerning the tenuousness of interracial ties. This story also is an inversion of white folklore concerning the black man as a sexual predator. It admonishes, "Beware of the white temptress." This story discourages trustful black-white relations.

The stories of racial violence create a mythology that can help or hinder progress in race relations. This narrative reveals the multifaceted character and the potential for ambiguity of the stories we pass on. A single lynching in a county is an act of terror that continues to touches generations. The full story of integration should not overlook these violent, complicated, and emotionally charged legacies.

Despite these memories, Lewis has not lost her drive and sense of hope. "When we have Martin Luther King's birthday, we march from Grandy to past the courthouse to Camden High School. I could see a difference in that day and the day that we walked last year. So what I'm saying is I think they [whites in Camden] are trying. My sister said she thinks they are trying. She said about the principal that she didn't like him ever since he treated my son the way he did [he gave academics honors to whites but ignored her son's high achievements]." Lewis identified the slights to black children's academic achievements as part of the ongoing legacy of white domination in integrated education.

"I said, 'Well, you've got to forgive him'... I said, 'because he's trying to change.' I said, 'God forgives.' And she said, 'Oh Lord, you always try to forgive.' I said, 'He had cancer...' I told my son. I said, 'Son, I shook his hand with a smile.' I said, 'He shook my hand back.' My son laughed and said, 'Mama, you did?' I said, 'Yeah. I really meant it, but he reached his hand out to me and I could not, not shake it.'"

"Camden is a little sneaky. That's what I always tell them [her children]. Because my son he has principles and all that and now he says, 'Mama, I still don't trust them.' And I say, 'Well, they're changing there, baby.' And he says, 'Mama, you can say all you want to. I still don't trust them.'"

Lewis' unyielding hope and faith are driven by her propensity to forgive. Her children may not always agree with every part of her worldview. But they do agree with her passion for social change. After all, they were the ones who hung up the Martin Luther King Jr. blanket with his visionary gaze and powerful dreams. Through her stories of the black community organizing for an integrated kindergarten, Lewis became a model for her children. Her tale of collective activist persistence and ultimate victory demonstrates the power of black activism, so rare in this rural, conservative county in North Carolina.

CHAPTER 9

Memory, Pedagogy, and Social Change

> When a community loses its memory, its members no longer know one another. How can they know one another if they have forgotten or have never learned one another's stories?
>
> —Wendell Barry
>
> The duty to remember is a duty to teach, whereas the duty to forget is a duty to go beyond anger and hatred.
>
> —Paul Ricoeur

During the celebration of the fiftieth anniversary of *Brown v. Board of Education*, the dominant national narrative focused on moments of school integration: one little black girl with remarkable courage, federal marshals enforcing the law, black and white children sitting together in a classroom.[1] For some Americans, these iconic episodes confirm their belief that the struggle for school desegregation is over, the Civil Rights era finished. Yet a sampling of the memories in Camden County uncovers a remarkably different history of school desegregation that reveals how the relationships between individuals and institutions were altered by *Brown*.

These local oral histories show vividly the profound impact of school integration on the families, churches, and fabric of the community. They also reveal the often-ignored power of all kinds of memories in social change and the unanticipated consequences of these policies.

The memories detailed in this book are formed through stories and other cultural artifacts such as Leary's Camden Museum. These memories serve as sites of belonging within specific communities. In Camden, such stories are often race-specific and sustain segregated communities. Storytelling—an art at which Leary and Hughes excel—continues to transmit and alter traditions as a way of preserving group-specific memories in changing contexts. While top-down histories are a powerful part of the national narrative, the oral histories in this book show the power and persistence of grassroots memory.

Winter points out, "History and memory overlap, infuse each other, and create vigorous and occasionally fruitful incompatibilities."[2] Oral histories such as those of Revelle and Lewis reveal how people combine diverse, sometimes conflicting memories of the experience of school desegregation with their life narrative. The tensions in these memories reveal the complex, multivocal, and changing nature of memories.

This chapter explores these overlaps and their "fruitful incompatibilities," reflecting on what these different forms of remembering can reveal about race and education. Throughout the book, different people employ diverse forms of remembering. Both the content and the form of their memories offer insights into ongoing attempts to address race, public education, and equity.

These memories raise and sometimes answer key questions: How do the practices of social memory work differently in the white and black communities? How does each narrator construct and use memory in their narratives? As listeners to these stories, what kinds of memory are we being invited into and what are the attendant ethical bonds? Finally, can we experience and respond to these memories in ways that enrich our understanding of our collective history and our world today?

Counter-Memory

Hughes' stories illustrate the connection between oral history and counter-memory. His memories, born of local experience, provide a depth of understanding from sources, as Jamaica Kincaid writes, "not yet a part of history."[3] These stories challenge the national narratives that racial equality has consistently progressed, with such systems as graded education and de jure school integration. In this sense his oral history proves to be, "more democratic than other historiographical methodologies because it provides an alternative viewpoint from below, a viewpoint that conventional methodology disenfranchises."[4]

The memories of Hughes offer a long view of school segregation and integration from his perspective, first as a black student and then later as a parent. They create counter-memories—"that differ from, and often challenge, dominant discourses"[5]—by highlighting the domestic nature of education, both in terms of the vital parental role in "learning" children to work and the connected relationship of schooling and labor. These memories challenge larger narratives of educational and economic improvement by revealing the costs of the relationship between education and capitalism—both in terms of informal economies and a diminished sense of community.

Another powerful legacy Hughes leaves is his unyielding positive attitude. As he says, "I try to think positive" (*in an energetic tone*). This positive energy initiates a forward motion (both his own and that which he passed on to his children) that flies in the face of the numerous structural and social barriers that many black people faced. When I asked his daughter if he had passed this positive attitude on to her, she replied, "Don't have time for a negative thought. Too busy."

This positive approach to life shaped how Hughes remembered the past, educated his children, lived his life, and inscribed the future. In this way, his memories may not represent the broader black experience. He is a survivor and he tells survival tales. But this positive attitude, combined with strategic use of counter-memories, succeeded in propelling his children toward a similarly successful, bright future, in part because his stories laid out paths to success that are not commonly told.

Communication scholar J. Robert Cox's work on "critical memory" explains why this form of memory matters. Critical memory uses the past as a mode of invention to warrant a better future.[6] Critical memory, as Cox conceives it, "becomes an awareness of history and the possibilities for change within a culture... it constitutes a critical horizon, the memory of possibilities that transcend the 'given' of received premises for argument."[7] In other words, by re-examining the past one may find unrecognized sites of meaning.

Memories, inherently conservative, draw on *doxa*, cultural interpretations, to create arguments—relying necessarily on once-important versions. Critical memory subverts the currently accepted memory and fosters ethical discussions of alternate versions. For example, Hughes constructs a critical memory when he challenges the hegemonic cultural stories of unequivocally beneficial school desegregation. His counter-memories of informal learning, barter economies, and black pride in segregated education open a deliberative space where desegregated contemporary education can be reconsidered.

White Laughter, Domesticating Strangeness

As a historian, Leary remembers some of what is left out of history, what we cannot find in books. He brings to life the struggle between history, searching for the truth of the past, and story, which regardless of its factual nature may be more real to the life of the community because "so many people know this story." Leary, a "teller of silly tales which of course no kind of history keeps track of," taught me about some of the pleasures and entrapments of lived history.[8]

Leary's stories arise from his experiences as a teacher and a white community member. His memories show the ways that people reinvent the past: through practices that are alive and inseparable from traditions; through carefully controlled narratives that reaffirm the legitimacy of particular power relations; and through dialogue intended to improve relations.

Leary's narratives provide insight into memories of the white community. As Leydesdorff et al. point out, "focusing exclusively on the dominated makes a full understanding even of the origins and maintenance of their subordination impossible."[9] Leary's memories offer insights into dominant forces in the community during segregation and desegregation and into how oppression was maintained. They shed light on what school desegregation meant to the white community, from forced teacher integration to changed mascots and increased interracial contact—topics that are often edited out of contemporary conversations as they reflect past racial attitudes now judged.

Oral histories, particularly when told from the perspective of those historically in power, rarely offer alternate forms of knowing. Leary's memories hint at underexamined stories of what whites lost and gained from school integration. They do contain important details of the process of integration—from ways some whites disciplined other whites that were more receptive to integration to emerging interracial understanding and friendship. But these personal memories are often eclipsed by the dominant public memories of desegregation as only progress and a thing of the past. Storytelling is a double-edged sword—capable of transforming race relations or of maintaining the status quo or open spaces for transformation of race relations.

As historian David Lowenthal contends, and as Leary's stories reveal, remembering the past is an exercise in domesticating strangeness. This is doubly true in the case of school desegregation, which was a domestic endeavor: it occurred at the levels of home, family, and community. Desegregation changed schools from familiar racially homogeneous spaces into discomforting places.

They became strangely diverse settings and lost their symbolic value as the center of raced communities.

Domestication of strangeness offers a frame for interpreting Leary's collection of Civil War artifacts, his stories of the land, and his approach to history. Although Civil War artifacts are familiar historical relics, their ubiquitous presence in Leary's contemporary home presents a past that is strangely distant to many people. The shed in Leary's back yard, named the "Alder Branch Museum," provides another example of a literal as well as figurative domestication of the past (the past is housed in a mundane domestic shed and is domesticated in the form of a museum).

Throughout his narratives, Leary's humor worked to domesticate the strangeness and release the underlying tension of my Yankee interpretation of race and the Civil War. Through humor Leary effectively took some of the questions I asked him about desegregation, and turned them back toward me, implicating me in his restructuring of whiteness. As a guest in a context that required norms of hospitality, I sometimes felt strange participating in the homely nature of our shared whiteness. Even though his use of humor invited me to feel at home, I felt that I could not call attention to the extent to which I was sometimes ill at ease.

Throughout our conversations, Leary controlled the turbulent memories of school desegregation through the use of humor. Freud, in his discussion of the "uncanny," explores the tension between the words "homely" (alternately meaning "belonging to the house, not strange, familiar, tame, intimate, friendly, etc.")[10] and "unfamiliar" (that which is "concealed and kept out of sight").[11] The uncanny, employed through Leary's use of strategic narrative and humor, worked on me as a listener and a researcher. Despite the value of humor and the necessity of laughter that I found in my encounters with Leary, I remain troubled by my own participation in these powerful forms of familiarity, which ultimately tamed difference. I failed to challenge certain comments that while often normalized in white conversation contained racist assumptions and a narrow white perspective on history.

The assumed intimacy of this white laughter drew me in. The iterative performance of stories such as the one of the black cafeteria worker maintained the dominance of whiteness. As a part of the conversation, I, too, participated in its reinstantiation: laughing at jokes, being cajoled into affirming certain norms of whiteness. My hopes for more vigorously dialogic communication about issues of race and power were pushed to the margins of our conversation. What was all this laughter about? Some of the things we laughed about were not funny but belied serious instances of violence, racism, and injustice. Are these stories of the first attempts to desegregate Camden County, especially as they met with resistance and found their radical potential foiled, a laughing matter?

Jokes can be insidious. And yet they are necessary for survival. In Leary's stories, humor works as a way to stabilize his version of history. Leary's willingness to examine himself and his family's past, to be open and reflexive in conversation, contains certain contradictions. His desire to tell history and to be an authority operates in tension with his resistance to reflecting deeply on race and the volatility of desegregation in Camden. He is not alone in this conundrum. Many whites struggle with narrating their place in a condemned history of segregation, which allows for nostalgia and fond recollection and not evoking ethical questions and guilt. This tension may arise in part because of the competing pulls of past and present assessments of white supremacy. Leary holds tightly, with pride, to a past that is dear to him, one largely a tale of white success and victory. Yet, he lives in a time that is not as charitable in its interpretations of past race relations, a world in which he is also at home.

Leary's humor has a monologic quality. In each story he tells, Leary deftly controls the punch line and, to some extent, the listener. Jokes become a part of domesticating the history of school desegregation and containing, rather than opening up, the radical possibilities of his memories. The stories about Tom Jones, Martin Luther King, and Witherspoon unsettled me. As I listened with bated breath to these intensely dramatic moments of community conflict, racial tension, and corporal punishment, I felt our discussions could have led to a powerful dialogue. But just before the meaning of these histories could open to discussion and reinvention, Leary, the master storyteller, would resolve the stories with humor. Leary leaves me with an uncomfortable legacy of laughter. Bergson writes, "However spontaneous it seems, laughter always implies a kind of secret freemasonry, or even complicity, with other laughters, real or imaginary."[12]

The live spirit of the comic has been important for me as I delved into the painful history of intransigence, injustice, and sorrow. Paradoxically, as Bergson notes, "the comic demands something like a momentary anesthesia of the heart."[13] Thus, the comic allows us to live in and through pain.

Leary's collections of Civil War artifacts, dominated by instruments of death, and his many narratives demonstrate both the desire to preserve and to perform. Lowenthal argues, "The past is a foreign country whose features are shaped by today's predilections, its strangeness domesticated by our preservation of its vestiges."[14] Preservation of the past in the form of select and organized artifacts and carefully polished and controlled narratives does not offer an intimate, vital understanding of the past. As Lowenthal concludes, "we also preserve...because we are no longer intimate enough with that legacy to rework it creatively."[15] Leary's stories also work as a caution that however potentially liberating the oral history may be, they present the possibility of reinforcing dominance. Memories remain vulnerable to domestication for present purposes as can be seen both in Leary's narratives and in contemporary public remembrance of school desegregation.

Leary's memory performances demonstrate how his identity as a member of the white community creates tensions that he resolves through humor. Yet Leary's domesticated racial memories fall short of offering ways to eliminate racism in the present or create historical sites of meaning for heterogeneous communities. This is one of the more challenging aspects of white memories from that time.

Collective Memory and Resistance

Because he "passed over" a week before I first arrived in Camden County, the memories of Whittier Crockett Witherspoon are not from, but about, him.[16] Like a social ghost, Witherspoon turns up time and again in memories of blacks and whites in the county and nearby Elizabeth City. What does his ghostly presence mean and how do these stories work within the broader collective memory of the communities? Jay Winter writes, "Collective remembrance is another matter entirely: it points to time and place and above all to evidence, to traces enabling us to understand what groups of people try to do when they act in public to conjure up the past."[17]

The black community in Camden and Elizabeth City continues to act in public—to remember Witherspoon and the glories of Marian Anderson School. They do this though such events as the annual Elizabeth City State University Witherspoon-Martin Luther King Jr. basketball tournament, the Witherspoon-Harris scholarship fund, and the Marian Anderson School reunions. Bellah and co-authors argue that "Communities...have a history—in an important sense are constituted by their past—and for this reason we can speak of a real community as a 'community of memory,' one that does not forget its past."[18]

The retelling of the stories of Witherspoon is a key part of the black community's narrative of achievement. The selection of Witherspoon, a paragon of the black community, serves a function beyond commemoration. Olick and Robbins write, "Collective memory does not merely reflect past experiences (accurately or not); it has an orientational function...As Schwartz puts it, 'collective memory is both a mirror and a model for society.'"[19] Witherspoon's memory, free of human blemishes and lovingly embellished by those committed to protecting and preserving it, remains a consummate model for the black community.

Witherspoon is also present in the white community memory—as a model black educator, bridgebuilder, and leader. But the orientational function of these memories is slightly different. He is remembered in part because of his exceptionalism. For some in the white community Witherspoon did not cause them to alter their negative stereotypes. Instead, they talk about him as an exception to their prejudice. In this light his strict discipline was admired in part because it instilled order in what whites considered an unruly or lesser black community.

While both the black and the white communities remember Witherspoon, the meanings of these memories function differently. As Foucault put it, "Since memory is actually a very important factor in struggle...if one controls people's memory, one controls their dynamism."[20] For the black community, their control of Witherspoon's memory is a part of a long legacy of struggle for equal education and political power. For some in the white community, he is remembered as a leader, anointed by the white community to maintain order in the black community. For some in the black community he is remembered as an Uncle Tom. For some members of the white and black communities, he is remembered for his commitment to bridge both communities—with an unwavering dedication that few in either community matched.

Historian David Thelen writes, "The struggle for possession and interpretation of memory is rooted in the conflict and interplay among social, political, and cultural interests."[21] These interests in both the black and white communities shape the way Witherspoon is remembered. The ubiquity of Witherspoon in the memory of many blacks is not a coincidence but an act of will by many individuals. Irwin-Zarecka argues that collective memory "is a product of a great deal of work by large numbers of people."[22] Collective memory represents "the past within social imagination...as collectively shared representations."[23] The collective representations of Witherspoon serve both the white and black version of the past. For blacks, the memories of Witherspoon attest to their communities' united dedication to education and the potential of black achievement, particularly in a period rife with oppression.

Solidarity through Memory

My many visits with Revelle provided me with insights into both what a lonely endeavor it was to be a white man working for economic and social justice and to be an "integrationist" in a time of popular support for de jure and de facto school segregation. His memories highlight the consolidated and tightly guarded white authority over education, a white power that remains secretive and unrecognized even by most whites in the community. Even Revelle, as a principal, did not have input into such choices as changes in the school name or its colors.

Revelle's stories detail the challenges of bringing about equality and justice during the early stages of integration. His memories brought home the intense, entrenched nature of prejudice as it is constantly being organized and reorganized by those who derive benefit from structures of whiteness, either economically or through some sense of racial superiority. His memories bring to life a powerful white backlash against any symbols of school desegregation.

Initially, I did not understand Revelle's self-proclaimed desire to forget the process of school desegregation, an extremely stressful time in his life. I also detected ambivalent feelings of that time by Revelle. Memory can be full of ambivalent judgments, especially when the past did not unfold in the way he might have hoped for or when retrospectively he wished he had acted differently. Revelle's ambivalent memories are an uncommon type of remembering that he engages in frequently.

Zembylas and Beckerman write, "Getting 'to know' the past does not mean 'controlling' it. Instead, 'knowing' requires an act which 're-cites' and re-sites what one has learned—not only about what happened to others... but also (and this is key) what one has learned of and within the disturbances and disruptions inherent in comprehending the substance and significance of these events."[24] In contrast to Leary's domesticating forms of memory, Revelle does not attempt to control the past through his stories. Instead, he resituates what he has experienced in the past with his present understanding of racial inequality. Still an unequivocal supporter of integration as a socially just position, Revelle reflects, with ambivalence, on the implementation of school desegregation as well as concerns with race and equity.

This ambivalence, which might be misinterpreted by some as weak or not fully supportive of integration, provides a vital way of understanding that has allowed Revelle to help build fragile forms of interracial solidarity. Revelle introduced me to Jones and Hughes as two valuable sources of knowledge on desegregation in Camden County. He was fondly regarded by Lewis. In his own memories, he recalls understanding why the black community would be angered by desegregation and empathizes with their resistance.

The feelings Revelle demonstrates is discussed by Zembylas and Bekerman: "What constitutes such a solidarity is empathizing with the sufferings of others, grounded in 'feeling with' the others' suffering. The conditions of possibility for solidarity must also be interrogated because empty empathy... threatens to slide through the doors." The cultural circulation of others' suffering does not always result in formations of solidarity. Revelle's desire that I interview Jones so that her story of voter disenfranchisement could be documented as an important historical lesson constitutes one such act of solidarity. He knew of the story because he and Jones had worked together on poverty and community issues, and she had shared it with him. This act, along with his own recollections of school desegregation, illustrate Revelle's propensity for "feeling with" others' suffering.

In these cases, memory becomes an avenue for interracial solidarity. Zembylas and Bekerman draw a distinction between being a spectator or a witness to others' pain: "in our view, to learn to hear the Other's pain and respond to this pain as witnesses and not as spectators... is precisely what creates new openings for solidarity."[25] Through hearing and witnessing the pain of the blacks, Revelle uses memory to critically understand the past in ways that because of his position as a white community member he personally could not fully experience at the time.

This is a demanding form of remembering for whites committed to racial justice. It requires jeopardizing one's privileged position in history to better know another perspective, even one that implicates you in processes and institutions that continue oppression. As Zembylas and Bekerman note:

> On a personal level, this solidarity requires a constant openness and criticality to one's self and transformation and a willingness to recognize our connections to another's suffering—through attention to their memories of suffering such as listening to their stories and working with them to alleviate suffering. In this way, we begin to see ourselves as interdependent and vulnerable to injustices.[26]

Revelle's engagement with painful memories appears driven by a desire to take a different path toward social justice. This hope for a different present and future, one not constrained by racism and inequality, helps explain

Revelle's desire to forget. The forgetting Revelle desires is not motivated by a desire to erase evidence of past inequality, which he consistently acknowledges and works to end. Zembylas and Bekerman explore the function of the forgetting Revelle desires: "Forgetting is usually criticized for...denying foundational memories...However, is it possible perhaps that some forms of forgetting...might provide new insights into solidarity with the Other?"[27] As Leary uses humor as anesthesia of the heart, Revelle uses forgetting to bring about the future he has long worked to achieve. This forgetting allows him and others not to be constrained by bitter memories that can support racial hatred for generations.

Forgetting becomes a way to quiet the "fussing" and racist comments of the past, to reduce the pain of remembering an oppressive past, and to forget past enmities.[28] In this way Leary and Revelle reveal two different forms of memory practiced by whites to deal with oppression and racism.

Zembylas and Beckerman clarify the motivation: "It is not that the unjust past and the suffering are being forgotten. Rather it is the anger and the hatred that are being forgotten, so as to enable space for reconciliation."[29] In his letter to the editor Revelle wrote about moving beyond past racism. He has worked hard so that people forget enmity, embrace their better selves, and work for a just and equal society. His forms of remembering for solidarity and forgetting for reconciliation provide a model for whites and blacks to engage in the process of remembering as they move toward community reconciliation and integration.

Dangerous Memories

The way Revelle introduced me to Jones opened a space for her to share her "dangerous memories" with me, a white outsider. Dangerous memories are "those memories that are disruptive to the status quo, that is, the hegemonic culture of strengthening and perpetuating existing group-based identities."[30] Without my introduction from her friend Revelle, she might not have so willingly shared these memories in the single interview I was able to arrange before her passing.

Dangerous memory, a concept developed by different scholars of memory and education, possesses several defining qualities. The term "dangerous" is not a judgmental assessment. Any memory can be considered dangerous if it challenges dominant historical narratives.[31] Jones' narratives demonstrate how black memories of integration resist dominant white memories, especially as they recover lost points of authority and pride, such as the contribution of I.M. Trafton and the community fundraising for black schools. These memories, as well as Jones' recollections of everyday racism, work as dangerous memories by challenging the white historical narrative of segregated schools as inferior; integrated schools as progress; and racism as a thing of the past.

Dangerous memory "enables solidarity by not appealing to past understandings of identity or ideological narratives but by recognizing shared historical experiences as well as the heterogeneity of those experiences."[32] Such memories constitute "a people's history of resistance and struggle in the face of oppression."[33] One way in which Jones achieves this resistance is through remembering the personal and institutional effects of racism in her life. By recalling these everyday indignities and showing how they continue in the present, Jones disrupts the ideological narrative that race relations and inequality have substantially improved with the Civil Rights Movement and can be considered complete. Through dangerous memories, Jones reveals a broader and more sustained struggle against racial oppression.

These political memories, "in the sense that they involve power relations, revealing the patterns of violence and suffering at work," constitute "a disruptive practice of and from memory."[34] By recalling black memories of segregation and desegregation, Jones resists the racist practices of the present, which persist in schools (both institutionally—through a culture of power—and for students who are not taught the history of segregation) and in community institutions (both against individuals and in structural practices).

As Zembylas and Beckerman write, "All humans as subjects are located in suffering; thus, through the memories of suffering—that is, dangerous memories—the taken-for-granted narratives are interrupted."[35] These memories are necessary "if we are to find and sustain the strength, resilience, courage and hope required for resisting the forces of evil."[36] Such disruptive memories take "seriously a non-totalizing view of the past without the naïve acceptance that the past determines who we ought to be."[37]

Jones' memories of the vital segregated schools could benefit everyone. Through her memories of Marian Anderson School she reveals a viable way in which education can be seen as a collective endeavor; not just concerned with individual needs to do well on tests and compete with peers. The value of these dangerous memories is that they disrupt the prevailing viewpoints and may facilitate integration.

By returning to forgotten black memories—not only the important and shocking narratives of racist practices—but those of black strength and commitment to education, we create narratives and social memories that could more fully represent the goals of school integration. Black memories access alternative ways of "doing community," such as using the school for parties and funerals. They also could challenge contemporary racist practices, such as letting white parents excuse their children from Black History Month activities.

Dangerous Memories and Emotional Legacies

Memories and histories of desegregation and integration course with emotion. In Camden County these emotional legacies—the feelings handed down from previous generations through narration—are fraught with contradiction and paradox. The stories are intimate—bound up with complex histories of family, cultural, and political feelings, conveyed in discussions, comments, jokes, and even gestures. They are also one of the most powerful reminders of the ongoing community struggles toward integration in substantive way. These stories provide touchstones for exploring the larger paradoxes and politics of emotional legacies: "The point of memories, then, is less to tell us what 'exactly' happened than what it felt like to experience an event."[38]

Emotion, as Nussbaum argues, is not necessarily any more reliable than "any other set of entrenched beliefs."[39] It is, however, like other entrenched beliefs, worthy of careful attention. Emotional systems shaped and continue to shape histories and the stories. Why are certain memories inherited and others forgotten?

Emotional legacies often elude careful examination because of their links with imagination and storytelling (areas sometimes perceived as lacking "authenticity" or "veracity").[40] As Madison suggests, the black oral tradition of remembering calls up "the interiors of ancestral lives enabling both storyteller and listener to remember and experience those lives intimately. Calling up these lives intimately meant that their yearnings, pleasures, heartaches, humor, contemplations, rage, and deeds were truer than facts."[41] These oral performances color the emotional landscape of future generations. To consider affective legacies is: to call up "the interiors" of historical lives; to track the emotional intimacies that bind storytellers and listeners; and to regard "yearnings, pleasures, and heartaches" as meaningful and probably more important as any complementary "facts."

Critical consideration of efforts to understand the past through stories is particularly important in race relations.[42] Emotional legacies continue to guide race relations on personal, cultural, and political levels, and remain under-examined. The power of emotion exceeds individual life spans and standard histories.[43] Contemporary stories of ongoing struggles toward integration cannot be told in full without highlighting the persistent power of emotional legacies.

Lewis' stories center on the role of the home and domestic intimacies as they related in profoundly emotionally charged ways to school desegregation. They offer fertile ground for exploring legacies—from the emotional to the political. Lewis tells stories full of hope, pride, and determination, while simultaneously revealing the challenges of parenting children in a society with many forms of residual segregation and deeply rooted legacies of pain, anger, and fear.

Emotional legacies are highly social, often familial inheritances. These legacies charge the next generation's emotional circuitries. As Trinh writes, "what is transmitted from generation to generation is not only stories, but the very power of transmission."[44] Lewis took charge of this power, even as it charged her, to shepherd her children through school integration.

The stories she tells, such as the one about the iceman and the irrevocable injuries to the black student at the beginning of desegregation, convey powerful emotions. These emotions travel across generations. Such memories are open to multiple interpretations. Memories such as that of the iceman possess two dimensions—"that of hope and that of suffering..."[45]

The fear of miscegenation travels through her stories, boosting her determination, and yet adding a tremor to triumph. The school integration, for which she fought so hard, led to the interracial "mixing" that still makes her son's marriage dangerous. She shows no regret, but the proximity of her stories of pride and fear strike a note of ambivalence.

Emotional evocation in oral history presents an inspiring and mobilizing possibility. Emotion is something that is part of rational thought. It is not juxtaposed to reason, but as Lewis' story points out, emotion can be engaged in reason. As Kenneth Plummer points out, there continues to be "the need to understand the emotional basis and history of much talk... Much conversation and argument then is not simply a matter of rational debate: it speaks to us from depths we do not understand."[46]

Such memories contain hope for a different future, including the one her son and daughter-in-law, and her interracial granddaughter affirm. The hope of emotional legacies is that they inspire survival, resistance, and social change. These memories become a form of cultural capital and contain a protective force as they teach future generations. As storyteller Leslie Silko writes, "I will tell you something about stories... They aren't just entertainment / Don't be fooled / They are all we have, you see / All we have to fight off / Illness and Death. You don't have anything / If you don't have stories."[47] Storyteller Thomas King adds, "If we stopped telling stories…we would discover that neglect is as powerful an agent as war and fire."[48] Lewis' stories, ranging from lynching to black activism in education, keep memories alive. And they inspire her son to continue to fight oppression and engage in social activism himself. Because they propel emotions into the present, memories become an important part of the future.

Memories continue to influence race relations on personal and societal levels. They shape our communities—such as where we choose to live and to send our children to schools. One generation passes their racial attitudes to the next, although the young children themselves have few problems relating to each other. In other words, through emotional legacies parents can perpetuate their own race problems or plant the seeds for solutions to them.

In our journey toward justice in race relations, the emotional legacies in narrative memories are passed down intimately from generation to generation, like a fractured heirloom that has been broken and put back together. As the inheritors of these heirlooms, as a nation with this fractured inheritance, we must recognize the scars and the fissures. Lewis' stories illustrate unresolved issues of reconciliation and justice. At the same time, her narratives evoke emotions that fuel passions in the next generation for social change and racial justice.

CONCLUSION

Moving On

> Until we can see the world as others see it, all the educational reforms in the world will come to naught.
>
> —Lisa Delpit

Many scholars of *Brown v. Board of Education* agree that the promises of this Supreme Court decision have yet to be achieved. Communities to this day are haunted by questions about its implementation left open by the Court decision, such as: "Is the national obligation just to dismantle racial classifications or to dismantle the more complex and difficult problem of racial subordination and inequality?"[1] The black community hoped that by desegregating schools and guaranteeing equality under the law, broader socioeconomic equality and opportunity would ensue.[2] But half a century after *Brown,* educational historian James D. Anderson argues, "The troubled legacy that has become *Brown*'s heritage... is the long-standing struggle to bridge the fundamental contradiction between legal or formal racial equality and the day-to-day institutionalized segregation and its underlying cultural norms."[3]

Also, as Anderson argues, "the continuing structure of educational inequality... remains virtually unmoved by the *Brown* decision."[4] Many also argue that *Plessy v. Fergusson*, which promised separate but equal funding, has yet to be realized in many contemporary de facto resegregated schools. For the segregated schools in Camden, as well as most schools throughout North Carolina, unequal funding was a fact of life. But the broader and arguably more harmful issue is the relationship between race and capitalism that continues to shape public education today.

Education, Race, and Economic Inequality

Capital, a core economic concept that is purportedly "color-blind," exerts profound race-specific consequences in education. Looking back at desegregation in Camden County, schools and education were inextricably intertwined with the social and economic realities of class, race, and the region's declining agricultural economy. The diminishing of racial inequalities and cultural difference—privatizing economic and social inequities and ignoring the influences of social barriers—was a common strategy used to diffuse issues of race, education, and inequality.

The continuing impact of the "culture of privatization" on race and education policy reflects broader American values, especially in communities and individuals favored by the historical power structure. As Katherine Newman observes,

> American culture plucks out of the many conceivable explanations for an individual's fate those that center on individual decisions that we control, at least in theory...We *could* focus on how history carved up the social landscape in ways that all but determined the fate of particular individuals. We tend not to however. Instead, the culture of individualism and self-determination that has been the country's hallmark almost since its inception locates blame and credit in the character and actions of individuals and for the most part subtracts the history that has shaped their options...Individuals are supposed to "get over" the road blocks, despite the fact that those obstacles may be inherently unfair or excessively debilitating even for very talented and driven people.[5]

As Newman points out, this American cultural belief is "not just a 'white' point of view" but also a powerful subtext of successful people in communities of color.[6]

Various stories of formal and informal education throughout this book highlight the ways the economics of capitalism are inherent in white pedagogy and dominant forms of schooling. White pedagogy reinforces race-based "systems of advantage and disadvantage." This remains one of the major critiques of Brown:

> *Brown* fell considerably short in the structural vision of equality and redistributive justice sought by African American litigants and many black parents. Instead, what triumphed through Brown's interpersonal logic of

eliminating separateness by placing black and white students in proximity to one another was attenuated formal equality that failed to address the inequitable distribution of resources and opportunities...Despite the transformative significance attached to it, the decision remained tethered to the profound social and cultural divisions it seemed to resolve.[7]

As the oral histories in this book reveal, profound divisions in memory, pedagogy, power, and community persist.

Pedagogy, often presented as color-blind,[8] is "a form of political and cultural production deeply implicated in the construction of knowledge, subjectivities, and social relations." School pedagogies continue to reify white themes and "subjects" and disguise fundamental cultural and social biases through the logic of meritocracy.[9] Yet whiteness is neither natural, nor normal; it is a set of relational processes that maintain privileges of power through politics and economic practice.[10] Whiteness also involves language and ideologies that benefit whites while systematically oppressing others.[11] White pedagogy dominates our schools and our memories, particularly concerning school desegregation.

The various stories in this book provide possibilities for rethinking pedagogy and accounting for persistent inequalities. When social problems are articulated though economic language, the social and cultural language of equality and freedom often falls silent in educational institutions.[12] Bridging social and cultural capital requires new terms of debate that address the persistent inequities of social and economic justice.

Education, Memory, and Integration

Public education policy touches so many parts of society—from culture to curriculum and social change. Some of the powerful shaping forces with which it must reckon include the economy, racism, and inequality. In the everyday experience of desegregation, education policy is entangled in these broader issues. Formal education and legal policy can be part of social change and greater racial equality. But narrow vision, monologic and monocultural thinking, and historical narratives that serve the interests of those in power will not achieve lasting social change.

This book explores the critical roads to integration (including the many hidden paths around residual segregation) through detailed oral histories of local players. National policies of school desegregation can be well-intentioned catalysts, but their success depends on their implementation in families and communities. The recognition of these oral histories and traditions are part of the underpinnings for lasting bridges between the races. Bridges built by white-dominated school boards and administrators with selective memories are fissured and contain elements of de facto segregation. As long as the stories remain segregated, superficial appearances of integration cannot suture the larger cultural divides or heal the wounds of racial inequality that persist in the nation.

Delpit points out the difficulties and the need for greater understanding:

> Two groups of people living side by side, smiling and greeting each other every morning and evening, yet, holding completely different views of the realities surrounding them—one group never conceiving of the other's sense of powerlessness and rage... When we teach across the boundaries of race, class, or gender—indeed when we teach at all—we must recognize and overcome the power differential, the stereotypes, and other barriers which prevent us from seeing each other... Until we can see the world as others see it, all the educational reforms in the world will come to naught.[13]

Understanding each other's memories requires a willingness to feel pain and move in solidarity toward the educational buttress of an equitable, democratic society.

Notes

Introduction

1. Jeffrey J. Crow, Paul D. Escott, and Flora J. Hatley, *A History of African Americans in North Carolina* (Raleigh: North Carolina Office of Archives and History, 2002): 152.
2. A number of court cases, as well as continued resistance to school desegregation, have resulted in increasing trends toward school resegregation (Irons, 2002). Irons contends, "Between 1988 to 1998, most of the progress toward integration of the previous two decades had disappeared" (p. 291). Various strategies to avoid full integration, including "white flight" into the suburbs, has led to resegregation of urban schools and continuing segregation of suburban schools.
3. Bland Simpson, *The Great Dismal: A Carolinian's Swamp Memoir* (Chapel Hill: University of North Carolina, 1990): 4.
4. Bland Simpson tells the story of the Great Dismal Swamp Canal and its development in great detail in his book *The Great Dismal*. The swamp, even before the development of the canal, held great significance for blacks in the area, some of whom escaped enslavement by using the Swamp as a path to freedom or as an area to live (Crow, Escott, and Hatley, *A History of African Americans in North Carolina,* 24). After the Revolutionary War, when British land became state property and all available land was claimed, swamp land, although uninhabitable, was quite fertile and could be used for agriculture. In 1763, George Washington along with eleven other investors created a company to drain and farm 1,100 acres of the Swamp (Simpson, *The Great Dismal,* 41–2). By 1812, a canal running through Camden County connected the port of Norfolk, Virginia, to Elizabeth City and the North Carolina Sound. The dirt removed to form the canal is the roadbed for today's Highway 17. This road, along with the swamp, contributed to the economic development of Camden as traveling and commerce became much easier.
5. In the two decades from the beginning of desegregation to 1980, Camden lost 10 percent of its black community, which continues to decrease.
6. Crow, Escott, and Hatley, *A History of African Americans in North Carolina*.

7. I use both the term desegregation and integration but by no means do I take them to be synonymous. Throughout the book, I will explore the symbolic and material differences between these two terms. For now, I mark the difference between the rhetoric of desegregation, an undoing of the separation of the races, and integration, "the bringing of together of different racial groups in free and equal association" (*Webster's New World Dictionary*, 1982). As an undoing, desegregation contains a greater potential for oppression than integration, a bringing together in free and equal association. I consider desegregation to be largely a topic of the two decades following *Brown* and integration as an ongoing project that is still far from complete.
8. Several studies serve as exemplars of local studies with broad implications. See, e.g., David Cecelski, *Along Freedom Road: Hyde County North Carolina and the Struggle for Black Freedom* (New York: Oxford Press, 1994); Carol Stack, *A Call to Home: African Americans Reclaim the Rural South* (New York: Basic Books, 1996); and Timothy Tyson, *Blood Done Sign My Name* (New York: Three Rivers Press, 2004).
9. For a discussion of the "long Civil Rights movement," see Jacquelyn Dowd Hall, "The Long Civil Rights Movement and the Political Uses of the Past." *Journal of American History* 91 (2005).
10. Jack Bass and Walter Devries, *The Transformation of Southern Politics: Social Change and Political Consequence since 1945* (New York: Basic Books, 1976).
11. For this book project, I analyze oral histories collected in Camden County from 2002 to 2004 as part of a Spencer Foundation research grant. In this study, I will consider in depth the memories of a select group of individuals who provide unique insights into school desegregation.
12. See Richard Bauman, *Story, Performance, Event: Contextual Studies of Oral Narrative* (New York: Cambridge University Press, 1986); Della Pollock, *Remembering: Performance and Oral History* (New York: Palgrave Macmillan, 2005); Samuel Schrager "What is Social in Oral History?" *International Journal of Oral History* 4 (1983); Hugo Slim and Paul Thompson, eds, *Listening for a Change: Oral Testimony and Development* (London: Panos Publications, 1995).
13. The goal of this project is not to theorize about citizenship. However, I should clarify that while other scholarship has explored citizenship as a *role* within democratic states that is contracted, this definition may be too limited for the purposes of this project as well as perhaps for the United States, which seems to be experiencing the collapse of the role of the democratic citizen (e.g., the decrease in the number of people voting).
14. Norman Denzin, *Performance Ethnography: Critical Pedagogy and the Politics of Culture* (Thousand Oaks, CA: Sage, 2003): xii.
15. See, e.g., Jonathan Kozol, *The Shame of the Nation: The Restoration of Apartheid Schooling in America* (New York: Crown Publishers, 2005).

16. Dr. Martin Luther King as quoted in James M. Washington, *A Testament of Hope: The Essential Writings and Speeches of Martin Luther King, Jr.* (New York: HarperCollins, 1991): 87.
17. This is the case not only of blacks and whites in the United States but also in a number of colonized nations. By World War II the connection between segregation and the oppression of people around the world had been widely recognized. For quotation, see Mark McPhail, in Rob Anderson, Leslie. A. Baxter, and Kenneth. N. Cissna (eds), *Dialogue: Theorizing Difference in Communication Studies* (Thousand Oaks, CA: Sage, 2004): 221.

Chapter 1

1. Over the last three decades, many have gone bankrupt or sold their land to developers. According to data from the *USA Counties 1998 CD-ROM*, in 1978 Camden had 138 family farms and by 1992 that number dropped to 69.
2. When young Hughes was pulled from school to work the farm, removing a child to work on the farm was not an uncommon practice in rural North Carolina. A number of white interviewees said that their education was stopped because of the demands of farm work.
3. North Carolina slang for "large."
4. For a discussion of deficit-storytelling, see Daniel G. Solorzano and Tara J. Yosso, "A Critical Race Counterstory of Race, Racism, and Affirmative Action," *Equity & Excellence in Education* 35 (2002): 155–68.
5. Jacquelyn Dowd Hall, "The Long Civil Rights Movement and the Political Uses of the Past," *Journal of American History* 91 (2005): 123–63.
6. James Leloudis, *Schooling the South: Pedagogy, Self, and Society in North Carolina* (Chapel Hill: University of North Carolina Press, 1996): 19–20.
7. Ibid., 19.
8. Ibid., 6.
9. At the time, North Carolina ran a triracial education system for American Indians, blacks, and whites.
10. Ibid., 13.
11. Ibid.
12. This section provides a cursory glance at the transition from common to graded school and the characteristics of both. Here, I highlight a few of the main threads that pertain most to this research. For an in-depth treatment of this topic, see ibid. For the quoted material, see ibid., 20.
13. Ibid., 21.
14. One reason North Carolina embraced the importance of citizenship was, as Superintendent Wiley noted, because the common school promoted a "united citizenry," bonded by their observance of common law. See ibid., 21.

During slavery, this mission played an important role in maintaining—within the white community—a discipline about race relations and the legitimacy of slavery. After abolition, the role of education and politics in maintaining a united citizenry and peaceful race relations continued to be a powerful force in North Carolina history.

15. Ibid., 20.
16. Robert I. Rotberg, "The Interdisciplinary Study of Political History," in *Politics and Political Change* (Cambridge, MA: MIT Press, 2001): 14.
17. David Douglas, *Reading, Writing, & Race: The Desegregation of the Charlotte Schools* (Chapel Hill: University of North Carolina Press, 1995): 9.
18. Statistics from the *Biennial Report of the Superintendent of Public Instruction of North Carolina 1922–1923 and 1923–1924*, Part I, 39. At the same time the cost of the average new white school was $22,297 while that of the new black school was $3,830. See Part III, 120. For a detailed discussion of black education in North Carolina from 1910 to 1960, see Sarah Thuesen, "Classes of Citizenship: The Culture and Politics of Black Public Education in North Carolina, 1910–1960," unpublished dissertation.
19. Theusen, "Classes of Citizenship," 112.
20. Robert D.W. Connor and Clarence Poe, *The Life and Speeches of Charles Brantley Aycock* (Garden City, NY: Doubleday, Page, & Co, 1912): 247–51.
21. One of the many ways the black community formed pockets of resistance and support was through social, fraternal, and service organizations such as the Masons, the Odd Fellows, the Eastern Star, and the Sons of Hamm [Jeffrey J. Crow, Paul D. Escott, and Flora J. Hatley, *A History of African Americans in North Carolina* (Raleigh: North Carolina Office of Archives and History, 2002): 97]. For the quoted material, see Leloudis, *Schooling in the New South*, 180.
22. The general assembly passed a state constitutional suffrage amendment in 1900 that created a poll tax and a literacy test for voters, effectively disenfranchising most black people. See Crow, Escott, and Hatley, *A History of African Americans in North Carolina*, 115–17; Douglas, *Reading, Writing, & Race*, 12.
23. Crow, Escott, and Hatley, *A History of African Americans in North Carolina*, 181.
24. See ibid., 156.
25. According to a black former Camden Elementary School teacher, seventy-one-year-old Eva Maryland Watson, eventually Camden ran five schools for blacks,

> There were five black schools in three parts of Camden County: Rosenwald School, grades 1–11 in South Mills; Sawyer's Creek School, grades 1–11 near the middle of Camden; Trotman Road School, grades 1–8 in between Belcross and Shiloh; Wickham School, grades 1–11 in Shiloh; and Ivy

Neck School. Black segregated schools were responsible for educating all [black] kids. In the early 1950s, 1951 or 1952, the black schools were consolidated to three: Rosenwald, Sawyer's Creek, and Wickham School.

According to Vivian Jones, who attended Ivy Neck School, between Shiloh and Camden/Belcross, "There were only two teachers in the school, two teachers taught the whole one through seventh grade. Then high school [Sawyer's Creek], eighth through twelfth, there was only three teachers in the school."

26. See James R. Grossman, *Land of Hope: Chicago, Black Southerners, and the Great Migration* (Chicago: University of Chicago Press, 1989); Leloudis, *Schooling the South*.
27. Crow, Escott, and Hatley, *A History of African Americans in North Carolina,* 125.
28. Leloudis, *Schooling in the New South*, 213.
29. As I will discuss later, this massive change in the education system was implemented and experienced differently in the white and black communities.
30. Ibid., 212.
31. Ibid., 225.
32. Ibid., 226.
33. See Crow, Escott, & Hatley, *A History of African Americans in North Carolina,* 138.
34. In a later interview, Hughes explained to me why big farming was so costly and risky:

> Fertilizer and gas bill about $10,000 year. $46,000 for a tractor. 18% interest. And it ain't many people got a hundred thousand dollars to go out there and buy stuff...And you go pay that interest and everything...you ain't got much left. But if I lose some off of the little bit I'm messing with now, it won't break me. But you got a hundred thousand dollars out there...and if you lose it...you...can't do it many years. You're too broke! That's what I went through. The labor bills and the upkeep of the equipment.

35. Henry A. Giroux, "Cultural Studies, Public Pedagogy, and the Responsibility of Intellectuals," *Communication and Critical/Cultural Studies* 1 (2004): 69.
36. Hughes' narrative refigures debates over home schooling. Historically some parents have expressed dissatisfaction with graded education, but more often as it is implicated in secularizing children (and not so much training them to be good capitalists). See Michael W. Apple, *Educating the "Right" Way: Markets, Standards, God, and Inequality* (New York: Routledge/Falmer, 2001). Alternately, arguments focus on home schooling as a way to resist the hegemony of standardized test scores and achievement. In contrast, Hughes emphasizes home schooling as a vital supplement to school knowledge.

His approach preempts contemporary dynamics of schools legislating and bemoaning the lack of minority involvement in children's education.
37. Barbara Shircliffe, "'We Got the Best of that World': A Case Study of Nostalgia in Oral History of School Segregation," *Oral History Review*, 2 (2001): 59–84.
38. This argument originates in Shircliff's work. Specifically, she argues for shifting away from oral historians interpreting nostalgic recollections as unreliable and instead embracing a meaning-centered understanding in the context of black education. Such nostalgia may occlude the injustices and inequalities of Jim Crow and forward potentially simplistic understandings of the value of "separate but equal" education in the context of the increasing resegregation of contemporary education. But nostalgic memories, although selective and often romanticized, work both to "illustrate the construction of a historical consciousness," and to critique the present. See Shircliff, "We Got the Best of that World," 84.
39. Hall, "The Long Civil Rights Movement," 26.
40. Giroux, "Cultural Studies, Public Pedagogy, and the Responsibility of Intellectuals," 68–9.
41. John T. Warren, "Doing Whiteness: On the Performative Dimensions of Race in the Classroom," *Communication Education* (2001): 91–108
42. Henry Giroux, *Border Crossing: Cultural Workers and the Politics of Education* (New York: Routledge, 1992): 2.
43. This way of thinking about whiteness comes from a talk given by Dr. Aimee Carrillo Rowe at the National Communication Association Annual Convention in Chicago, Illinois, November 2004. See also Ruth Frankenberg, *White Women, Race Matters: The Social Construction of Whiteness* (Minneapolis: University of Minnesota Press, 1993); Dreama Moon, "White Enculturation and Bourgeois Identity," in *Whiteness: The Communication of Social Identity*, ed. Thomas Nakayama and Judith Martin (Thousand Oakes, CA: Sage, 1999): 177–97; Thomas Nakayama and Robert L. Krizek, "Whiteness as Strategic Rhetoric," in *Whiteness*; Raka Shome, "Whiteness and the Politics of Location: Postcolonial Reflections,"' in *Whiteness*, 107–28; and Warren, "Doing Whiteness."
44. Dr. Julia Johnson made this argument at the National Communication Association Annual Convention in Chicago, Illinois, November 2004.
45. Solorzano and Yosso, "A Critical Race Counterstory."
46. Ibid., 28.
47. This claim is based on my reading of the performance of memory as somehow fundamentally resistant—even if its after effects are not guaranteed to be counterhegemonic. As a performance, a community then is responsible for making this alternative telling de facto disobedient or subversive.
48. See, e.g., Lisa Delpit, *Other People's Children: Cultural Conflict in the Classroom* (New York: W.W. Norton 1995); Ruben Donato, *The Other*

Struggle for Equal Schools: Mexican Americans during the Civil Rights Era (Albany, NY: State University of New York Press, 1997); Theresa McCarty, *A Place to be Navajo: Rough Rock and the Struggle for Self-Determination in Indigenous Schooling* (Mahwah, NJ: Lawrence Earlbaum Associates, 2002); Vanessa Siddle Walker, *Their Highest Potential: An African American School Community in the Segregated South* (Chapel Hill: University of North Carolina, 1996).

Chapter 2

1. Peter Irons, *Jim Crow's Children: The Broken Promise of the Brown Decision* (New York: Viking, 2002): 188. The intent of *Brown II* was to speed up implementation of *Brown I*, which had not provided a clear time frame for desegregation. The ambiguity of the phrase "all deliberate speed" left open too much room for interpretation in resistant communities and allowed them to continue their gradual approach that essentially maintained the status quo.
2. While integrated, the three blacks on the eighteen-member committee were all employees of the state.
3. David Douglas, *Reading, Writing, & Race: The Desegregation of the Charlotte Schools* (Chapel Hill: University of North Carolina Press, 1995): 25.
4. William Chafe, *Civilities and Civil Rights: Greensboro, North Carolina, and the Black Struggle for Freedom* (New York: Oxford University Press, 1981): 7.
5. Ibid.; and James Leloudis, *Schooling the South: Pedagogy, Self, and Society in North Carolina* (Chapel Hill: University of North Carolina Press, 1996).
6. See Douglas, *Reading, Writing, & Race*, 266.
7. While these legal forms of obstruction demonstrate a general unwillingness to desegregate North Carolina schools, it is worth noting that North Carolina was the only southern state not to take any of the following actions: abolishing constitutional amendments requiring public education, withholding money from schools that desegregated, and passing legislation to limit the work of the NAACP (ibid., 33). In addition, the Pearsall Plan satisfied militant segregationists while avoiding any of the actions mentioned earlier.
8. See Juan Williams, *Thurgood Marshall: American Revolutionary* (New York: Random House, 1998): 31.
9. Ibid.
10. See Douglas, *Reading, Writing, & Race,* 26.
11. See Jeffrey J. Crow, Paul D. Escott, and Flora J. Hatley, *A History of African Americans in North Carolina* (Raleigh: North Carolina Office of Archives and History, 2002): 172.
12. See Sherick Hughes, *Pedagogy of Struggle and Hope: Black Families Responding to Desegregation,* doctoral dissertation (University of North Carolina, 2004): 222.

13. Ibid.
14. Because of the undergrowth and the swamp, people traveled mostly by waterway.
15. "Kindly" is a word used in North Carolina colloquial conversation and here means "pretty."
16. While the black Buffalo soldiers that fought in the Indian Wars are better known, the over fourteen hundred men from Northeast North Carolina that fought for the Union were also called Buffalo soldiers. These white southerners joined the Union in order to oppose the wealthy landowners and their black slaves and advance the economic position of poor southern whites. During the Civil War, approximately ten thousand white North Carolinians and five thousand black North Carolinians served Union regiments.
17. As discussed in the introduction, storytelling, while not the same as first-hand oral history, can gain a social truth and influence people's thoughts, feelings, and action, as does historical fact.
18. Patrick Chamoiseau, *Texaco* (New York: Vintage International, 1997): 43.
19. Later I discussed this with Mr. Leary when he read this chapter and he said his point was that the white community had enough wealthy white families that they were able to purchase these amenities for the white school and the blacks did not have enough wealthy families to do the same.
20. See Ruth Frankenberg, *White Women, Race Matters: The Social Construction of Whiteness* (Minneapolis: University of Minnesota Press, 1993): 228–9.
21. Pamela Grundy, *Learning to Win: Sports, Education, and Social Change in Twentieth-Century North Carolina* (Chapel Hill: The University of North Carolina Press, 2001): 262.
22. Ibid.
23. See ibid., 5.
24. J.E. Thomas, "Innocence and After: Radicalism in the 1970s," in *Radical agendas? The politics of adult education*, ed. S. Westwood and J. E. Thomas (Leicester, UK: NIACE, 1991): 11.
25. Peter Mayo, "A Rationale for a Transformative Approach to Education," *Journal of Transformative Education* 1.1 (2003): 38–57.

Chapter 3

The first epigraph has been taken from Lisa Delpit, *Other People's Children: Cultural Conflict in the Classroom* (New York: The New Press, 1995): 11; and the second from George W. Noblit and Thomas W. Collins, "Patience and Prudence in a Southern High School: Managing the Political Economy of Desegregated Education," in *Particularities: Collected Essays on Ethnography and Education,* ed. G.W. Noblit (New York: Peter Lang, 1999): 157–8.

1. Some scholars have criticized the use of capital in these two sociological concepts for good reason; the use of capital normalizes capitalism and its attendant values—competition, individualism, and wealth; these terms serve to legitimize the role of economic capital in social and political relationships; using economic discourse to explain political participation undermines democratic action; and such terms serve to privatize public communication. See, e.g., Stephen Samuel Smith and Jessica Kulynych, "It May be Social, But Why is it Capital? The Social Construction of Social Capital and the Politics of Language," *Politics Society* 30 (2002): 149. While I agree with these critiques, I argue that the term capital—economic, social, and cultural—has a heuristic value in analyzing and explaining dynamics of race, education, and equity, which are increasingly shaped by capitalist forces. While capitalist assumptions may lead to less than optimal metaphors and ways of thinking about education, they have dominated the educational landscape for decades and need to be examined.
2. Erin McNamara Horvat, Elliot B. Weininger, and Annette Lareau, "From Social Ties to Social Capital: Class Differences in the Relations Between Schools and Parent Networks," *American Educational Research Journal* 40 (2003): 323.
3. V.P. Franklin, "Introduction," in *Cultural Capital and Black Education: African American Communities and the Funding of Black Schooling, 1865 to the Present*, ed. V.P. Franklin and Carter Julian Savage (Greenwich, CT: Information Age Publishing, 2002): xi–xx, 177.
4. Bordieu argues that to understand the social world, capital must be examined, "in all of its forms and not solely in the form recognized by economic theory." He presents economic, cultural, and social capital as interconnected. While Bordieu attends to how other forms of capital may be converted into economic currency, this chapter focuses on the broad social value of these relationships and networks embodied in individuals in communities.
5. See, e.g., Jonathan Kozol, *The Shame of the Nation: The Restoration of Apartheid Schooling in America* (New York: Crown Publishers, 2005).
6. Katherine S. Newman, *A Different Shade of Gray: Midlife and Beyond in the Inner City* (New York: The New Press, 2003): 44.
7. Ibid.
8. Lauren King, "Farmer Cultivated Crops—and Friends," *The Virginian-Pilot*, July 30, 2006.
9. Ibid.
10. Jeffrey S. Hampton, "Camden Grower Cultivates Farmers Market Customers," *The Virginian-Pilot*, December 1, 2003.
11. Lauren King, "Farmers Market Set To Open Despite Absence of Beloved Produce Vendor," *The Virginian-Pilot*, April 6, 2007.
12. Paul C. Gorski, "Good Intentions Are Not Enough: A Decolonizing Intercultural Education." (September 13, 2007). http://www.edchange.org/publications/intercultural-education.pdf.: 5.

13. Prudence L. Carter, *Keeping it Real: School Success Beyond Black and White* (New York: Oxford Press, 2005): 10.
14. Ibid.
15. Robert D. Putnam, *Bowling Alone: The Collapse and Revival of American Community* (New York: Simon & Schuster: 2000). Although inspired by Putnam, the form of bridging social capital I propose differs in the way the metaphor of the bridge is invoked.
16. Barbara Arneil, *Diverse Communities: The Problem with Social Capital* (New York: Cambridge University Press: 2006): 181.
17. Carter, *Keeping it Real*, 15.
18. Tara J. Yosso, "Whose Culture Has Capital?: A Critical Race Theory Discussion of Community Cultural Wealth," *Race Ethnicity and Education* 8 (2005): 75.
19. Delpit, *Other People's Children*, 28.
20. Franklin, "Introduction," xiv.
21. Carter Julian Savage, "Our School in Our Community: The Collective Economic Struggle for African American in Franklin, Tennessee, 1890–1967," in *Cultural Capital and Black Education*, ed. Franklin and Savage, 50.
22. Ibid., 52.
23. Ibid., 66.
24. Ibid., 72.
25. Jean Ann Madsen and Etta R. Hollins, "African American Teachers' Roles in School Desegregation: At the Dawn of a New Millennium," *Urban Education* 35 (2000): 6. See also W.H. Watkins, "Can Institutions Care? Evidence from Segregated Schooling of African American Children," in *Beyond Desegregation: The Politics of Quality in African American Schooling*, ed. M.J. Shujaa (Thousand Oaks, CA: Corwin Press, 1996): 5–27.
26. Carter, *Keeping it Real*, 51–2.
27. Yosso, "Whose Culture Has Capital?" 77.
28. Ibid., 89.
29. Ibid.
30. The idea of 'ancestral wisdom' as a valuable aspect of cultural capital comes from Sarah Lawrence-Lightfoot, *I've Known Rivers: Lives of Loss and Liberation* (New York: Penguin Books, 1994).
31. Shernaz B. García and Patricia L. Guerra, "Deconstructing Deficit Thinking: Working with Educators to Create More Equitable Learning Environments," *Education and Urban Society* 36 (2004): 150–68. See also Etta R. Hollins, *Culture in School Learning: Revealing the Deep Meaning* (Mahwah, NJ: Erlbaum, 1996).
32. Delpit, *Other People's Children*, 23.
33. Ibid., 17.
34. Ibid., 25.
35. Ibid.

36. Ibid.
37. Carter, *Keeping it Real*, 47.
38. Wendell Berry, "The Work of Local Culture," *What Are People For?* (San Francisco: North Point Press, 1990): 154.
39. This book itself is a performance that brings together the stories of Hughes and Leary for an integrated audience.
40. Della Pollock, "Telling the Told, Performing like a Family," *The Oral History Review* 18 (1990): 69.
41. Ibid.
42. Berry, "The Work of Local Culture," 166.
43. See, e.g., Delpit, *Other People's Children*; Ruben Donato, *The Other Struggle for Equal Schools: Mexican Americans during the Civil Rights Era* (Albany, NY: State University of New York Press, 1997); Theresa McCarty, *A Place to be Navajo: Rough Rock and the Struggle for Self-Determination in Indigenous Schooling* (Mahwah, NJ: Lawrence Earlbaum Associates, 2002); Vanessa Siddle Walker, *Their Highest Potential: An African American School Community in the Segregated South* (Chapel Hill: University of North Carolina 1996).

Chapter 4

1. In many of this book's narratives, Witherspoon appears as someone that substantially influenced the lives and memories of people, supporting Gergen's insight about social ghosts that "In all our present relationships, we carry the essences of the past." Mary Gergen, *Feminist Reconstructions in Psychology: Narrative, Gender, and Performance* (Thousand Oaks, CA: Sage, 2001): 12.
2. Jeff Hampton, "He Lives to Help Others with all his Might: Retired Educator has Devoted a Life to Public Service," *The Virginian-Pilot*, March 11, 1996.
3. Funeral program.
4. Mr. Spence and Mr. Vaughn, two good friends of Witherspoon, were the major sources for this chapter. I interviewed them each alone and once together. Their interviews were particularly important in that they provided an intimate look at a public figure. While many people knew Mr. Witherspoon and recalled their experiences of his exceptional oratory or outstanding penmanship, few knew his personal side as Spence and Vaughn did—as close friends, fraternity brothers, and colleagues.
5. Diana Crane, *Fashion and its Social Agendas: Class, Gender, and Identity in Clothing* (Chicago: University of Chicago Press, 2000): 191. See also Vetta L. Sanders Thompson, "The Complexity of African American Racial Identification," *The Journal of Black Studies* (November 2001): 155–65.
6. Funeral program.

7. Hampton, "He Lives to Help Others."
8. The exchange occurred in a joint conversation with Mr. Vaughn and Mr. Spence.
9. Hampton, "He Lives to Help Others."
10. Ibid.
11. http://www.jcsu.edu/friends/about.htm.
12. Hampton, "He Lives to Help Others."
13. Ibid.
14. Boss Hoggs was a fictional character on the television show the Dukes of Hazard. He was the wealthy white southern local county commissioner that ran the town, using his authority as he pleased and exerting influence throughout the entire community. Coach Vaughn transposes this concept into the black cultural context, showing how educational leaders in the black community were de facto leaders with significant influence and social status. As Vaughn uses the term, it possesses different shades of meaning, revealing how such power can be used for good or abused.
15. Leary is making the point that at Marian Anderson there were three couples in which both spouses was a teacher at the school. If these teachers were to lose their job, then that family unit would lose its entire income. As a result the principal exerted extra influence on their family welfare.
16. Out-of-state tuition grant programs covered tuition but not travel or living expenses. See Michael J. Klarman, *From Jim Crow to Civil Rights: The Supreme Court and the Struggle for Racial Equality* (New York: Oxford University Press, 2006): 149.
17. Founded in 1910, North Carolina Central University in Durham, North Carolina, was a historically black university. The 1939 North Carolina General Assembly authorized the university to offer graduate courses in Arts and Sciences, then a School of Law (1940) and a School of Library Science (1941). Hampton University is a historically black university in Hampton, Virginia. Hampton began offering master's programs in 1928.
18. As documented by Delpit, Cecelski, and others, black teachers and families went to great efforts to provide their children with a high quality education, emphasizing education as a path toward emancipation. However, the material inequalities limited the abilities of black schools to compete with the substantially better funded white schools. Despite the many strengths of segregated black school, especially exemplary schools such as Marian Anderson, the significant extra effort required on behalf of the black community because of this systemic inequality cannot be underestimated.
19. Ibid.
20. Sherick Hughes, "Theorizing Oppressed Family Pedagogy: Critical Lessons from a Rural Black Family in the Post-Brown South," *Educational Foundations* (Jersey City, NJ: New Jersey City University, American Education Studies Association, 2005): 65.

21. "Thank You Mr. Witherspoon," *Camden County Free Press*, February 6–12, 2003: 1.
22. Lauren King, "Elizabeth City retailer, activist Cader Perry Harris Jr. dies," *The Virginian-Pilot*, January 1, 2008.
23. Hampton, "He Lives to Help Others."
24. Ibid.
25. Pasquotank County Board of Commissioners Minutes, February 2, 2004: 2.
26. Ibid., 3.
27. Ibid.

Chapter 5

1. De facto segregation, "segregation that resulted from nongovernmental factors such as housing patterns," was not addressed directly through *Brown* [Joseph Crespino, "The Best Defense Is a Good Offense: The Stennis Amendment and the Fracturing of Liberal School Desegregation Policy, 1964–1972," *The Journal of Policy History* 18 (2006): 310]. Efforts to redress de facto segregation would need to correct "racial imbalances" (a term that arose during discussions of the Civil Rights Act) more broadly (ibid., 305). But the Nixon administration opted to enforce compliance with the law and highlighted its politically palatable commitment to public education [Gareth Davies, "Richard Nixon and the Desegregation of Southern Schools," *The Journal of Policy History* 19 (2007)]. Many politicians stayed away from the politically unpopular choice of addressing pernicious racial imbalances.
2. The phrase "progressive mystique" comes from historian William Chafe [*Civilities and Civil Rights: Greensboro, North Carolina, and the Black Struggle for Freedom* (New York: Oxford University Press, 1981): 7]. A few counties moved promptly toward integration, e.g., such urban areas as Charlotte, Greensboro, and Winston-Salem. In addition, not all blacks welcomed integration [David S. Cecelski, *Along Freedom Road: Hyde County, North Carolina, and the Black Struggle for Freedom.* (New York: Oxford Press, 1994)]. For details on pupil placement laws, the Pearshall Plan, and the Freedom of Choice policy, see Chafe, *Civilities and Civil Rights*; Jeffrey J. Crow, Paul D. Escott, and Flora J. Hatley, *A History of African Americans in North Carolina* (Raleigh: North Carolina Office of Archives and History, 2002); David Douglas, *Reading, Writing, & Race: The Desegregation of the Charlotte Schools* (Chapel Hill: University of North Carolina Press, 1995); and George W. Noblit, "North Carolina School Desegregation: The Intersection between Law, Tradition, and Transition," paper presented at the 2002 annual meeting of the American Education Research Association in Pittsburgh, PA.

3. See Chafe, *Civilities and Civil Rights*; James Leloudis, *Schooling the South: Pedagogy, Self, and Society in North Carolina* (Chapel Hill: University of North Carolina Press, 1996).
4. See Douglas, *Reading, Writing, & Race*, 26.
5. Ibid., 25.
6. Because of various, competing political interests, Presidents Johnson and Nixon as well as numerous politicians were troubled by HEW, not the Justice Department, enforcing desegregation. At the same time, the Justice Department had failed to desegregate the majority of schools a decade after *Brown*.
7. Davies, "Richard Nixon and the Desegregation of Southern Schools," 370.
8. Because of the political consequences of a federal government withholding funds for education, federal funds were only withheld from entirely noncompliant districts on rare occasions (ibid., 370). However, by 1966 HEW had cut off aid to forty-six segregated southern districts, showing the dire consequences of noncompliance (Dean Kotlowski, "With All Deliberate Delay: Kennedy, Johnson, and School Desegregation," *The Journal of Policy History* 17 (2005): 170). See also HEW news release, May 14, 1966, Folder: Civil Rights Enforcement 1966, Box 194, Office Files of the Commissioner of Education, RG 12, NA; "6 Areas in South Lose School Aid," *New York Times*, December 6, 1966, 24.
9. Kotlowski, "With All Deliberate Delay," 170.
10. Crespino, "The Best Defense," 310.
11. T.W. Burton and R. Moody, *Reply to Dr. Charles Carroll, Superintendent of Public Instruction concerning North Carolina School Desegregation*. Raleigh, NC: North Carolina State Archives, Gov. Dan Moor MSS, Box 26, Government, Federal—U.S. Commission on Civil Rights, 1965.
12. Crespino, "The Best Defense," 174. See also HEW news release, March 7, 1966, Folder: Civil Rights Act-Guidelines-Press Releases Only, Box 196, Office Files of the Commissioner of Education, RG 12, NA.
13. As a result of *Greene*, 159 southern school districts were required to abandon freedom of choice plans and pursue a more effective means of integration (Kotlowski, "With All Deliberate Delay," 178). In the Supreme Court case *Alexander v. Holmes*, the Justice Department argued unsuccessfully for a twelve-month delay in the implementation of *Greene*: The Supreme Court declared, "continued operation of segregated schools under a standard of allowing 'all deliberate speed' for desegregation is no longer constitutionally permissible. Under explicit holdings of this Court the obligation of every school district is to terminate dual school systems at once and to operate now and hereafter only unitary schools" (Davies, "Richard Nixon and the Desegregation of Southern Schools," 372–3). The Department of Justice had no alternative but to enforce the law immediately.
14. Crespino, "The Best Defense," 177. See also HEW Memorandum, "Policies on Elementary and Secondary School Compliance...," February 1968, Folder: School Guidelines March 1968, Box 75, Clark Papers, LBJL.

15. Davies, "Richard Nixon and the Desegregation of Southern Schools," 368.
16. See, e.g., George Lewis, *Massive Resistance: The White Response to the Civil Rights Movement* (New York: Hodder Arnold, 2006).
17. Northampton County was also one of the poorest counties in the state of North Carolina and in the nation in the 1960s. See Mollie Allick, "The Poor versus the Powerful: A Shared Concern A Rural and Urban Communities," in Working Paper Series (Durham, NC: Terry Sanford Institute of Public Policy, Duke University, 2002): 1–26.
18. Robert R. Korstad and James Leloudis, "The North Carolina Volunteers and the War on Poverty," *Law and Contemporary Problems*, 62 (Durham, NC, 1999): 177–97.
19. Ibid., 177.
20. Ibid., 196.
21. Ibid., 188.
22. Robert Kelly-Goss, "In 1963, at the height of the Civil Rights Movement, Elizabeth City was site of protests and sit-ins," *The Daily Advance*, February 30, 2008.
23. Cecelski, *Along Freedom Road*, 38.
24. Korstad and Leloudis, "The North Carolina Volunteers," 197.
25. No one that I spoke with in the black community recalled being consulted about Witherspoon's replacement. I could not confirm a source for the superintendent's claim.
26. Although this was technically during the time of desegregation under the freedom of choice program, the school had no white students and only a few white teachers.
27. This is a multi-tailed whip used for punishment, including, historically, in the British Royal Navy.
28. Kenneth Plummer, *Intimate Citizenship: Private Decisions and Public Dialogues* (Seattle: University of Washington, 2003): 47.
29. Roy Rosenzweig and David Thelen, *The Presence of the Past: Popular Uses of History in American Life* (New York: Columbia University Press, 1998): 6.

Chapter 6

The epigraph has been taken from Vanessa Siddle Walker, *Their Highest Potential: An African American School Community in the Segregated South* (Chapel Hill: University of North Carolina, 1996): 212.

1. Loren Miller, *The Petitioners: The Story of the Supreme Court of the United States and the Negro* (New York: Pantheon Books, 1966).
2. Charles V. Willie and Sarah S. Willie, "Black, White, and Brown: The Transformation of Public Education in America," *Teachers College Record* 107 (2005): 481.

3. Ibid., 479.
4. Witherspoon had left Camden but he still served as an advisor to the black community and supported integration in principle.
5. Derrick P. Alridge, "Conceptualizing A Du Boisian Philosophy of Education: Toward A Model for African-American Education," *Educational Theory* 49 (1999): 363.
6. Jerome E. Morris, "Research, Ideology, and the Brown Decision: Counter-narratives to the Historical and Contemporary Representation of Black Schooling," *Teachers College Record Volume* 110 (2008): 719.
7. Ibid., 719.
8. Alridge, "Conceptualizing A Du Boisian Philosophy," 369.
9. Ibid., 372.
10. Linda Moore, "Toward Politics of Body and Conscience," in *Body Movements: Pedagogy, Politics, and Social Change,* ed. S. Shapiro and S. Shapiro (Cresskill, NJ: Hampton Press Inc, 2002): 255–6.
11. Luce Irigaray, "Interview," in *Women Analyze Women in France, England, and the United States,* ed. E.H. Baruch and L. Serrano (New York: New York University Press: 1988): 159.
12. Ibid., 159.
13. Gloria Ladson-Billings, "Landing on the Wrong Note: The Price We Paid for Brown," *Educational Researcher* 33 (2004): 5.
14. Robert Crain, *The Politics of School Desegregation* (Garden City, NJ: Doubleday, 1969): 6.
15. Karen Lebacqz, *Six Theories of Justice* (Minneapolis: Augsburg Publishing House, 1986): 86.
16. Moore, "Toward Politics of Body and Conscience," 10.
17. August B. Hollingshead, *Elm Town's Youth* (New York: John Wiley and Sons, 1949): 125.
18. Ibid.
19. Donna M. Davis, "Merry-Go-Round: A Return to Segregation and the Implications for Creating Democratic Schools," *Urban Education* 39 (2004): 398.
20. Tara J. Yosso, Laurence Parker, Daniel G. Solórzano, and Marvin Lynn, "Critical Race Discussion of Racialized Rationales and Access to Higher: From Jim Crow to Affirmative Action and Back Again," *Review of Research in Education* 28 (2004): 9–10.
21. Vann Dempsey and George Noblit, "Cultural Ignorance and School Desegregation," in *Beyond Desegregation: The Politics of Quality in African American Schooling,* ed. Mwalimu J. Shujaa (Thousand Oaks, CA: Corwin): 119–37.
22. See J.D. Anderson, *The Education of Blacks in the South, 1860–1935* (Chapel Hill: University of North Carolina Press, 1988); Dempsey and Noblit, "Cultural Ignorance and School Desegregation," 115–37; Russell Irvine

and Jackie Irvine, "Impact of the Desegregation Process on the Education of Black Students: Key Variables," *Journal of Negro Education* 52 (1983): 410–22; Siddle Walker, *Their Highest Potential*.
23. Anderson, *The Education of Blacks*.
24. Michelle Foster, *Black Teachers on Teaching* (New York: New Press, 1997); Ladson-Billings, "Landing on the Wrong Note," 3–13; Jennifer J. Beaumont, "Implementation of Court-Ordered Desegregation by District-Level Administrators," in *Beyond Desegregation,* ed. Shujaa, 75–90.
25. Jerome E. Morris, "American Schooling and Community in the Urban South and Midwest Can Anything Good Come From Nazareth? Race, Class, and African American Schooling and Community in the Urban South and Midwest," *American Education Research Journal* 41 (2004): 101.
26. In Camden, black teachers were not fired. They were replaced, upon their departure, with white teachers.
27. Jerome E. Morris, "A Pillar of Strength An African American School's Communal Bonds With Families and Community Since *Brown*," *Urban Education* 33 (1999): 585.
28. Ibid., 588.
29. Ibid.
30. Ibid.
31. Ladson-Billings, "Landing on the Wrong Note," 7.
32. See, e.g., Morris, "A Pillar of Strength"; Siddle Walker, *Their Highest Potential*; Sherick A. Hughes, *Black Hands in the Biscuits, Not in the Classrooms: Unveiling Hope in a Struggle for Brown's Promise* (New York: Peter Lang, 2006); and Ruben Donato, *The Other Struggle for Equal Schools: Mexican Americans during the Civil Rights Era* (Albany, NY: State University of New York Press, 1997).
33. Morris, "Research, Ideology, and the Brown Decision," 727.

Chapter 7

1. bell hooks, "Homeplace (a site of resistance)," in *Woman That I Am: The Literature and Culture of Contemporary Women of Color,* ed. Madison, D. Soyini (New York: St. Martin's Press, 1994): 451.
2. Raka Shome, "Space Matters: The Politics and Practice of Space," *Communication Theory* 13 (2003): 43.
3. Notable exception is Vanessa Siddle Walker's *Their Highest Potential: An African American School Community in the Segregated South* (Chapel Hill: University of North Carolina, 1996); and David Cecelski's *Along Freedom Road: Hyde County, North Carolina, and the Black Struggle for Freedom* (New York: Oxford Press, 1994).

4. This was the name of Marian Anderson School before Witherspoon renamed the school.
5. Siddle Walker, *Their Highest Potential*, 5. For discussion of black teachers, see Michelle Foster, *Black Teachers on Teaching* (New York: The New Press, 1997).
6. See the *Durham Morning Herald*, April 17, 1951, "State School Program Narrowing Gap between White and Negro Facilities."
7. Siddle Walker, *Their Highest Potential*, 1–3.
8. Russell Irvine and Jackie Irvine, "Impact of the Desegregation Process on the Education of Black Students: Key Variables," *Journal of Negro Education* 52, no. 4 (1983): 410–22, p. 416.
9. For discussions of deficit discourse and race, see Daniel G. Solorzano and Tara J. Yosso, "Critical Race Methodology: Counter-Storytelling as a Framework for Education Research," *Qualitative Inquiry* 8, issue 1 (2002): 23–44; Kate Willink, "Economy & Pedagogy: Laboring to Learn in Camden County, North Carolina," *Communication and Critical/Cultural Studies* 5, no. 1 (March 2008): 64–86; and Paul C. Gorski, "Good Intentions Are Not Enough: A Decolonizing Intercultural Education" (September 13, 2007). http://www.edchange.org/publications/intercultural-education.pdf. For discussions of deficit discourse more broadly, see Nana Osei-Kofi, "Pathologizing the Poor: A Framework for Understanding Ruby Payne's Work," *Equity & Excellence in Education* 38 (2005): 367–75; James Collins, "Language and Class in Minority Education," *Anthropology & Education Quarterly* 19 (1988): 299–326; Mark R. Rank, *One Nation, Underprivileged: Why American Poverty Affects Us All* (New York, NY: Oxford University Press, 2004); Carolyn Shields, Bishop Russell, and Andre E. Mazawi, *Pathologizing Practices: The Impact of Deficit Thinking on Education* (New York: Peter Lang, 2005); Steve Tozer, "Class," in *Knowledge and Power in the Global Economy: Politics and the Rhetoric of School Reform,* ed. David Gabbart (Mahwah, NJ: Lawrence Erlbaum Associates, 2004): 149–59.
10. In his discussion of *Brown*, Kluger addresses black community resistance to desegregation as does David Cecelski in his book *Along Freedom Road* about the African American community in Hyde County, North Carolina. As Siddle Walker concludes, "This small body of material suggests that schooling for African American children during the era of legal segregation may have been more highly valued by some of its constituents than has been generally considered" (*Their Highest Potential*, 4).
11. One of the ongoing patterns of integration nationally, and locally according to some in the black community, is tracking of children. This tracking includes filling almost all the honors classes with whites and all special educations classes with blacks. But this example brings to light subtle ways in which black students might be excluded from certain educational opportunities that would be important for white collar career advancement. Speaking with black parents, some felt as if important decisions were made before they

had an opportunity to provide input, such as the schedule of Jones' daughter or important decisions at the integrated PTA.
12. Lisa Delpit, *Other People's Children: Cultural Conflict in the Classroom* (New York: W.W. Norton, 1995): 24.
13. Carter Julian Savage, "Our School in Our Community: The Collective Economic Struggle for African American in Franklin, Tennessee, 1890–1967," in *Cultural Capital and Black Education: African American Communities and the Funding of Black Schooling, 1865 to the Present,* ed. V.P. Franklin and Carter Julian Savage (Greenwich, CT: Information Age Publishing, 2002): 72.
14. Nathan Wright Jr., *What Black Educators Are Saying* (New York: Hawthorne Books, 1970): v.
15. Siddle Walker, *Their Highest Potential*, 3–4.
16. James C. Scott, *Domination and the Arts of Resistance: Hidden Transcripts* (New Haven, CT: Yale University Press, 1990): 7.
17. bell hooks, "Eating the Other: Desire and Resistance," in *Media and Cultural Studies: Keyworks,* ed. Meenakshi Gigi Durham and Douglas M. Kellner (New York: Blackwell Publishing, 2006): 249.
18. Mab Segrest, *Born to Belonging: Writings on Spirit and Justice* (New Brunswick NJ: Rutgers University Press, 2002): 169.
19. Ibid., 171.
20. Howard Winant, "Racial Dualism at Century's End," in *The House that Race Built,* ed. Wahneema Lubiano (New York: Vintage Press, 1998): 108.
21. For a discussion of this phenomemon, see Sofia Villenas, "Latina Mothers and Small-Town Racisms: Creating Narratives of Dignity and Moral Education in North Carolina," *Anthropology & Education Quarterly* 32 (2001): 3–28; and Gorski, "Good Intentions Are Not Enough."
22. Michael Fultz, "Overcoming Historical Amnesia: The Displacement of Black Educators Post-Brown," *History of Education Quarterly* 44 (2004): 11–45.

Chapter 8

1. Gloria Ladson-Billings, "Landing on the Wrong Note: The Price We Paid for Brown." *Educational Researcher* 33 (2004): 7. As Ladson-Billings notes, in 1971 half a million white southern children attended segregated private academies.
2. Sean Spano, *Public Dialogue and Participatory Democracy: Cupertino Community Project* (Cresskill, NJ: Hampton Press, 2001): 25.
3. Michael Apple and James Beane, eds., *Democratic Schools* (Alexandria, VA: ASCD, 1995).
4. Donna M. Davis, "Merry-Go-Round: A Return to Segregation and the Implications for Creating Democratic Schools," *Urban Education* 39 (2004): 394–401.

5. Gloria Ladson-Billings, "From the Achievement Gap to the Education Debt: Understanding Achievement in U.S. Schools" *Educational Researcher* 35 (2006): 7.
6. Ladson-Billings, "Landing on the Wrong Note," 6.

Chapter 9

The first epigraph has been taken from Wendell Berry, "The Work of Local Culture." *What Are People For?* (San Francisco: North Point Press, 1990): 153–69; and the second from Paul Ricoeur, "Memory and forgetting," in *Questioning Ethics: Contemporary Debates in Philosophy,* ed. R.K. Earney and M.D. Ooley (New York: Routledge): 5–11.

1. To be clear, I am not arguing that we should not commemorate *Brown*, discounting the effort to arrive at the decision, or underestimating its substantial impact on the United States. I am arguing for a more inclusive, introspective, and ongoing interrogation into the memory of desegregation as it continues to impact present and future policies and lives.
2. Jay Winter, *Remembering War: The Great War and Historical Memory in the Twentieth Century* (New Haven, CT: Yale University Press, 2006): 5–6.
3. Jamaica Kincaid, *My Brother* (New York: Farrar, Straus, & Giroux, 1997).
4. Jeffrey K. Olick, and Joyce Robbins, "Social Memory Studies: From 'Collective Memory' to the Historical Sociology of Mnemonic Practices," *Annual Review of Sociology* 24 (1998): 126.
5. Ibid.
6. J. Robert Cox, "Cultural Memory and Public Moral Argument." Presented as the Van Zelst Lecture. Northwestern University, Evanston, 1987.
7. J. Robert Cox, "Argument and Usable Traditions," in *Argumentation: Across the Lines of Discipline,* ed. F.H. van Eerermen et al. (Providence, RI: Foris Publications, 1987): 93–99.
8. Patrick Chamoiseau, *Texaco* (New York: Vintage International, 1997): 43.
9. Selma Leydesdorff, Luisa Passerini, and Paul Thompson, *Gender and Memory* (Oxford: Oxford University Press, 1996).
10. Sigmund Freud, *Psychological Writings and Letters* (Sendra Gilman, ed.) (New York: Continuum, 1995): 123
11. Ibid., 126.
12. Henri Bergson, *Laughter: An Essay on the Meaning of the Comic* (C. Brereton & F. Rothwell, trans.) (Los Angeles: Green Integer, 1911): 12.
13. Ibid., 11.
14. David Lowenthal, *The Past is a Foreign Country* (Cambridge, UK: Cambridge University Press, 1985): xvii.
15. Ibid., xxiv.

16. I did view a charming video of Witherspoon that captured his poetic delivery, his prodigious memory, and his touch of wit.
17. Winter, *Remembering War,* 5.
18. Robert N. Bellah, et al., *Habits of the Heart: Individualism and Commitment in American Life* (Los Angeles: University of California Press, 1985): 153.
19. Jeffrey K. Olick and Joyce Robbins, "Social Memory Studies: From 'Collective Memory' to the Historical Sociology of Mnemonic Practices," *Annual Review of Sociology* 24 (1998): 124.
20. Michel Foucault, *Language, Counter-Memory, Practice: Selected Essays and Interviews* (Ithaca, NY: Cornell University Press, 1977): 126.
21. Roy Rosenzweig and David Thelen, *The Presence of the Past: Popular Uses of History in American Life* (New York: Columbia University Press, 1998): 127.
22. Olick and Robbins, "Social Memory Studies."
23. Ibid.
24. Michalinos Zembylas and Zvi Bekerman, "Education and the Dangerous Memories of Historical Trauma: Narratives of Pain, Narratives of Hope," *Curriculum Inquiry* 38 (2008): 125–54, 144.
25. Ibid., 131.
26. Ibid., 132.
27. Ibid., 139.
28. For brief discussion of enmity, see ibid., 140.
29. Ibid., 130.
30. Ibid., 125.
31. Ibid., 130.
32. Ibid., 126.
33. Ibid., 132.
34. Steven T. Ostovich, "Epilogue: Dangerous memories," in *The Work of Memory: New Directions in the Study of German Society and Culture,* ed. A. Confino and P. Fritzsche (Urbana and Chicago: University of Illinois Press, 2002): 239.
35. Zembylas and Bekerman, "Education and the Dangerous Memories," 130.
36. Ibid.
37. Ibid.
38. Ibid., 129.
39. Martha C. Nussbaum, *Upheavals of Thought: The Intelligence of Emotions* (New York: Cambridge University Press, 2002): 2.
40. Ibid.; Thomas King, *The Truth about Stories: A Native Narrative* (Toronto, ON: House of Anansi Press, 2003); Trinh T. Minh-ha, "Grandma's Story," in *The Woman that I Am: The Literature and Culture of Contemporary Women of Color,* ed. D.S. Madison (New York: St. Martin's Griffin, 1994): 462–84.
41. D. Soyini Madison, "'That Was My Occupation': Oral Narrative, Performance, and Black Feminist Thought," in *Exceptional Spaces,* ed. D. Pollock (Chapel Hill: University of North Carolina Press, 1998): 319–42.
42. King, *The Truth about Stories*; Minh-ha, "Grandma's Story."

43. Minh-ha, "Grandma's Story," 473.
44. Ibid.
45. Zembylas and Bekerman, "Education and the Dangerous Memories," 105.
46. King, *The Truth about Stories*, 89–90.
47. Ibid., 92.
48. Ibid., 98.

Conclusion

The epigraph has been taken from Lisa Delpit, *Other People's Children: Cultural Conflict in the Classroom* (New York: W.W. Norton 1995): 134.

1. James D. Anderson, "The Jubilee Anniversary of *Brown v. Board of Education*: An Essay Review," *History of Education Quarterly* 44 (2004): 153.
2. George W. Noblit and Thomas W. Collins, "Patience and Prudence in a Southern High School: Managing the Political Economy of Desegregated Education," in *Particularities: Collected Essays on Ethnography and Education*, ed. George W. Noblit (New York: Peter Lang, 1999): 157–8.
3. James D. Anderson, "Still Desegregated, Still Unequal: Lessons From Up North," *Educational Researcher* 35 (2006).
4. Anderson, "Still Desegregated," 31.
5. Katherine S. Newman, *A Different Shade of Gray: Midlife and Beyond in the Inner City* (New York: The New Press, 2003): 145; emphasis in the original.
6. Ibid.
7. Kevin Gaines, "Whose Integration Was It? An Introduction," *The Journal of American History* 91 (2004): 2.
8. Henry Giroux, "Education, Pedagogy, and the Politics of Cultural Work," in *Cultural Pedagogy: Art, Education, Politics,* ed. David Trend (Westport, VT: Bergin and Garvey (1992): vii.
9. Henry Giroux, *Border Crossing: Cultural Workers and The Politics of Education* (New York: Routledge, 1992): 2.
10. This way of thinking about whiteness comes from a talk given by Dr. Aimee Carrillo Rowe at the National Communication Association Annual Convention in Chicago, Illinois, November 2004. See also Ruth Frankenberg, *White Women, Race Matters: The Social Construction of Whiteness* (Minneapolis: University of Minnesota Press, 1993); Dreama Moon, "White Enculturation and Bourgeois Identity," in *Whiteness: The Communication of Social Identity,* ed. Thomas Nakayama and Judith Martin (Thousand Oakes, CA: Sage Publishing, 1999): 177–97; Thomas Nakayama and Robert L. Krizek, "Whiteness as Strategic Rhetoric," in *Whiteness: The Communication of Social Identity*, 87–106.; Raka Shome, "Whiteness and the Politics of Location: Postcolonial Reflections," in *Whiteness: The Communication of Social Identity*, 107–28; and John T. Warren, "Doing Whiteness: On the Performative

Dimensions of Race in the Classroom," *Communication Education* 50 (2001): 91–108.
11. Dr. Julia Johnson made this argument at the National Communication Association Annual Convention in Chicago, Illinois, November 2004.
12. Linda Moore, "Toward Politics of Body and Conscience: A Critique of Rights and the Limits of Reason," in *Body Movements: Pedagogy, Politics, and Social Change,* ed. Sherry Shapiro and Svi Shapiro (Creskill, NJ: Hampton Press, 2002): 237–64.
13. Delpit, Other People's Children, 134.

Bibliography

Allick, Mollie. "The Poor versus the Powerful: A Shared Concern Among Rural and Urban Communities." In Working Paper Series, Terry Sanford Institute of Public Policy. Durham, North Carolina: Duke University, December 2002. http://www.publicpol.duke.edu/courses/ncf/final_paper/molie.pdf.

Alridge, Derrick P. "Conceptualizing a Du Boisian Philosophy of Education: Toward a Model for African-American Education." *Educational Theory* 49 (1999): 359–79.

Anderson, James D. *The Education of Blacks in the South, 1860–1935.* Chapel Hill: University of North Carolina Press, 1988.

———. "The Jubilee Anniversary of Brown v. Board of Education: An Essay Review." *History of Education Quarterly* 44 (2004): 149–57.

———. "Still Desegregated, Still Unequal: Lessons from Up North." *Educational Researcher* 35 (2006): 30–33.

Apple, Michael W. *Educating the "Right" Way: Markets, Standards, God, and Inequality.* New York: Routledge/Falmer, 2001.

Apple, Michael, and James Beane, eds. *Democratic Schools.* Alexandria, VA: ASCD, 1995.

Arneil, Barbara. *Diverse Communities: The Problem with Social Capital.* New York: Cambridge University Press, 2006.

Bass, Jack and Walter Devries. *The Transformation of Southern Politics: Social Change and Political Consequence since 1945.* New York: Basic Books, 1976.

Bauman, Richard. *Story, Performance, Event: Contextual Studies of Oral Narrative.* New York: Cambridge University Press, 1986.

Beaumont, Jennifer J. "Implementation of Court-ordered Desegregation by District-Level Administrators." In *Beyond Desegregation: The Politics of Quality in African American Schooling,* edited by Mwalimu J. Shujaa, 75–90. Thousand Oaks, CA: Corwin Press, 1996.

Bellah, Robert N. et al. *Habits of the Heart: Individualism and Commitment in American Life.* Los Angeles: University of California Press, 1985.

Benjamin, Walter. *Illuminations.* New York: Schocken Books, 1968.

Bergson, Henri. *Laughter: An Essay on the Meaning of the Comic.* Translated by C. Brereton and F. Rothwell. Los Angeles: Green Integer, 1911.

Berry, Wendell. *What Are People For?* 153–69. San Francisco: North Point Press, 1990.

Carter, Prudence L. *Keeping It Real: School Success Beyond Black and White*. New York: Oxford Press, 2005.

Cecelski, David S. *Along Freedom Road: Hyde County, North Carolina, and the Black Struggle for Freedom*. New York: Oxford Press, 1994.

Chafe, William. *Civilities and Civil Rights: Greensboro, North Carolina, and the Black Struggle for Freedom*. New York: Oxford University Press, 1981.

Chamoiseau, Patrick. *Texaco*. New York: Vintage International, 1997.

Collins, James. "Language and Class in Minority Education." *Anthropology & Education Quarterly* 19 (1988): 299–326.

Connor, Robert D.W. and Clarence Poe. *The Life and Speeches of Charles Brantley Aycock*. Garden City, NY: Doubleday, Page, and Co, 1912.

Crain, Robert. *The Politics of School Desegregation*. Garden City, NJ: Doubleday, 1969.

Crespino, Joseph. "The Best Defense Is a Good Offense: The Stennis Amendment and the Fracturing of Liberal School Desegregation Policy, 1964–1972." *The Journal of Policy History* 18 (2006): 304–25.

Crow, Jeffrey J., Paul D. Escott, and Flora J. Hatley. *A History of African Americans in North Carolina*. Raleigh: North Carolina Office of Archives and History, 2002.

Davies, Gareth. "Richard Nixon and the Desegregation of Southern Schools." *The Journal of Policy History* 19 (2007): 367–94.

Davis, Donna M. "Merry-Go-Round: A Return to Segregation and the Implications for Creating Democratic Schools." *Urban Education* 39 (2004): 394–401.

Delgado Bernal, Delores. "Learning and Living Pedagogies of the Home: The Mestiza Consciousness of Chicana Students." *Qualitative Studies in Education* 14 (1998): 623–39.

Delpit, Lisa. *Other People's Children: Cultural Conflict in the Classroom*. New York: W.W. Norton, 1995.

Dempsey, Vann and George Noblit. "Cultural Ignorance and School Desegregation: A Community Narrative." In *Beyond Desegregation: The Politics of Quality in African American Schooling*, edited by Mwalimu J. Shujaa, 115–37. Thousand Oaks, CA: Corwin Press, 1996.

Denzin, Norman. *Performance Ethnography: Critical Pedagogy and the Politics of Culture*. Thousand Oaks, CA: Sage, 2003.

Donato, Ruben. *The Other Struggle for Equal Schools: Mexican Americans during the Civil Rights Era*. Albany: State University of New York Press, 1997.

Douglas, David. *Reading, Writing, & Race: The Desegregation of the Charlotte Schools*. Chapel Hill: University of North Carolina Press, 1995.

Foster, Michelle. *Black Teachers on Teaching*. New York: The New Press, 1997.

Frankenberg, Ruth. *White Women, Race Matters: The Social Construction of Whiteness*. Minneapolis: University of Minnesota Press, 1993.

Franklin, V.P. Introduction to *Cultural Capital and Black Education: African American Communities and the Funding of Black Schooling, 1865 to the Present*, edited by V.P. Franklin and Carter Julian Savage, xi–xx. Greenwich, CT: Information Age Publishing, 2002.

Freud, Sigmund. *Psychological Writings and Letters*. Edited by Sendra Gilman. New York: Continuum, 1995.

Fultz, Michael. "Overcoming Historical Amnesia: The Displacement of Black Educators Post-Brown." *History of Education Quarterly* 44 (2004): 11–45.

Gaines, Kevin. "Whose Integration Was It? An Introduction." *The Journal of American History* 91 (2004): 2.

García, Shernaz B. and Patricia L. Guerra. "Deconstructing Deficit Thinking: Working with Educators to Create More Equitable Learning Environments." *Education and Urban Society* 36 (2004): 150–68.

Gergen, Mary. *Feminist Reconstructions in Psychology: Narrative, Gender, and Performance*. Thousand Oaks, CA: Sage, 2001.

Giroux, Henry A. *Border Crossing: Cultural Workers and The Politics of Education*. New York: Routledge, 1992.

———. "Education, Pedagogy, and the Politics of Cultural Work," in *Cultural Pedagogy: Art, Education, Politics*, edited by David Trend, vii–xii. Westport, VT: Bergin and Garvey, 1992.

———. "Cultural Studies, Public Pedagogy, and the Responsibility of Intellectuals." *Communication and Critical/Cultural Studies* 1 (2004): 59–79.

Gorski, Paul C. "Good Intentions Are Not Enough: A Decolonizing Intercultural Education." September 13, 2007. http://www.edchange.org/publications/intercultural-education.pdf.

Grossman, James R. *Land of Hope: Chicago, Black Southerners, and the Great Migration*. Chicago: University of Chicago Press, 1989.

Grundy, Pamela. *Learning to Win: Sports, Education, and Social Change in Twentieth-Century North Carolina*. Chapel Hill: The University of North Carolina Press, 2001.

Hall, Jacquelyn Dowd. "The Long Civil Rights Movement and the Political Uses of the Past." *Journal of American History* 91 (2005): 123–63.

Hampton, Jeffrey S. "He Lives to Help Others with all his Might: Retired Educator has Devoted a Life to Public Service." *Norfolk (VA) Virginian-Pilot*, March 11, 1996.

———. "Camden Grower Cultivates Farmers Market Customers." *Norfolk (VA) Virginian-Pilot*, December 1, 2003.

Hollingshead, August B. *Elm Town's Youth*. New York: John Wiley and Sons, 1949.

Hollins, Etta R. *Culture in School Learning: Revealing the Deep Meaning*. Mahwah, NJ: Erlbaum, 1996.

hooks, bell. "Homeplace (A Site of Resistance)." In *Woman That I am: The Literature and Culture of Contemporary Women of Color*, edited by Madison D. Soyini. New York: St. Martin's Press, 1994. 448–54.

———. "Eating the Other: Desire and Resistance." In *Media and Cultural Studies: Keyworks*, rev. edn, edited by Meenakshi Gigi Durham and Douglas M. Kellner, 366–80. New York: Blackwell, 2006.

Horvat, Erin McNamara, Elliot B. Weininger, and Annette Lareau. "From Social Ties to Social Capital: Class Differences in the Relations Between Schools and Parent Networks." *American Educational Research Journal* 40 (2003): 319–51.

Hughes, Sherick A. "Pedagogy of Struggle and Hope: Black Families Responding to Desegregation." PhD dissertation, University of North Carolina, 2004.

———. "Theorizing Oppressed Family Pedagogy: Critical Lessons from a Rural Black Family in the Post-Brown South." *Journal of Educational Foundations* 19 (Summer 2005): 45–72.

———. *Black Hands in the Biscuits, Not in the Classrooms: Unveiling Hope in a Struggle for* Brown's *Promise*. New York: Peter Lang, 2006.

Irigaray, Luce. "Interview." In *Women Analyze Women in France, England, and the United States,* edited by E.H. Baruch and L. Serrano, 149–66. New York: New York University Press, 1988.

Irons, Peter. *Jim Crow's Children*. New York: Viking, 2002.

Irvine, Russell and Jackie Irvine. "Impact of the Desegregation Process on the Education of Black Students: Key Variables." *Journal of Negro Education* 52 (1983): 410–22.

Jackson, John. *Harlemworld: Doing Race and Class in Contemporary Black America*. Chicago: University of Chicago Press, 2001.

Kelly-Goss, Robert. "In 1963, at the Height of the Civil Rights Movement, Elizabeth City was Site of Protests and Sit-ins." *Elizabeth City (NC) Daily Advance*, February 30, 2008.

Kincaid, Jamaica. *My Brother*. New York: Farrar, Straus, and Giroux, 1997.

King, Lauren. "Farmers Market Set To Open Despite Absence of Beloved Produce Vendor." *Norfolk (VA) Virginian-Pilot*, April 6, 2007.

King, Thomas. *The Truth about Stories: A Native Narrative*. Toronto, ON: House of Anansi Press, 2003.

Kluger, Richard. *Simple Justice: The History of Brown v. Board of Education and Black America's Struggle for Equality*. New York: Random House. 1977.

Korstad, Robert R. and James Leloudis. "The North Carolina Volunteers and the War on Poverty." *Law and Contemporary Problems* 62 (Durham, NC, 1999): 177–97.

Kotlowski, Dean. "With All Deliberate Delay: Kennedy, Johnson, and School Desegregation." *The Journal of Policy History* 17 (2005): 155–92.

Kozol, Jonathan. *The Shame of the Nation: The Restoration of Apartheid Schooling in America*. New York: Crown Publishers, 2005.

Ladson-Billings, Gloria. "Landing on the Wrong Note: The Price We Paid for Brown." *Educational Researcher* 33 (2004): 3–13.

———. "From the Achievement Gap to the Education Debt: Understanding Achievement in U.S. Schools." *Educational Researcher* 35 (2006): 3–12.

Lareau, Annerr, and Erin McNamara Horvat, "Moments of Social Inclusion and Exclusion: Race, Class, and Cultural Capital." *Sociology of Education* 72 (1999): 37–53.

Lawrence-Lightfoot, Sarah. *I've Known Rivers: Lives of Loss and Liberation*. New York: Penguin Books, 1994.

Lebacqz, Karen. Six Theories of Justice. Minneapolis: Augsburg Publishing House, 1986.

Leloudis, James. Schooling the South: Pedagogy, Self, and Society in North Carolina. Chapel Hill: University of North Carolina Press, 1996.

Lewis, George. *Massive Resistance: The White Response to the Civil Rights Movement*. New York: Hodder Arnold, 2006.

Lowenthal, David. *The Past is a Foreign Country*. Cambridge, UK: Cambridge University Press, 1985.

Madison, D. Soyini. "'That Was My Occupation': Oral Narrative, Performance, and Black Feminist Thought." In *Exceptional Spaces*, edited by D. Pollock, 319–42. Chapel Hill: University of North Carolina Press, 1998.

Madsen, Jean Ann and Etta R. Hollins. "African American Teachers' Roles in School Desegregation: At the Dawn of a New Millennium." *Urban Education* 35 (2000): 5–30.

McCarty, Theresa. *A Place to be Navajo: Rough Rock and the Struggle for Self-Determination in Indigenous Schooling*. Mahwah, NJ: Lawrence Earlbaum Associates, 2002.

McPhail, Mark. "Race and the (Im)possibility of Dialogue." In *Dialogue: Theorizing Difference in Communication Studies*, edited by Rob Anderson, Leslie. A. Baxter, and Kenneth. N. Cissna, 209–24. Thousand Oaks, CA: Sage, 2004.

Miller, Loren. *The Petitioners: The Story of the Supreme Court of the United States and the Negro*. New York: Pantheon Books, 1966.

Minh-ha, Trinh T. "Grandma's Story." In *The Woman that I Am: The Literature and Culture of Contemporary Women of Color*, edited by D.S. Madison, 462–84. New York: St. Martin's Griffin, 1994.

Moon, Dreama. "White Enculturation and Bourgeois Identity." In *Whiteness: The Communication of Social Identity*, edited by Thomas Nakayama and Judith Martin, 177–97. Thousand Oakes, CA: Sage Publishing, 1999.

Moore, Linda. "Toward Politics of Body and Conscience: A Critique of Rights and the Limits of Reason." In *Body Movements: Pedagogy, Politics, and Social Change*, edited by Sherry Shapiro and Svi Shapiro, 237–64. Cresskill, NJ: Hampton Press Inc, 2002.

Morris, Jerome E. "A Pillar of Strength: An African American School's Communal Bonds with Families and Community Since *Brown*." *Urban Education* 33 (1999): 584–605.

———. "Research, Ideology, and the Brown Decision: Counter-narratives to the Historical and Contemporary Representation of Black Schooling." *Teachers College Record* 110 (2008): 713–32.

Nakayama, Thomas and Robert L Krizek. "Whiteness as Strategic Rhetoric." In *Whiteness: The Communication of Social Identity*, edited by Thomas Nakayama and Judith Martin, 87–106. Thousand Oaks, CA: Sage, 1999.

Nasir, Na'ilah Suad and Victoria M. Hand. "Exploring Sociocultural Perspectives on Race, Culture, and Learning." *Review of Educational Research* 76 (2006): 449–75.

Newman, Katherine S. *A Different Shade of Gray: Midlife and Beyond in the Inner City*. New York: The New Press, 2003.

Noblit, George W. "North Carolina School Desegregation: The Intersection between Law, Tradition, and Transition." Paper presented at the 2002 annual meeting of the American Education Research Association in Pittsburgh, PA.

Noblit, George W. and Thomas W. Collins. "Patience and Prudence in a Southern High School: Managing the Political Economy of Desegregated Education." In *Particularities: Collected Essays on Ethnography and Education*, edited by George W. Noblit, 157–80. New York: Peter Lang, 1999.

Noblit, George W. and Vann O. Dempsey. *The Social Construction of Virtue: The Moral Life of Schools*. Albany: State University of New York, 1996.

Nussbaum, Martha C. *Upheavals of Thought: The Intelligence of Emotions*. New York: Cambridge University Press, 2002.

Olick, Jeffrey K. and Joyce Robbins. "Social Memory Studies: From 'Collective Memory' to the Historical Sociology of Mnemonic Practices." *Annual Review of Sociology* 24 (1998): 105–40.

Oliver, Melvin and Thomas Shapiro. *Black Wealth/White Wealth: A New Perspective on Racial Inequality*. New York: Routledge, 1997.

Osei-Kofi, Nana. "Pathologizing the Poor: A Framework for Understanding Ruby Payne's Work." *Equity and Excellence in Education* 38 (2005): 367–75.

Ostovich, Steven T. "Epilogue: Dangerous Memories." In *The Work of Memory: New Directions in the Study of German Society and Culture*, edited by A. Confino and P. Fritzsche, 239–56. Urbana and Chicago: University of Illinois Press, 2002.

Plummer, Kenneth. *Intimate Citizenship: Private Decisions and Public Dialogues*. Seattle: University of Washington, 2003.

Pollock, Della. "Telling the Told, Performing like a Family." *The Oral History Review* 18 (1990): 1–36.

———. *Remembering: Performance and Oral History*. New York: Palgrave Macmillan, 2005.

Putnam, Robert D. *Bowling Alone: The Collapse and Revival of American Community*. New York: Simon & Schuster, 2000.

Rank, Mark R. *One Nation, Underprivileged: Why American Poverty Affects Us All*. New York, NY: Oxford University Press, 2004.

Rosenzweig, Roy and David Thelen. *The Presence of the Past: Popular Uses of History in American Life*. New York: Columbia University Press, 1998.

Savage, Carter Julian. "Our School in Our Community: The Collective Economic Struggle for African American Education in Franklin, Tennessee, 1890–1967." In *Cultural Capital and Black Education: African American Communities and the Funding of Black Schooling, 1865 to the Present*, edited by V.P. Franklin and

Carter Julian Savage, 49–80. Greenwich, CT: Information Age Publishing, 2002.

Schrager, Samuel. "What is Social in Oral History?" *International Journal of Oral History* 4 (1983): 76–98.

Scott, James C. *Domination and the Arts of Resistance: Hidden Transcripts.* New Haven, CT: Yale University Press, 1990.

Segrest, Mab. *Born to Belonging: Writings on Spirit and Justice.* New Brunswick, NJ: Rutgers University Press, 2002.

Shields, Carolyn, Bishop Russell, and Andre E. Mazawi. *Pathologizing Practices: The Impact of Deficit Thinking on Education.* New York: Peter Lang, 2005.

Shome, Raka. "Whiteness and the Politics of Location: Postcolonial Reflections." In *Whiteness: The Communication of Social Identity*, edited by Thomas Nakayama and Judith Martin, 107–28. Thousand Oakes, CA: Sage Publishing, 1999.

———. "Space Matters: The Politics and Practice of Space." *Communication Theory* 13 (2003): 39–56.

Siddle Walker, Vanessa. *Their Highest Potential: An African American School Community in the Segregated South.* Chapel Hill: University of North Carolina, 1996.

Simpson, Bland. *The Great Dismal: A Carolinian's Swamp Memoir.* Chapel Hill: University of North Carolina, 1990.

Slim, Hugo and Paul Thompson, eds. *Listening for a Change: Oral Testimony and Development.* London: Panos Publications, 1995.

Smith, Stephen Samuel and Jessica Kulynych. "It May be Social, But Why is it Capital? The Social Construction of Social Capital and the Politics of Language." *Politics Society* 30 (2002): 149–86.

Solorzano, Daniel G. and Tara J. Yosso. "A Critical Race Counterstory of Race, Racism, and Affirmative Action." *Equity & Excellence in Education* 35 (2002): 155–68.

———. "Critical Race Methodology: Counter-Storytelling as a Framework for Education Research." *Qualitative Inquiry* 8 (2002): 23–44.

Spano, Sean. *Public Dialogue and Participatory Democracy: Cupertino Community Project.* Cresskill, NJ: Hampton Press, 2001.

Stack, Carol. *A Call to Home: African Americans Reclaim the Rural South.* New York: Basic Books, 1996.

Timothy Tyson. *Blood Done Sign My Name.* New York: Three Rivers Press, 2004.

Tozer, Steve. "Class." In *Knowledge and Power in the Global Economy: Politics and the Rhetoric of School Reform,* edited by David Gabbart, 149–59. Mahwah, NJ: Lawrence Erlbaum Associates, 2004.

Villenas, Sofia. "Latina Mothers and Small-town Racisms: Creating Narratives of Dignity and Moral Education in North Carolina." *Anthropology & Education Quarterly* 32 (2001): 3–28.

Warren, John T. "Doing Whiteness: On the Performative Dimensions of Race in the Classroom." *Communication Education* 50 (2001): 91–108.

Watkins, William H. "Can Institutions Care? Evidence from Segregated Schooling of African American Children." In *Beyond Desegregation: The Politics of Quality in African American Schooling*, edited by Mwalimu J. Shujaa, 5–27. Thousand Oaks, CA: Corwin Press, 1996.

Williams, Juan. *Thurgood Marshall: American Revolutionary*. New York: Random House, 1998.

Williams, Patricia J. "The Ethnic Scarring of American Whiteness." In *The House that Race Built*, edited by Wahneema Lubiano, 253–63. New York: Vintage Press, 1998.

Willie, Charles V. and Sarah S. Willie. "Black, White, and Brown: The Transformation of Public Education in America." *Teachers College Record* 107 (2005): 475–95.

Willink, Kate. "Economy & Pedagogy: Laboring to Learn in Camden County, North Carolina." *Communication and Critical/Cultural Studies* 5 (2008): 64–86.

Winant, Howard. "Racial Dualism at Century's End." In *The House that Race Built*, edited by Wahneema Lubiano, 87–115. New York: Vintage Press, 1998.

Winter, Jay, *Remembering War: The Great War and Historical Memory in the Twentieth Century*. New Haven, CT: Yale University Press, 2006.

Wright, Jr. Nathan, ed. *What Black Educators Are Saying*. New York: Hawthorne Books, 1970.

Yosso, Tara J. "Whose Culture Has Capital? A Critical Race Theory Discussion of Community Cultural Wealth." *Race Ethnicity and Education* 8 (2005): 69–91.

Yosso, Tara J., Laurence Parker, Daniel G. Solórzano, and Marvin Lynn. "Critical Race Discussion of Racialized Rationales and Access to Higher Education: From Jim Crow to Affirmative Action and Back Again." *Review of Research in Education* 28 (2004): 1–25.

Zembylas, Michalinos and Zvi Bekerman. "Education and the Dangerous Memories of Historical Trauma: Narratives of Pain, Narratives of Hope." *Curriculum Inquiry* 38 (2008): 125–54.

Index

abolition of slavery, 14
Alexander v. Holmes (1969), 101
Aycock, Governor Charles, 16

barter economy, 21, 22–4, 25, 30, 52, 57, 64, 66, 169
black historical framework, 7, 14
blackness, 5, 6, 164
black power movement, 3
black-white power relations, 5
Boss Hoggs, 78, 91, 94, 198
Brennan, Justice William, 1
Brown v. Board of Education of Topeka, Kansas, 1, 3, 7, 8, 33, 34, 35, 44, 48, 49, 99, 101, 119, 123, 124, 125, 129, 130, 138, 139, 158, 167, 183, 184, 188, 193, 198, 199, 200, 201, 202, 203, 204, 205, 206, 208
Brown II, 33, 49 119, 193
Burgess
   Dempsey, 37, 53, 102, 106, 115
   Peter, 41

Camden County Press, 85
Camden High School, 2, 36, 44, 53, 54, 86, 87, 88, 139, 140, 145, 147, 161, 166
Camden Middle School, 83, 86, 87, 107, 114, 132
capital
   cultural, 7, 51, 52, 55, 56, 58, 59, 60, 63, 64, 65, 66, 67, 68, 69, 70, 71, 128, 180, 185
   social, 51, 52, 53, 54, 55, 56, 57, 58, 59, 61, 62, 63, 64, 65, 66, 67, 69, 71, 128, 195, 196
capitalism, 20, 22, 23, 25, 30, 31, 169, 183, 194, 195
churches, 11, 12, 14, 18, 41, 64, 65, 73, 76, 90, 144, 151

black, 16, 40, 56, 60, 90
   integrated, 39
   white, 52
citizenship, 6, 15, 16, 18, 188, 189
civil rights, 4, 35, 135, 152, 193, 199, 200
   Act of 1964, 35, 100, 101, 199, 200
   advocate, 95, 134
   era, 5, 167, 193, 197, 198, 203
   long civil rights movement, 7, 14, 188, 189, 192
   movement, 1, 4, 7, 14, 16, 125, 178, 201
   struggle, 1, 4
Civil War, 14, 36, 37, 40, 42, 43, 54, 55, 171, 172, 194
College of Albemarle, 30, 58
common school system, 15, 16, 18, 189
corporal punishment, 27, 28, 117
County Commission, 38, 91, 93, 96, 105, 112, 121, 163, 198
culture of privatization, 184
curriculum, 15, 31, 68, 70, 134, 137, 185
   black, 2, 143
   white, 68, 129
Currituck, 77

Davis, Barbarette, 77, 82, 83
deficit
   narrative, 14
   storytelling, 14
   thinking, 58, 59, 61, 63–6, 137
Department of Health, Education, and Welfare (HEW), 35, 100, 101, 200
Du Bois, W.E.B., 121–2, 124
dialogue, 6, 9, 20, 45, 70, 114, 117, 129, 141, 170, 172
discipline, 5, 6, 8, 25, 27, 28, 39, 80, 82, 83, 84, 85, 87, 88, 108, 109, 117, 126, 127, 133, 145, 174, 190
Dismal Swamp Canal, 2, 14, 36, 55, 187

Division of Negro Education, 15, 17
double taxation, 15

East Carolina University, 103
Economic Improvement Council (EIC), 102, 104, 106, 111, 123, 148, 149, 152, 159
education
    black, 8, 16, 17, 18, 28, 38, 39, 58, 64, 65, 76, 77, 86, 87, 88, 113, 120, 122, 128, 134, 135, 136, 190, 192
    formal, 22, 24, 25, 30, 31, 57, 64, 65, 133, 189
    informal, 5, 7, 12, 13, 21, 30, 184
    public, 1, 6, 7, 14, 31, 34, 126, 130, 146, 154, 155, 168, 183, 185, 190, 193, 199, 201
education policy, 6, 69, 184, 185
Elementary and Secondary Education Act of 1965, 35, 100
Elizabeth City, 2, 8, 10, 30, 61, 72, 77, 85, 86, 88, 91, 95, 96, 102, 103, 104, 120, 121, 127, 139, 149, 159, 163, 173, 187, 199, 201
    State University, 85, 88, 121, 127
emancipation, 14

Ferebee, Nancy, 87
Ferrari, Suzanne, 122
Franklin, Rev. William, 73
freedmen, 14, 76
Freedom of Choice, 7, 35, 48, 49, 100, 101, 102, 103, 163
funding for schools, 15, 16, 18, 35, 100, 102, 109, 183

Gallup, Joyce, 88
Gates Foundation, 3
graded school system, 15, 17, 30, 168, 189, 191
gradualism, 34, 138
Grandy Elementary School, 3
Greensboro Daily News, 34
Green v. County School Board of New Kent County (1968), 48, 49, 100
Griffin v. County School Board of Prince Edward County (1964), 49

history, 6, 36, 40, 42, 48, 55, 70, 119, 145, 168, 169, 170, 171, 172, 173, 176, 178, 180, 184

black, 31, 63, 68, 88, 145, 147
    of desegregation, 167, 172
    educational, 144
    hidden, 40
    lived, 42, 170
    local, 55, 82, 145, 171
    national, 70
    oral, 4, 6, 7, 45, 168, 173, 180, 188, 192, 194, 197
    of segregation, 172, 178
    social, 3
    violent, 42, 149, 163
    white, 31, 36, 38, 39, 40, 68, 147
Hodges, Governor Luther H., 33
Hughes, Charlie, 7, 11–31, 51, 55–8, 62–3, 70, 169, 176, 189, 191, 193

individualism, 15, 31, 68, 143, 184, 195
interracial progress, 14

Johnson C. Smith College, 76
Jones, Vivian, 8, 129, 177–9, 191

King, Martin Luther, Jr., 2, 4, 9, 35, 46, 93, 94, 120, 147, 148, 157, 166, 172, 173, 189
Klu Klux Klan, 2, 35, 104, 105, 111

labor, wage, 14
Leary, Alex, 7, 14, 16, 19, 32–49, 51–5, 60–3, 67, 68, 69, 70, 79, 82, 87, 101, 146, 148, 168, 170–2, 177, 194, 197, 198
legacies
    emotional, 179–31
    of violence, 162–5
Lewis, Fannie Mae, 8, 73, 123, 157–66, 168, 176, 180, 181
Lowenthal, David, 170, 172, 173

Malcolm X, 3
Marian Anderson School, 4, 7, 8, 35, 39, 44–9, 53, 54, 60, 61, 65, 73, 77, 78, 79, 81, 82, 86, 87, 88, 101, 102–13, 116, 124, 126, 133, 135, 136, 137, 138, 141, 143, 144, 145, 146, 148, 154, 162, 173, 178, 198, 204
Marshall, Thurgood, 35
Martin, Governor James, 96

mascots, 3, 4, 30, 78, 134, 145, 146, 173
memory, 3, 30, 39, 46, 61, 66, 69, 70, 75, 109, 115, 116, 136, 137, 145, 146, 163, 168, 169, 171, 173, 174, 175, 176, 177, 178, 185, 206
  collective, 4, 6, 138, 173, 174
  community, 69, 167, 173
  counter-memory, 168–9
  critical, 169
  dangerous, 177–81
  historical, 206
  performances, 30
  racial, 8
  social, 168, 206
  and social change, 167–81
Miller, Judge Loren, 119
money age, 14, 15
multiple-room schools, 15

narrative, 14, 42, 43, 46, 58, 69, 70, 134, 135, 137, 140, 141, 158, 165, 166, 171, 173, 181, 191
  cultural, 31
  historical, 178
  ideological, 178
  life, 168
  national, 4, 167, 168
  progress, 14, 30
  traditional, 14
national progress narrative of the Civil Rights movement, 14
Neibuhr, Reinhold, 125
Newbold, Nathan Carter, 15, 17
nineteenth century, 15
Norfolk, Virginia, 2, 3, 55, 187
Norfolk Virginia-Pilot, 56, 58, 74, 76, 78, 84, 90
North Carolina Fund, 104, 105

obstructionism, 34, 100
Office of Economic Opportunity, 102, 104
Old Trap, 16, 36, 40, 53, 158
one-room school house, 18
oral history, *see* history
oral traditions, 6
Order of the Long Leaf Pine, 99
Outer Banks, 2–3
Owens, W.C. "Bill," Jr., 91

parent, 5, 6, 7, 8, 9, 13, 15, 24, 26, 30, 34, 39, 44, 45, 54, 60, 63, 65, 66, 68, 73, 74, 76, 82, 83, 85, 88, 102, 105, 108, 109, 113, 114, 128, 129, 133, 135, 136, 137, 138, 139, 140, 141, 142, 143, 145, 147, 151, 152, 153, 158, 159, 160, 161, 162, 169, 181, 184, 191, 204
  …association, 60
  organizations, 162
  parental involvement, 6
  parent-child interaction, 6
  parenting, 6, 180
  parent-teacher, 129, 142
  Parent-Teachers' Association (PTA), 5, 63, 129, 136, 150, 161, 162
Parents Involved in Community Schools v. Seattle School District No.1 (2007), 7, 9
Pasquotank County, 2, 11, 91, 96, 99
Pearsall Plan, 34, 193
pedagogies, 6, 25, 30, 31, 68, 69, 71, 101, 121, 125, 128, 133, 134, 135, 137, 142, 147, 160, 185
  black, 79, 82, 88, 101, 109
  memory, and social change, 167–81, 185
  and social change, 119–31
  white, 30, 31, 70, 128, 154, 184, 185
Perquimans, 77, 105
Plummer, Kenneth, 180
policy
  education, 6, 69, 184, 185
  federal, 2
  power and, 6, 133
  public education, 6
pride, 5, 8, 16, 20, 21, 24, 25, 26, 27, 28, 36, 65, 87, 103, 133, 157, 172, 178, 180
  black, 137, 169
principals
  black, 7, 38, 61, 63, 73, 124, 125
  white, 5, 8, 60, 106, 107, 108, 113, 124, 129
professionalism, 15

racial equality, 5, 9, 16, 31, 41, 102, 103, 109, 114, 115, 124, 127, 134, 157, 159, 163, 168, 175, 183, 184, 185
railroad, 14
reciprocity, 23, 57
Revelle
  Billy, 8, 39, 60, 87, 98–117, 119–31, 145, 168, 174–7

Revelle—*Continued*
　Earlene, 102, 103
rhetoric, political, 16, 34, 46, 99, 188

Sawyer's Creek School, 77, 103, 106, 135, 190, 191
school board, 34, 36, 48, 49, 63, 67, 87, 107, 114, 115, 123, 125, 126, 129, 138, 146, 150, 162
Schoolmasters Club, 60, 79, 80
segregation, 1, 3, 9, 14, 16, 31, 42, 43, 44, 49, 59, 62, 78, 79, 113, 114, 121, 126, 138, 139, 148, 149, 159, 163, 165, 170, 172, 178, 180, 183, 185, 187, 189, 199, 202, 204, 205
　de facto, 1, 7, 44, 48, 60, 123, 126, 147, 163, 186, 199
　de jure, 1, 7, 44, 49, 60, 99, 100, 101, 155, 163, 168, 175
　school, 44, 101, 119, 131, 137, 143, 169, 175, 192
self-determination, 16, 18, 64, 184
separate but equal, 1, 14, 18, 19, 46, 56, 183, 192
Shiloh, 11, 16, 17, 40, 57, 62, 190, 191
Slavery, 14, 42, 95, 117, 190
Spence, J.R., 57, 74, 75, 76, 77, 79, 80, 82, 84, 86, 87, 89, 90, 91, 92, 94
standardization, 15
Stanford, Terry, 34, 35, 104
story, 6, 14, 19, 21, 28, 29, 30, 41, 42, 43, 44, 47, 54, 69, 70, 75, 83, 115, 131, 141, 152, 158, 159, 162, 163, 164, 165, 166, 170, 172, 176, 180, 187, 188
storytelling, 6, 14, 69, 70, 168, 170, 179, 194
　deficit, 14

student-teacher relations, 6
suburbanization, 3
Supreme Court, 2, 3, 7, 27, 35, 99, 119, 130, 183, 200
　see also individual cases

Thirteenth Amendment, 14
Trafton, I.M., 135–6, 145, 178

unanticipated consequences, 8, 167
Uncle Tom, 42, 94–6
underground railroad, 160
University of North Carolina, 103

Vaughn, Bobby "Coach," 74, 75, 77, 78, 80, 85, 86, 88, 89, 91, 92, 93, 94, 95, 120, 121, 197, 198
VISTA volunteers, 104, 123, 159

Washington, Booker T., 80, 81, 121
W.C. Chance High School, 77
whiteness, 5, 6, 30, 44, 45, 46, 104, 125, 137, 155, 171, 175, 185, 192
white privilege, 7, 30, 46, 52
white supremacy, 16, 75, 82, 109, 123, 125, 129, 139, 172
Wilkins, Buster, 91
Witherspoon, Whittier Crockett, 7, 8, 38, 39–46, 61–3, 72–97, 102, 108, 109, 119, 120–30, 141, 144, 145, 172, 173–4, 197, 199, 204, 207
　the bridge builder, 60–2, 75, 89–90, 96, 174
work
　ethic, 21, 24, 25, 57
　skills, 14